ANNOUNCING SUSAN REINTJES' NEW BOOK

THROUGH THE FAIRY DOOR

A magical adventure for all ages

"A fantasy romp with life lessons tagging along for the ride."

available now @www.thruthefairydoor.com

Also available from **Third Eye Publishing**:

AUDIO RECORDINGS to enhance your emotional, physical, mental, and spiritual well-being:

PAST LIVES REVISITED: Experience firsthand a past life regression to heal present problems and relationships.

TIME FOR THE INNER CHILD: Meditations to reconnect and communicate with the inner child and facilitate spiritual opening.

TIME TO LET GO AND RECEIVE: Meditations to make space for abundance and joy by releasing fear and limitations.

HEALING EATING DISORDERS FROM THE INSIDE OUT: Meditations to uncover the origin of eating problems and to feel and heal the emotional issues.

TIME FOR BIRTHING AND TIME FOR PARENTING: Lessons and Meditations to prepare for a healthy birth experience and tips for conscious parenting.

See details @ www.susanreintjes.com

NEW YORK TIMES BESTSELLER

PROOF of HEAVEN

A Neurosurgeon's Journey into the Afterlife

by Eben Alexander, MD

"Communicating with a coma patient," she {Susan Reintjes} later told me, "is a little like throwing a rope down a deep well. How deep the rope needs to go depends on the depth of the comatose state. When I tried to contact you, the first thing that surprised me was how deep the rope went. The farther down, the more frightened I became that you were too far away- that I wouldn't be able to reach you because you weren't coming back." After five full minutes of mentally descending via telepathic "rope" she felt a slight shift, like a fishing line deep down in the water getting a small but definite tug.

More Praise for THIRD EYE OPEN

"If you're up to the challenge of growth and delightful perspectives, read THIRD EYE OPEN. Be ready to see life, love, laughter and spirit with a fresh view, designed to provide tools to manage thinking and feeling in the 21st century. Susan Reintjes writes in a captivating fashion, offering guidance with substance and simplicity. THIRD EYE OPEN is a primer for the healthy life of the future. You'll refer to it often."

~Merrily Neill, psychotherapist and author of *A New Blueprint of Marriage*

"The ancient stirrings in the belly call for us to come inside and rediscover our true selves. THIRD EYE OPEN-*Unmasking Your True Awareness* helps us in this process. Following the yogic ways of recognizing that all that has been created is part of our own being, Susan Reintjes' book shows us how to reconnect with the psychic nature of our world."

~Angela Farmer and Victor van Kooten, authors of *From Inside Out 1 & 2* and the video *The Feminine Unfolding*

"THIRD EYE OPEN offers a spiritual interpretation of daily events and encounters. Susan Reintjes' book is an intriguing and innovative guidebook for raising consciousness. Through recognizing and completing unfinished inner work, the reader can develop psychic abilities and gain spiritual knowledge to navigate the accelerating intensity of the new millennium."

~Elise Browning Miller, Iyengar yoga teacher, author of *Life is a Stretch*

Third Eye Open

Unmasking Your True Awareness

Susan Reintjes

Third Eye Publishing

Front cover photograph by Muriel Mandel
Back cover photograph by Adam Siegel
Cover Design by FJ Ventre
Book Design by Julie Evans

Second Printing, December 2012

ISBN: 0-9726159-0-3

www.thirdeyeopen.com

Printed in the United States of America

To my daughter, Sarah,
whose kindness, consciousness and comedy
have delighted me for sixteen years.

"Close both eyes to see with the other eye."
—Rumi

Little Green Goblin

The little green goblin sat one day
Trying to think of something to say.
He thought and thought and thought a lot,
Until his brain was in a knot.
He thought in bed.
He thought and said,
"Oh, what shall I do?"
Then he thought of the little word "boo".
He said it over.
He read it over.
Then over and over again.
Then he saw a maiden coming down the road
With quite a load.
He shouted and shouted and shouted real loud.
But nothing did she do.
So he forgot about the little word "boo".

Susan Reintjes, age 9

Tangential

At once, radiant and despairing

    The still kinetic girl-woman weaves the net

        that cradles and encases her

    She dips ever nearer the water's mirror-top

Not reaching, not resisting

    the journey is timeless and eternal

    Awake, she knows her descent is her life

    Asleep, she dreams of her arrival

Mist from the lake brushes her cheek

At once, she looks up and down

    The net meets the water

    Alive and unknown, she tips forward.

Susan Reintjes, age 30

Acknowledgments

Heartfelt thanks to all of my teachers, clients, friends and family who have helped me know myself better and who shared their lives with me. A special thank you to Merrily Neill, my therapist, and Rebecca Whitaker, my high school English/Drama teacher, for encouraging me to express myself and to write.

Special thanks to Mike Johnson, Jennie Chamberlin and Jini Gute for support along the way. My warm appreciation goes to my personal editor, Katie Haywood and to Catherine Kerr for her support in final editing, publishing and publicity.

Contents

Preface

I was born on July 2, 1954, a controversial year of rising integration and UFO sightings. The third child of four, I grew up in a small coastal town of North Carolina with a clinical psychologist mother and a marine biologist father. The ocean was a constant source of fun and comfort for me. I spent hours at the beach and in the water. I would hold fast to the floats attached to the thick ropes marking the swimming areas. The current would pull me under and the float would bounce me back to the surface for air. I imagined I was riding my pet sea serpent. I was very drawn to dolphins and could call them into the shore. I would chant "Dolphins, dolphins, dolphins of the sea. Dolphins, dolphins come to me." I repeated the chant until I saw the tips of the dorsal fins over the crests of the waves. When I would spy a pod of dolphins, I would concentrate on communicating with them.

One day, a dolphin swam in closer than the others. I kept asking her to come closer and closer hoping she would swim near enough for me to wade out to her. It was January, and the air was raw and cold. I waded into the frigid water ready to swim with her. She was so close I felt I could reach out and touch her. The numbness in my feet and legs warned me not to go further into the waves. Reluctantly, I backed out. She stayed in the shallows near me before she rejoined her pod and swam out to sea. I remained on the shore shivering with both cold and excitement at the close encounter.

My childhood was both magical and troubled. With freedom to roam in acres of woods and a liberal upbringing, I experienced the joys of nature and embraced the diversity of the world. I rode my bike for hours and played outside with my sisters and brother until nightfall. I recall coming into the house tired and spent with cheeks pink from the evening chill and "potato rows" of dirt under my chin as evidence of the rough and tumble nature of our play. I was always surprised how dark it seemed from the inside of the house. Our eyes had gradually adjusted to the decreasing light, giving us the night vision of nocturnal creatures.

Nature was very important to me. I spent hours in the woods, communing with the trees and plants, building pine straw huts and adopting stray or injured animals. I was fascinated by stories of fairies and elves and spent time imagining and interacting with a family of elves that lived in the hollow of a tree. I took them small offerings of food and left acorn tops for them to wear as hats. As a child, I wrote and illustrated books of elves and a family of owls.

Maternal feelings blossomed in me at a very tender age. I cared for a large family of dolls, each with their own formulas and sleeping and bathing schedules. As a child, I remember the feeling of falling into bed after an especially trying day filled with doll baths and feedings. Now after a hard day of balancing my role as a mother and a therapist, I collapse into bed with the same feelings of relief and satisfaction.

On the darker side, I was frequently plagued by vivid nightmares and years of bedwetting. My parents were dedicated to their physical and mental parental roles, but very lacking in an awareness of their emotions and psyches. As a sensitive child, I soaked up their fears and neuroses. My father was hard-working, imaginative and intense. He made up stories when we were young and entertained us by eating fire and doing magic tricks. One afternoon when my mother needed some quiet time, we "ran away from home" and cooked hotdogs on sticks in the woods. When he was in a good mood he was playful and funny, and when he was angry, his mood came across just as strongly. His unresolved sexual issues came out as control and inappropriate boundaries. At night, I remember my father putting me to bed. He would lay down beside me, pressed so closely I could feel the pressure of an erection. Even as a small child I knew something was wrong. I lay very still, my arms pinned under me and my body turned away from his. I held my breath as I silently willed myself to fall asleep. My nightmares often featured a "bad daddy" who would get me out of bed in the middle of the night and take me to a darkened room. I would wake up terrified, my heart pounding. This reoccurring nightmare plagued me for years. I could always tell when it was coming and would try to stay awake as long as possible to delay the dream. I have logged hundreds of dreams about my father, from early childhood to the present; all include sexual pursuit and being held hostage. I wanted my relationship with him to be different. I wanted to feel safe and playful, but instead I was guarded, confused, scared and shameful. Like many sexual abuse survivors, I chose to hurt myself. From the age of eight through high school I burned my genitals with scalding water, calling out my father's name. I am aware now how I blamed and shamed myself for his sexual advances. I was punishing myself for being chosen as a victim. My family's denial system tried to push the truth out of my reality. After years of examining my deep fear and mistrust of men, flashbacks of sexual encounters with my father came to the surface. These memories brought floods of pain as well as the relief of uncovering the truth. It has taken years of hard work to process the pain, betrayal and loss, and to reclaim my innocence.

When it came to dealing with my numerous emotional and physical symptoms, my mother was at a loss. The family's impenetrable denial system made it impossible for my sexual abuse symptoms to be recognized and treated. In spite of the denial, my mother was a good provider of necessities and fun. A favorite memory is coming home to a tea party after school, a warm pot of sugared tea with small squares of cinnamon toast on a cold, wintry afternoon. Willing to sew a costume or help with a school project, she possessed true energy and enthusiasm.

Eager to be seen and loved, I used my quick wit, humor and vivacity in an attempt to charm my parents into a deeper rapport. As my repeated attempts failed, I retreated into an inner world where I could find comfort and create my own fantasies of relating. Even when I was alone, I felt the presence of other beings. Although these energies were invisible, I established a connection that comforted me. In my adult life, I have had to unlearn my uncanny ability to cloak myself. This habit served me in retreating from painful and frightening childhood events, but handicaps me in adult communicating and relating.

An awareness of past lives presented itself to me at an early age. As a young child, I was terrified of airplanes flying overhead. Since we lived near a military base, it was a common occurrence. I would hide under my bed until they passed, holding my breath as if waiting for a bomb to drop. In my mind, I could hear the high-pitched whistle of the falling missile. I was in the first grade when my embarrassed sisters walked me home from the bus one afternoon. They told our mother that I was telling everyone at school that I was Jewish. We lived in a rural coastal town in North Carolina, so we had little or no contact with Jewish people. I remember thinking that I did not know what Jewish was, only that it was important to let people know I was Jewish. Many times, I would awaken terrified from dreams of hiding from soldiers and barely escaping imminent danger. Some years later, I discovered *The Diary of Anne Frank*, which I read over and over again—reading it aloud until I had nearly memorized it. Later in my life, when I developed an eating disorder, I wondered if my starvation was a reenactment of memories of Nazi concentration camps.

My fascination with self-hypnosis blossomed when I was very young. My parents bought us a recording of a Colorado housewife named Ruth Simmons. Hypnotized by a therapist, she began to reveal memories of an earlier existence in Ireland as Bridey Murphy. I listened to this recording over and over again, mesmerized by the techniques used by the doctor and the unusual voice of the young woman in trance. During naptime, I recall sitting on the floor of my room before the window. Without blinking, I would stare at the glass until the window began to move into the distance. I would telescope away from the room, leaving my physical body. I often saw spirits and forms move by me. I heard singing and voices in conversation. I realized later that I was putting myself into a trance.

My parents enjoyed traveling, and took the family on many trips in the States and in Europe. As a child, I was fascinated with other cultures. I got a pair of wooden shoes from Holland when I was in the second grade. I loved these shoes with a passion. One day, I wore them to school for show and tell. I clacked down the hall to my class, out to recess and to lunch. I told the other children about the wetlands of Holland and how the shoes kept their feet high and dry. I felt compelled to tell them that although the children in Holland wore different shoes, they were like us. They had recess, families and pets. At a young age, I felt my mission was to educate people on the similarities among different cultures. For example, when I heard a Polish joke, I would tell the person that Reintjes was a Polish name. It is really a Dutch name, but I was trying to jolt the jokester into an awareness of his put-down. It was difficult for me to understand cultural prejudice and the human tendency to put others down. This calling led me to work with the mentally and physically handicapped during my teens and twenties. Spiritually, I felt a kinship with these special populations. Unable to throw themselves fully into the human game of competition and performance, I found them to be refreshingly open, loving and truly filled with spirit. Although unable to perform certain mental and physical tasks, they were gifted in the areas of faith and compassion.

During college in the early 70s, I began to experience a growing sense of anxiety and insecurity. The walls between my safe inner world and the changing outer world were thinning and rupturing. After gaining ten pounds my first semester in college, I became obsessed with exercise and limiting my food intake. I cut my hair very short and wore little boys' clothes. I was well into my first year of anorexia nervosa before I had a name for my behavior. I stumbled across an article that described me to a T—a sensitive young woman with perfectionist tendencies, often the third child of controlling, intellectual professionals. In the long years after the onset of anorexia and bulimia, I uncovered disturbing childhood feelings and memories. I faced my emotional and physical fear of my father and my distrust of my mother's denial about the family's dysfunction.

It was at this time, I became aware of my psychic abilities. I attended Silva Mind Control, a course for developing intuition. I was intrigued by the exercises, and one in particular caught my interest. We were each given a name of a stranger and asked to describe any impressions of physical ailments. Our partner knew this person and was ready to corroborate our impressions. I closed my eyes to better tune into the man's name. I saw some weakness around the liver and a history of headaches. My partner affirmed that the man had migraines and a history of liver disease. I saw an outline of his body in my mind's eye and the trouble areas showed up as dark, cloudy spots. I was having difficulty focusing in on the right leg of the individual. I frowned and redoubled my concentration, but failed to see the outline of his right leg. Finally, I opened my eyes and said in a puzzled voice, "I can't see his right leg." My partner smiled and said, "That's not surprising. He lost his right leg in the war. He is an amputee." After that experience, my psychic abilities expanded and I began to sense and know events before they occurred. Several weeks after finishing the course, I sat in a booth in a diner. I overheard two women talking about their grandchildren. As one proud grandma rustled in her purse for photos, I had a flash of two small boys named David and Charles. Several seconds after my insight, the woman pointed to the figures in the photo and said, "These are my grandsons, David and Charles." My confidence grew as I experienced more and more psychic incidents.

The next years found me studying French and traveling abroad. I spent two years in France learning the language and visiting other European cultures. I returned to America to complete a master's program in teaching French. I taught French and dance for several years in a private high school. As a youth, I had dreamt of being an interpreter at the United Nations. In a sense, I fulfilled my dream: as a medium I interpret messages from deceased loved ones, dreams, animals and nature. In my own spiritual context, I work to help disparate cultures to communicate and collaborate in the hopes of expanding compassion and unity.

In 1982, I married and discovered the Patricia Hayes School for Inner Sense Development (now Delphi University). I went to a weeklong mediumship training and knew I had found my true profession. My previous years of psychotherapy, meditation and yoga training merged compatibly with the classes on hypnosis, past-life regression, etheric healing and channeling. Several months after completing the intensive mediumship program, I opened the doors to my professional psychic practice. Simultaneously, a flood of psychic events washed into my life.

One event occurred in my first year of seeing clients. I had just completed the advanced study of communication with a discarnate being. I was meditating on my deck and I felt the presence of an elderly man's spirit. He identified himself as the father of a good friend. Although I knew her father was living, I felt this man was deceased. He said he had a message for her and asked if I would act as an intermediary.

Coincidentally, I was seeing her that afternoon. When I saw my friend later that day, I asked about her father. After a heavy silence, she said that he had died suddenly several days before. I told her about his visit and we decided to set up a time to communicate with him in-depth.

We met soon after and established contact by focusing loving attention on her father. She said his name aloud three times. I asked her to remember a loving, connected time with him. We both felt a collective chill as his energy swept into the room. First, he showed me a large, brilliant star of lights. I felt it had to do with Christmastime. My friend knew he was referring to the large star that the town placed on the mountain near their family home each year at Christmas. It is visible every holiday season from their home. He was giving me trivial information that was relevant to the family member to establish credibility. He gave other facts that comforted her and then his spirit quietly left the room. This visit helped to ease the sadness and loss she felt at her father's death. It also confirmed my wishes to practice as a medium and counselor. Another event happened soon after to further confirm my desire to heal.

I was walking through the crowded room of a dinner party when I began to get a strong message about a young couple chatting near the buffet table. I picked up their distress over making a difficult family decision. I was sensitive about approaching strangers with information, but the feelings were overwhelming. I approached and introduced myself as a psychic. Immediately they looked interested and asked me what I sensed about them. I told them that I sensed "a father, an illness and a difficult decision." The woman began to weep as she explained the situation. Her father-in-law was having a mental collapse and they were intervening to get him help. Unable to assess his own need, he was angry and belligerent at this invasion of privacy. On the eve of the intervention, the young couple had begun to doubt that they were making the right decision to force him to receive professional assistance. We found a private spot, and I began to receive information about the root of his mental anguish. I was able to give them historical information that helped them understand his peculiar behaviors. I felt they were right in arranging support for him; however, he needed to feel more informed during this transition. I received suggestions of methods to ease the father's anxiety. The sane part of him was able to tell me clearly what he needed and I was able to relay this to his caregivers. After our talk, the couple felt lighter and more relaxed. Due to their heightened clarity, they were able to communicate more easily with the father and ease the difficult passage. Once again, I felt the strong surge of my purpose to act as an intermediary and facilitate healing.

During this time, I knew that I needed to take a break from teaching school to write a book about healing anorexia nervosa and bulimia. Over the next four years, I compiled my journal writings and healing techniques to complete the manuscript for *The Running Angel—In Search of My Soul.* I balanced a psychic practice with my healing studies, taking my last class when I was several months pregnant with my daughter.

My marriage ended in an affair in the eighth month of my pregnancy. Simultaneously losing my marriage and becoming a mother catapulted me into a profound emotional clearing. Although the symptoms of the eating disorder had been healed, the issues of sexual abuse and abandonment were still salient. These were powerful and painful times—often bittersweet, as cherished moments with my daughter Sarah were fused with the pain and shame of losing my husband. The woman with whom my husband became involved was possessive and unbalanced; so the emotional climate remained highly charged for several years. During these trying years, I needed all of my spiritual connections to support and comfort me. It is true that adversity propels one to greater heights of achievement. Some of my most profound spiritual and psychic experiences happened during this time.

Two years after separating from my husband, my father died suddenly. This event catalyzed even more psychic phenomena in my daily life. I experienced a surge of incidents, including vivid dreams of interactions with my father, electrical anomalies, and unexplained noises in my house at night. During this time, I had a profound meditative experience. One evening while meditating, I felt a strong presence in the room. My father came to me in the form of a spirit holding his empty seabag from his days in the Navy. He told me that much of the shame I felt was from his actions, and he wanted to take it back. I began to sob as I pictured myself filling the seabag with my self-hate, shame and fear. He came often in the first year after his passing to take more of the pain from my psyche.

During this time, I traveled to Lilydale, New York, a unique and quaint town of spiritual teachers and mediums. I was attending a week of workshops while staying at a bed-and-breakfast perched on the edge of the canal. Upon arrival, I went immediately to the daily "meeting at the stump." Outside, under sturdy shade trees, we sat on rustic benches. The summer air was soft and cool as we sat facing the immense tree stump where a medium would stand to talk to deceased loved ones. I was tired from my trip and sat with my eyes closed, breathing deeply, enjoying the gentle breeze and peaceful atmosphere. The male medium arrived, greeted us and closing his eyes began to speak. "I see a man who speaks of his daughter. He has a deep love of books. I see a library filled with books around him." I opened my eyes when I heard this. My dad had died the winter before, and he was an avid reader. President of the local Friends of the Library, he rarely finished a meal without getting up to check a reference book or two.

A woman several rows away said, "It's my father." The medium continued, "I see him speaking of the phoenix rising from the ashes. A new life starting for you after many trials and tribulations. Don't despair, there is light coming for you." Again I sat up taller in my seat. The past several years had been very difficult adjusting to my new life as a single mother and weathering a traumatic divorce. The woman several seats away nodded her head in agreement. The medium stopped suddenly and looked out into the crowd. "Who is Susan?" he called loudly. Stunned, I raised my hand. "This is your father who is speaking." He pointed his finger at me. I nodded in agreement. He then explained a rare phenomenon where two entities will cross their lines of communication and that he could be channeling messages for both of us at once. I left the meeting grateful for my deceased father's continued interest and support in my emotional and physical healing.

My daughter Sarah arrived in my life during this time of deep releasing, opening and healing. The outcome of this timing was a deepened psychic bond that started in utero. I did not have a sonogram to detect the sex of the baby because my dreams and intuition clearly told me that she was a girl. Interestingly, neither my husband nor I could decide on a boy's name, although the name Sarah came immediately and strongly. When I was four months pregnant. I dreamt that I gave birth to a baby girl who spoke to me. Smiling, she looked deeply into my eyes and said, "I am Rising Vectarius." The word Vectarius did not mean anything to me, but I wondered if she was trying to say the astrological sign of Aquarius. The rising sign is the sign on the horizon at the exact time of birth. She nodded when I asked her if she meant "Rising Aquarius." Five months later, five days after her proposed due date in the sign of Capricorn, Sarah was born an Aquarius Sun with Aquarius Rising.

Children are naturally psychic and if encouraged can develop and increase their intuitive abilities. One evening was especially noteworthy. Sarah was eighteen months old and sitting in her car seat in the backseat. We arrived at the mailbox and I reached out and gathered up the few letters and magazines. I flipped through the mail and pulled out a letter from a friend who was visiting the avatar Meyer Baba's home in India. I was excited to get news of his trip. As I opened the envelope, Sarah pointed excitedly to the letter. "Baba! Meyer Baba!" she said distinctly. She knew of Meyer Baba. The office assistant at her father's office was a follower of the Indian avatar and Sarah had learned to say his name when she saw his photo on the assistant's desk. "Yes," I told her. "It is from Baba." I scanned the letter and put it aside to read when I had more time.

The next letter had no stamp or return address—my name was hand-written on the envelope. As I started to open it, Sarah said loudly from her seat, "Kathy!" Sure enough inside there was a card from our neighbor Kathy inviting us to a baby shower for a mutual friend. We then drove the rest of the way home and settled in for the evening. I was in the habit of zoning out by occasionally watching the television show *Wheel of Fortune*. After the intensity of clients and single parenting a toddler, I needed the distraction of a lightweight show. Sarah sat in my lap drowsy from her supper and ready for bed. I had mentally figured out that the puzzle read "Run for your money" and knew that the vowel to buy would be an "o." Just as I thought it, Sarah turned her head and said to me, "O." She repeated it several times as if to be sure I understood and then closed her eyes and fell asleep.

When the psychic circuits are open between two people, the opportunities for telepathic communication are infinite. This intuitive communication continued to grow between us. One afternoon I was in my bedroom chatting with a friend. As I talked, I doodled on a pad resting on my lap. I drew arrows and lines. Then I began to draw a little creature with a slinky, elongated body and a pointed nose. I gave him beady eyes and a black dot nose. I smiled to myself as I looked at the finished product. Five minutes later my young daughter burst into the house. She had spent the afternoon with her Dad and was excited to share her day with me. She bounded into the room and collapsed beside me on the bed. "Look, Mommy! Look what I have!" She held in her hand an exact replica of the very creature I had doodled on my page. Made of orange mesh, the creature was long, slinky and had a pointed snout. Black beady eyes and a dot of a nose completed his portrait. I showed her the doodle and she laughed. "You drew my new toy!" she exclaimed. Distracted by the phone call, my right brain had tuned into my daughter's approach and her excitement over her new toy. There is a natural psychic connection between a mother and her child. If nurtured, the bond can stay strong and build a connecting bridge of support and comfort. Often when I traveled without Sarah, she was comforted by the fact that she could "talk" to me without a telephone and I would answer. We could send psychic hugs and reassuring words back and forth across the miles.

I continued to run my private practice, teach classes on psychic development and related topics and hold a monthly channeling meeting. During the group channelings, I taught various lessons on past lives, inner child work or automatic writing. After the short lesson, I would go

into an altered state to answer questions for the group. The questions
varied from career changes to housing situations, from physical ailments
to financial worries. At times, my students needed important information
or emotional closure with a deceased loved one.

One evening the spirit of a man came unbidden. During a pause in
the individual questions, I felt the strong presence of a large man with a
hat and a hunting gun. I described him and relayed that he had come to
apologize to his daughter who was in the group. There was a heavy
silence and a young woman quietly identified the man as her father who
had died ten years earlier. Since he had come uninvited, I asked her if
she wanted me to continue with the communication. There was a
lengthy pause, and then she quietly said to continue. He proceeded to
apologize for his physical and sexual abuse during her childhood. He
knew that he had caused her great pain that continued to negatively
impact her adult life. He had come to ask if he could help her in her
healing process. The young woman sobbed as the others in the group
drew closer to her for support. The air was electric with the intensity of
the healing. She had kept the abuse a secret, and it was startling and
relieving at the same time to have it known. She did not speak to her
father, she only listened to his message. His energy left the room as
quickly as it had come. His admittance had lightened her load of shame
and guilt. With the secret disclosed, she could now move to a new level
of healing. We all sat stunned and moved by the the unexpected spirit
visitor.

During my workweek, I helped clients deepen their awareness of
issues about work, health and relationships. One fall afternoon, a woman
came to see me regarding her relationships. Her third marriage was ending, and she wanted to understand the unhealthy pattern she kept repeating. Each husband seemed different from the one before yet ended up
exhibiting the same dysfunctional behavior. As I tuned into her energy
by holding her hands, I felt the unfinished emotional work with her first
husband. I questioned her and she spoke lightly of him. "Oh, we're good
friends. Though I haven't talked to him for several years now." I knew
there was much more to the story.

Divorced from him for eight years and having been married twice in
the interim, her energy still seemed consumed by him. I encouraged her
to go more deeply into her true feelings. As she shared more of their
story, she began to realize that she had not faced her true feelings for
him. An "amicable" divorce had ended the marriage, yet she harbored
strong feelings of anger toward him. I helped her voice the anger. She
hated his drinking, his passive aggressive behavior and his affairs. These
behaviors had resurfaced in the men in her two subsequent marriages.

She ranted and raved while I witnessed her venting. She was amazed at how angry she was, and we spent the bulk of the hour releasing the rage. She called me that night with an interesting tale. When she arrived home after our session, there were five messages on her machine. Four of them were from her first husband and they were all made during the time of our session. He said that he did not know why he was calling but that he felt compelled to contact her. He asked her to call him back as soon as possible. After three years of silence he had suddenly resurfaced. On some very real level he felt the power of her communication from my office. We were amused and impressed with the concrete evidence of the psychic power of her words.

In another session, Hillary, a professor at a local university, came to me to communicate with her deceased father. I asked her to picture her father as I held her hands. With eyes closed, I saw an old Ford car and a portrait of Henry Ford. I asked her if this image had any significance to her. She told me that her father owned a car dealership. I then received the image of a rabbit and knew that this pet was very important to her as a child. She smiled and shared with me that she had been stricken with rheumatic fever as a child and her father had brought her the pet rabbit to liven up the sickroom. The bunny had kept her company during the long weeks of convalescence. The next impression was confusing. At first I saw a crescent moon. I asked her if she understood this image, and she shook her head. I closed my eyes again and took a deep breath. Suddenly the image changed into a half moon and then I heard the words "half-pint." She smiled at me with tears in her eyes as she told me that "half-pint" was her father's nickname for her.

This is a good example of the symbolic language of the intuitive mind. During my years in practice I learned to patiently trust and follow the obscure images to find the pertinent information for each client. Often, the clues given were not clear and had to be solved like a mystery. Each day was an adventure, not knowing who would walk into my office. One morning I came out of a session to find a rather dazed looking man in the waiting room. He asked if I was Susan Reintjes and wanted to know the nature of my work. I told him and then asked if he had been referred to me. He paused and explained that he had received my name in a dream—spelled correctly, which is no small feat! He had been directed to get a session. Synchronistically I had an opening that morning and gave him a psychic reading. I was very impressed with his unique method of selecting a psychic counselor.

Life was full with raising a daughter and running a busy practice. Regular massages, swimming, yoga classes and retreats kept me physically and mentally fit. I traveled several times a year with my daughter, one

year swimming with wild dolphins and another visiting the culture of
Bali. Our travel adventures were rich with psychic and synchronous
events. I spent my spare time compiling ideas and techniques into a
manuscript for this book. Due to the personal nature of the writing, my
childhood issues continued to come forth for deeper healing. My mother
and I used this time to work on healing our relationship. Her willingness
to listen to my story and her interest in my psychic work have helped to
keep the channels of communication open. In my daily life I continue to
nurture my relationships with myself, my daughter, family and friends,
clients and community.

Now I stand at the threshold of a new millennium and I feel open and
expectant. Contrary to popular belief, psychics do not always know
what is coming next. So, like the rest of you, I am keeping my inner
senses open to hear my next directives.

Susan Reintjes
Chapel Hill, NC

Introduction

At the turning of the millennium, our spiritual work is intensifying. Like students nearing graduation, our life courses are gaining in difficulty and in number. We are being catapulted into a time of accelerated awareness.

As a spiritual counselor and psychic, I offer insights, teachings, and exercises for completing some of the courses required for graduation— for mastering the millennium with awareness, compassion and strength. As living witnesses to the new age, we each face the challenge of awakening our consciousness in order to bring an integrated, whole self into the twenty-first century.

In spiritual endeavors, the familiar adage, "Old business before new," is apropos. Many of us know that we are repeating old patterns, yet we are uncertain how to break our habits and move forward. In daily life, we are surrounded by many clues and signposts that show us where our particular unfinished business lies. Once we know how to read these signals, we can enliven the unaware portions of ourselves. The third eye, the energy center in the forehead, can read and decipher the signals and symbols around us, bringing us into heightened consciousness. When the third eye is open we can know the future, see secrets about the past and feel the power of the present. This new awareness is vital for assimilating effective patterns for conscious living and relating.

In this handbook, I offer examples of common lessons, including exercises and practices that will help you complete the requisite work. Some courses will interest you more than others. Both your interest and your aversion are guides to what is necessary for graduation. A strong adverse reaction may indicate a particularly important area for you to explore. We are all fortunate at this time to have the opportunity to grow at such an intensified rate, yet the blessing may feel like a curse when we are frightened, overwhelmed and in pain. The dizzying rate of change and our heightened sensitivity collude to increase fear and doubt. In this book, I hope to ease the difficulty by providing guidance and support.

Since the Harmonic Convergence in August 1987, humanity has experienced an acceleration of spiritual growth. Many people's life situations have changed dramatically. The lessons in personal growth are flying thick and fast as we move into the new millennium. We are experiencing firsthand the true meaning of the Age of Aquarius—the astrological sign of individuality and revolution. The success of these changing times is dependent on each of us taking responsibility for this internal uprising. My focus in this book is to direct each individual toward a responsible inner revolution.

The new millennium is ushering in a period of quickened extrasensory perception. We have the opportunity to develop our innate capacity for clairvoyance (clear seeing), clairaudience (clear hearing) and clairsentience (clear feeling). These abilities are present in each of us but lie dormant until awakened and nurtured. Now is a propitious time to begin to develop these other senses.

We are also learning to transcend perceived limits of time, space and matter. We are becoming increasingly aware of the merging of past, present, and future. As we tap into our precognitive talents, we will find it commonplace to access information about future incidents. We will then be able to prethink our reactions to coming events and to choose more evolved responses. Precognitive dreaming will become a routine way to prepare for the future. These same abilities will enable us to recall past lives in order to more fully comprehend our present lifetime.

As we dissolve the former limits of time, we also alter our perception of space. We are realizing that physical distance does not restrict human communication and connection. Distant healing, telepathic communication and communing with deceased loved ones can be daily occurrences. We can access and utilize our psychic e-mail, depending less on external technology. We can merge the best of our intuitive skills with the best of our technological abilities.

Our relationship with matter is also changing. Matter of all kinds seeks interaction and communication. As we acknowledge the interconnectedness of animate and inanimate entities, we can interpret the shifts and conditions of animals, weather, machinery and material possessions. We can receive subtle, and not so subtle, messages from our surroundings as we fine-tune our senses. The more we seek these messages and support, the more we receive them. It is up to us to open ourselves to the infinite associations our world offers us.

By learning and accepting our spiritual lessons, we take a significant burden off our planet and its inhabitants. We have unconsciously asked our world to carry and release our unresolved fears and issues. Pollution, political strife and war are some of the outward manifestations of our inner conflicts and imbalances. The intensification of environmental and political issues is a wake-up call notifying each of us that we need to attend to the storms and battles within. Our collective decision to nurture inner awareness is pivotal in reducing the outer drama on Earth.

As human beings residing on planet Earth, we live in an expansive and complex classroom. The variety of teaching styles and materials is infinite. Our role as students is to use as much of this educational system as possible. The teaching materials are not clearly labeled and waiting patiently on bookshelves, as they are in a regular classroom. The lesson curriculum may await us in a garden, on a highway or in a grocery store. The teacher may be a child, a flat tire or a windstorm. This book will provide you with a tool for recognizing and employing the many resources available to you.

Chapter 1

The Power of the Present

The new millennium is ushering in an intensification of life experiences. Our inner and outer lives reflect an acceleration of growth and change. Many areas of our lives clamor for attention. As technology creates more time-saving devices, we end up spending more time learning how to operate them and having them repaired.

The increasing complexity of living in the twenty-first century is causing our levels of stress to soar. We feel constant and unrelenting pressure to manage our time. We find ourselves rushing unconsciously from task to task in an effort to maintain our schedules. Leisure time is lost in the push to meet our obligations. The inner realms of self-knowledge and emotion are neglected in the drive to meet the physical and mental demands of the outer world.

It is essential that we regain a sense of time and space in our lives. Our well-being depends on a spacious, peaceful environment—inside and out. By being in the present moment, we can find the peace we so desperately seek. By coming completely into the present, we can prepare more fully for the spiritual empowerment of the future.

Breathing into the Present

The more stressed and pressured we feel, the more we tend to hold our breath. Ironically, the opposite is required to maintain a sense of balance and calm. Our instinctual healing energy depends on the unrestrained flow of the breath. When we hold our breath, we diminish our life force.

Breath is the gateway to an awareness of the present. Awareness of the present can stretch and elasticize our sense of time and space. Therefore, by becoming more conscious of our breath, we can expand our perception of time and space.

Awareness of the Breath

Breathing is an automatic biological function. We breathe while awake or asleep, conscious or unconscious. We continue to breathe whether or not we consciously think about it. This physiological fact decreases our awareness of our breath.

Conversely, dolphins breathe consciously. These graceful sea mammals are cognizant of each breath. A dolphin must remember to breathe to stay alive. When a dolphin sleeps, only half of its brain rests. The other half regulates breathing and watches for predators. Because the dolphin stays underwater for extended periods, it learns to take deep, full breaths. It knows how to use its oxygen judiciously. The dolphin can teach us the importance of becoming more conscious of breathing. It is one of the optimal mascots of awareness.

With increased awareness, we can influence how we breathe. We can become conscious of holding our breath when we are stressed or anxious. We can explore our breathing to find areas of the lungs that we ignore. Often we breathe into only a small portion of our available lung tissue. By holding parts of the body tense and tight, we discourage oxygen replenishment of the cells and tissues. The cells become depressed from lack of oxygen. In turn, the mental body feels depressed. Proper use of the breath has the power to positively affect our mental, emotional, spiritual and physical well-being.

Assessing Your Breath

For this exercise, you can sit or lie down. If you sit, be sure your spine is well supported. If you lie down, use a firm, cushioned surface and elevate the head slightly. Be certain that you will not be disturbed. Unplug the phone and alert the household that you will be unavailable.

First, observe your breath. Is it shallow and quick? Slow and regular? Halting? Is it forced? Does the breath go into the belly or into the upper chest? Can you feel any breath in your sides or back? Are you holding your breath? Is there any space or pause between breaths? Find the nature of your breathing at this moment.

At this point, it is not necessary to change the breath. Just observe it and allow it to be. Since emotions ride on the waves of the breath, you may become aware of feelings. Let these feelings be present. Try not to judge or stop them. As you continue to breathe consciously, you will move the emotions through your body.

Following Your Breath

Now follow your breath with your mind. Watch it move in and out of your body. You can follow the breath consciously by saying silently to yourself, "Breathing in, breathing out," as you inhale and exhale. The practice of following your breath is a simple and effective way to relax and calm the body and mind. This technique is helpful in alleviating insomnia and easing chronic pain. Moving the breath opens emotional blockages that cause sleeplessness and pain.

Your mind may try to distract you from following your breath. Notice
and acknowledge any distracting thoughts, then return your focus to the
breath. Keep repeating to yourself, "Breathing in, breathing out." Start by
doing this practice in three to five minute intervals. As you become
more comfortable with the technique, you may extend the time. These
periods of conscious breathing will increase your ability to stay conscious in your daily life.

Altering Your Breath

After assessing and following your normal breathing pattern, you can
begin to explore new areas of the breath. Visualize yourself as a cylinder-
shaped container. A cylinder does not have a front or back. The shape is
equally round and full. This image will remind you to move the breath
equally into the front, back and sides of the torso. Habitually, we breathe
more into the front of our body, neglecting the sides and the back. In a
full and deep breath, you can feel movement in the front, sides and back.

Place your hands on your rib cage and notice where the breath goes.
Notice also where your body does not expand with the breath. Now try
bringing your attention to the parts of your torso that are still.
Consciously move the breath into those parts. Find movement in your
sides and back. Notice if you fill one side more than the other. It is common to breathe into one lung more than the other. Now bring more
breath into the neglected side. Give special attention to filling the back
of your body. The back is often neglected because we cannot see it. It
symbolizes the unknown parts of the self. The more you breathe into the
back of your body, the more you awaken the unconscious.

The Audible Sigh

Sighing is an easy and natural way to release and replenish your
breath. Whenever you feel tense or fatigued, try inhaling fully and releasing the air in a big sigh. Sighing is a physical and psychological signal of
surrender. The audible sigh alerts the senses that you are letting go. In
response, your physical body will begin to relax tightened muscles. Try
vocalizing as you sigh. Notice how your body and psyche feel as you use
sound with the sighing. Try different tones and volumes to see which
sounds help you release the most. Try sighing with your mouth open
and closed to see which feels more relaxing.

Slowing Down Time

The next time you are rushing around and feeling pushed for time, try
to focus on your breath. You may try to tell yourself that you do not have
the time. If you are too busy to take time to breathe with awareness,
then you have lost touch with yourself. Your actions and decisions will

reflect the separation of self. How often have you forgotten your keys, ruined something or hurt yourself in a rush to be on time?

This practice can be done anywhere and anytime. It takes only a couple of minutes. To begin, stop moving and sit or stand still. Let your jaw release so that it opens slightly, and close your eyes if possible. Give yourself time to release three audible sighs and to take five deep breaths. As you breathe you will get more in touch with your current mood and surroundings, thereby reducing the possibility of an accident or a lost temper. Conscious breathing brings you the awareness to move efficiently and gracefully through your day.

Taking Each Step

There are mandatory courses in each lifetime. These are the lessons we keep bumping into no matter how many different roads we take. They will reappear until each step is completed. It is common to try to skip the difficult steps. When we skip a step, however, the lesson eventually returns with more drama and intensity. If we adopt an attitude of taking each step as it appears, we can help reduce the drama and pain of the lesson.

"But I see other people skipping steps!" This is a common expression from spiritual students weary of the continual challenge of accelerated awareness. It is not possible to skip the spiritual steps necessary for growth. We may sometimes postpone them until the lesson returns in a new form to be addressed and mastered. The sooner we choose to take the steps of the present lesson, the more quickly we can complete the course. Answering the following questions will help you complete the steps as they present themselves.

HOW TO BEGIN

1. What am I feeling? Let yourself express your feelings of resentment, fear, resistance or frustration at the steps in front of you. Write, beat or talk out your anger and resistance. Spend some time addressing the feelings stimulated by the present situation. (See chapter 2.)

2. What does this remind me of? Identifying the current lesson can save you time and energy. Search your memory for the last time you had similar feelings in a similar situation. Analyzing the earlier incidents can help you avoid familiar pitfalls.

3. What am I learning? Analyze your present situation. Are you being asked to let go or to take action? To make a move or to stay put? What challenges are you facing in this situation?

4. What am I avoiding? Try to remember when in the past you may have chosen to postpone this step. Be honest with your fears related to this particular lesson. Ask yourself what you fear losing and what you may gain from completing this lesson. Release the feelings that arise. (See chapter 2.)

5. How can I navigate through this lesson? Once you have faced your resistance, you will be given advice to help you complete the lesson. This guidance can come through many sources—dreams, encounters, therapists, television shows, books, animals, etc. Stay open to the countless ways your inner counsel can communicate with you.

The more steps you take, the deeper you go into your spiritual self. Spiritual evolution has no end. The process unfolds and unwinds, taking you deeper and deeper into your soul. Affirming that each step is vital and sacred will help you move to the next level of awareness.

Creating the Day to Come

This exercise is beneficial for changing the habit of projecting negatively on an upcoming event or situation. It is typical for the mind to rehearse the future in an attempt to gain control. Our ego does not like to be reminded that it has little control over major portions of our lives. It therefore creates the illusion of control by running potential scenarios through the mind. The majority of these scenes are negative and disempowering. Rather than focusing on the lack of control we have in determining the future, we can harness our present power to influence the positive charge of life events.

HOW TO BEGIN

Think ahead to a planned event. It can be a meeting, an interview, a doctor's appointment, a road trip or an examination. First, focus on the negative scenario your mind may have created. Write it down to help it pass through your consciousness. You may exaggerate the negative qualities until the scene sounds implausible and ridiculous. In the next step, imagine an ideal outcome. Write it down as you would a short story. Let's look at an example:

* * *

You are nervous about meeting with an angry friend. You begin to rehearse his negative comments and your retorts. You feel the nervous tension in your stomach and the tightness of your jaw. Your body is physically rehearsing the traumatic situation. To interrupt this habitual pattern, you write out the negative scenario followed by a description of the positive encounter.

Negative Scenario: You feel scared and tense. Your friend storms in, yelling. Feeling defensive, you interrupt him and yell back. You both want to be right, but someone has to be wrong and it's not going to be you! If you do feel wrong, you become more scared, more mad. The room feels tense and full of sparks. You resent his anger and want to leave. You want to push him away. You bring up old resentments, and he reciprocates. Nothing gets resolved. You both feel worse at the end of your meeting.

After writing out the negative scene, take some time to vent your feelings. Write out your anger and resentment. Speak to your friend as if he were present, allowing yourself to say whatever you feel. Stay aware of any similarities this relationship shares with past ones. Own your commitment to clear the unfinished business. For further study see chapter 5. Now you are ready to write the positive scene.

Positive Scenario: Breathe deeply. Remember that you are not guilty. Affirm that you are both innocent and both right. Feel calm and centered so you can listen to his feelings and opinions. You do not have to agree, just listen. Breathe deeply and validate his feelings of anger, attending more to how he feels than to what he says. Remember that anger is an expression of fear. Send him love and understanding. If you feel angry, then you are feeling afraid. Comfort yourself. Listen and breathe as you each vent your feelings. Remind yourself that you can always leave if you feel too threatened. Commit to venting your feelings at a later time. The room feels calm and secure. There is a positive feeling of a healing encounter. Listen and breathe to stay centered. You may not even need to talk. Keep repeating silently that you are both right and innocent. You can then state your feelings and needs from a centered, nondefensive stance. You both find a peaceful resolution and leave feeling encouraged about your relationship.

* * *

In the above example, the behavior of the other person is not being controlled. A meeting is made up of two or more people, each of whom contributes to the outcome. However, we can all take charge of our part in any given situation and bring our contribution to the highest level of awareness and understanding possible. We have the power to change our role in an encounter, and our projected expectations can influence the outcome. Often by changing our reaction and role, we can influence how others behave toward us and thus how an encounter ends.

Rehearsing the Future

As we elect to grow and evolve spiritually, we confront uncomfortable and psychologically threatening situations. We are placed in positions that require us to face fears and to master new and difficult behaviors. The following technique is designed to help you rehearse before an actual performance. Interestingly, the physical body does not know the difference between a rehearsal and a performance. Every time we practice a new action, we acquire the confidence that comes from completing an actual performance. The more we rehearse, the more we are able to relax into the role and enjoy ourselves. You can do the following exercise alone or with a trusted friend or therapist.

HOW TO BEGIN

1. Choose an action that is difficult for you to perform.

2. Find a therapist or trusted friend to practice with you.

3. Write or talk out your fears and concerns.

4. Notice any memories from the past that come up as you own your fears. Work with any unfinished emotional business in order to help clear the path for increased self-confidence and self-esteem. (See chapters 2 and 4.)

5. Describe to your partner the negative scenarios running through your mind. She or he can then play any roles necessary to help you face your fears.

6. Allow yourself to try out as many different styles of communication as you wish. You have the opportunity to express many different sides of your personality in a safe arena.

7. Notice your physical body and how it reacts in rehearsal. Keep breathing to help relieve anxiety and tension. Use laughter and humor to lighten the situation. This exercise can easily turn into an improvised comedy routine!

8. Give yourself permission to practice several times before setting up the performance. It is normal to still feel fear and anxiety as you go on stage. Watch how rehearsing changes your performance.

Following is an example of how this technique works:

* * *

Scott is a reliable and hardworking employee who has worked for a sales company for seven years. He received one small raise four years ago. His workload has recently increased, and he feels the need to request another raise. When he thinks about addressing this issue with his supervisor, he becomes anxious and tense. He is afraid he will stammer and stutter and appear incompetent. He is nervous about being turned down, and feels embarrassed and angry. These fears keep him from setting up an appointment with his supervisor. Meanwhile, his resentment is growing and weighing him down. He feels stuck.

Scott decides to talk to his friend, Elaine. He tells her about his fears and needs. Elaine suggests that they role-play the meeting. Elaine will play the supervisor, and Scott can practice asking for the raise. They jot down some ideas before they begin. First, Scott shares the fearful scenes he sees in his mind. They decide to play out the different scenarios to give Scott an opportunity to face his fears.

As they begin, Scott notes how nervous he feels. His heart is pounding and his palms are sweaty. He takes a deep breath and swallows. He tries to speak, but his throat is tight and dry. He remembers feeling this way when he gave a report in fourth grade. He can feel the awkwardness and insecurity he felt as a nine-year-old. Even though he is just practicing, he is amazed that his body is reacting as if he were standing in his supervisor's office. He takes another breath and blurts out his need for a salary increase.

Playing the role of the supervisor, Elaine tries out different reactions—supportive, shocked, withholding and patronizing. Scott practices asking in different ways. Since he is just rehearsing, he is able to let himself try out different scripts. He can be outrageous and bold, quiet and reserved, or angry and aggressive. He experiments to see how the different approaches feel to him. With each practice his body relaxes and opens. By the end of the role-playing he feels more comfortable with the idea of confronting his boss.

The next day Scott is able to set up the appointment. He still feels nervous, but he is surprised at how prepared and confident he feels. The meeting goes well. Even though the supervisor is not able to finalize a raise, she is willing to investigate Scott's situation. She is impressed with Scott's assertiveness and ease. They both leave the office feeling positive about their encounter.

Loving Yourself

Our society is geared toward looking outside ourselves for fulfillment and comfort. We are constantly cruising for an outfit, car or romance to

bring us a sense of completeness. The surge of energy these external distractions provide seems to fill the empty places inside. However, the fix
is only temporary and soon fades, at which point we begin the search
again.

The following technique, which can be done anywhere and anytime, is simple and will help you develop the capacity to fill yourself
from the inside. Self-acceptance is the answer to the yearning for lasting love and security. Since your outer circumstances are constantly
changing and evolving, it is important to have access to a constant core
of self-love.

HOW TO BEGIN

Begin by silently repeating the statement, "I love myself." You may
feel resistance. You may feel as if the words are empty and meaning-
less. You may feel sadness as you remember lost loves and a lonely
childhood. You may feel silly and embarrassed to be actively loving
yourself.

Be aware of any feelings and memories that come up as you continue to repeat the statement. If you need a break, take one and then
return to repeating, "I love myself." It may help to put up reminders.
Write the statement on note cards and place the cards wherever you
can see them daily. For example, place one on your bathroom mirror,
in your work area and on the dashboard of your car. You may want to
mail yourself a loving and supportive card. The more you remember
and recite the statement, the more you absorb the concept.

You may also try reciting the statement aloud. When you are alone
in your car or in the shower, repeat aloud, "I love myself." Try singing it
or chanting it. You can record yourself and listen to your own voice
repeating the words. Relax and remember to breathe in order to allow
the words to penetrate deeply into your unconscious.

The effects of this exercise are deep and lasting. Try to let go of
expectations for immediate results and trust the process. You may be
undoing years and years of separation from the concept of self-love.
You are worth the time, focus and patience this technique requires.

When I Least Expected It...

I began working with the statement, "I love myself," while recovering from my divorce. I spent several years alone, facing the lessons
related to the ending of my marriage. When the intensity of my grief
faded, I felt a longing for a new love. I knew, however, that the timing
was not right for me to begin a new relationship. My longing stemmed

from my need to feel loved and desired, and I knew that my neediness would only result in another unsatisfying relationship. I wanted to find a way to satisfy my need for love from the inside.

When I began repeating the statement, I felt uncomfortable. It felt like a lie. I became more aware of the ways I judged myself. I saw how critical I was of myself and my life choices, and how difficult it was for me to love myself. I noticed how automatically I judged myself for not loving myself! The more I discovered about myself, the more reasons I seemed to find for not loving myself. For months, I kept repeating, "I love myself," through the waves of self-condemnation and judgment. I persisted even though I felt no connection with the concept.

Finally, as I was stretching out before yoga class one day, I took a deep breath to help me relax and suddenly felt a strong and over-whelming wave of love wash over me. I automatically looked up to see if someone had just walked into the class, but there was no one there. The feeling felt familiar, like the heady rush of new love. Yet there was no new love in my life. Or was there? I sat and felt the love move through me, aware of an inner voice telling me I was loved. I felt the joy of a spontaneous hug from a dear friend. After months and months spent repeating the statement, "I love myself," I was at last reaping the benefits.

This experience is a reminder that the dedication and patience required for spiritual growth is worth the effort. The rewards of spiritual growth are often revealed when we least expect them.

This Is a Test. This Is Only a Test...

Life lessons are coming so fast now, that we may feel like batters trying to hit balls from out-of-control pitching machines. We have come to this planet to learn new and challenging lessons, and we must make peace with our mistakes. A person who never errs is repeating old patterns. Mistakes are a sign of moving into uncharted territory. It is through the exploration and navigation of the unknown realms of the soul that spiritual growth occurs.

In a classic *I Love Lucy* episode, Lucille Ball starts her first day at work filling candy boxes on a factory conveyor line. All is well for the first few minutes, until the belt begins to move faster. More and more candies pile up in front of Lucy's station as she frantically tries to keep up with the rapid pace. Unable to do so, she begins to stuff the candies wherever she can—in her bosom, her hat, and even her mouth. When the line supervisor comes by to inspect her work, Lucy is caught trying desperately to succeed in an impossible situation. We all know this uncomfortable feeling.

In many ways we have been put in the same situation as Lucy. We are being asked to handle numerous and complex tasks at a faster and faster pace. The human tendency is to criticize ourself and to judge our performance as lacking. This inclination robs us of the necessary energy and resources needed to accomplish our lessons. The work is hard enough without a critical voice handicapping us.

One prevailing viewpoint of how to get through life is to roll with the punches and move on as quickly as possible after a fall. This approach is not helpful for someone whose goal is to master lessons. For optimal spiritual growth, we must completely traverse difficult passages in order to understand what we are being taught. There is no set amount of time for completing this process. Your soul will know when the lesson is over. It usually takes longer than the ego thinks necessary.

Let's look at a technique for building an inner voice that will validate our hard work:

The Bouncing Checks

I once found it tedious and troublesome to balance my checkbook. Needless to say, I often received overdrawn slips in the mail. Whenever I spied the telltale envelope in my mailbox, my stomach would sink. My pulse would quicken, and instantly a litany of critical words would spill into my mind. "Again! How could you?! You are so stupid! Don't you know anything about being a responsible adult?!" The critical voice was off and running. My self-esteem would dissolve under the barrage of self-criticism.

This pattern happened often enough to make me want to look for another way to react. I knew the fault-finding judgment was inside my own mind, waiting for an opportunity to erupt. Even if I never bounced a check again, I was certain to find myself in another situation that would provoke self-criticism. I began looking for a way to heal the self-judgment.

I realized that every situation is an opportunity to judge or to love. Life is a never-ending series of tests. Fortunately, there is only one answer to every test. That answer is to love oneself in every instant, in every situation. So I devised a card to carry with me to remind myself of this universal truth.

Borrowing the opening statement of the Emergency Broadcasting System, I wrote:

This is a test. This is only a test.

Turning the card over I wrote:

There is only one answer to this test: to say, "I love myself in this instant in this situation." This is the only answer to every test, no matter its form.

Several weeks later, I had an opportunity to try out the card. As I sat by my mailbox holding an envelope from the bank, I immediately started repeating the antidote to my self-judgment. I repeated it over and over again while breathing deeply. I felt myself calm down and relax. I became aware of the many areas of my life in which I was being very responsible and adult. I recalled the many difficult things I had managed to accomplish in recent months, and I was able to give myself credit for what I had done well and to feel proud of all that I had achieved. With support, I could give myself some time to acquire the new skill of balancing my checkbook.

I saw that I was making the banking error more important than my peace of mind. It was important that I take more responsibility for balancing my account, but not at the expense of my self-esteem. I realized that nothing is more important than my peace of mind. Each day I often traded it for little errors and mishaps. It became clearer to me that guarding my peace of mind was crucial to my well-being. I reminded myself that denying mistakes was not the answer. Only through honest and open assessment of my mistakes could I facilitate growth in my weak areas. I realized that I must face the consequences of bounced checks without compromising my self-esteem.

Protecting Your Peace of Mind

Make yourself a "This Is a Test" card to carry in your wallet. Make one for your bathroom mirror, dashboard and computer screen. Try using it the next time you forget an important meeting, scratch a car fender or burn your toast. As you recite the words, your mind will free up energy so that your inner guidance can deal with the situation. This tool does not permit you to abdicate responsibility—rather, it allows you to use your resources creatively in order to solve problems instead of wasting your energy in self-denigration. Give it a try! With practice it will become automatic and bring you a feeling of ease and well-being.

"Are We There Yet?"

It is easy to feel frustrated and disenchanted as we walk the difficult path of accelerated awareness. Just like young children after the first few miles of a long trip, we ask, "Are we there yet?" During my counseling sessions and in talking to friends, I repeatedly hear such heartfelt laments as, "I thought I already did this piece of mother work!" "How can I still be angry at my father?" "Has all this work been in vain?" "I feel more confused and defeated than when I began!"

Many of us have been toiling for years in therapy, and on our own to heal family wounds. We have gone deeply into the psychology of our relationships with our parents and siblings. We have courageously and conscientiously surveyed and studied the ruins of failed projects and relationships. Why, then, do we feel disheartened about our profound journey?

It is very important that we keep our perspective as we travel the path of self-healing. Seeing where we came from and where we are now is paramount. Without this view, we miscalculate the value of our journey. Many of us walking the path of accelerated awareness are asking ourselves to change centuries of entrenched family patterns and beliefs. We are unwilling to follow in our ancestors' footsteps and unconsciously perpetuate the family dysfunction. Instead, we are taking responsibility for our strengths and weaknesses. We are striving to reclaim and responsibly release our emotions. We are working to own our divinity and our shadow. We are facing our childhood shame and pain in order to keep our own children from inheriting it. We are endeavoring to lighten the load for our children by identifying and owning our projections. In short, we have decided to become conscious in the present moment. This is a momentous and daunting enterprise.

The enormity and complexity of this endeavor is one reason that the project of self-healing is taking so long. The fruits of our efforts cannot be realized in a short amount of time. It will take years of remediation to change our unhealthy patterns. Many of us are dedicating our current lifetime to this gargantuan task, hoping future generations will be able to love themselves without effort, and accept their natural inheritance of abundance and health. This brings us back to the questions at hand: What about me? What about my life and all that I have given in pain and suffering to change this world? How much more is there to do? And when do I get to feel the positive effects and rewards?

The rewards are found in awakening to the present moment. Whether it be filled with pain, joy or emptiness, the present holds the key to understanding the human experience. It is all we truly possess. Only in the present can we understand what it is to be human. As we look deeply into the present, our past fears and future goals become unimportant. We are moved to ask ourselves some revealing questions: How can we bring more Spirit into this moment? How can we breathe into our pain and confusion? How can we love ourselves more deeply? How can we understand and accept those who project pain and violence?

We never truly finish our family work or feel human pain for the last time. Yet in each of our encounters, we can endeavor to live in the present as fully as possible. There is no greater purpose for living on Earth than to contribute to our spiritual evolution. By living consciously in the present, we can rediscover the missing core of our humanity. When every human being chooses a path of awareness, universal peace is inevitable.

Chapter 2

Feel to Heal

We have four essential bodies—physical, mental, emotional and spiritual. In our culture we have the tendency to overwork the physical and mental bodies, while disregarding the emotional and spiritual ones. This imbalance is reflected in the proliferation of physical disease and mental imbalances in our society. Cultures that include regular spiritual practices have fewer illnesses and addictions. Likewise, cultures that honor the open expression of emotions have healthier and happier members.

For optimal health, each of the four bodies must operate efficiently and effectively. If one body is underdeveloped, another will pick up the unclaimed work and try to complete it. This results in the weaker body becoming less and less developed, while the rescuing body is overworked and stressed out. Ill-equipped to do the weaker body's job, the rescuing body suffers the consequences. Let's look at two examples:

Jack and Jill

Jack is four years old. Since his mother left him at age two, he has lived with his grandparents. His grandfather is gruff and impatient, spanking Jack whenever he makes too much noise. Jack feels anger and outrage at the spankings. Yet he has learned that freely expressing his feelings leads to more spanking and rejection. He is very fearful of being abandoned a second time, so he learns to swallow his anger and tears. It is not physically safe for Jack to release his emotions, so his physical body holds his emotions for him. Jack learns to hold his jaw and stomach very tight to restrain his hurt and rage. Like a secure bank, his physical body contains the emotions for him. In time, Jack develops migraine headaches and stomachaches. He has frequent nightmares and strongly resists going to his nursery school. In Jack's case, the healthy expression of emotions is arrested and rerouted to his physical and mental bodies.

Jill is seven years old and lives with her parents in a Chicago suburb. She is the only child of a high-powered professional couple. Jill is a sensitive child and has difficulty feeling comfortable in groups. When she talks with her parents about her hurt feelings and misunderstandings she has with her friends, they discount her feelings. Her tears are met with comments such as "That didn't hurt you!" or "Don't be upset about that!" Often in the company of adults, Jill soon learns to sublimate her childish feelings.

In time, Jill cries less and less. Her parents feel proud that she is getting a thicker skin. In reality, Jill has forced her emotions underground. She withdraws from her parents, friends and teachers. She spends more time alone in her own world. She develops chronic bronchitis that often turns into pneumonia. Severe hives accompany the bronchial distress. She hides snacks in her room and begins to gain weight. Her parents are puzzled by her behavior and her illnesses.

In both cases, the healthy, normal expression of emotions is arrested and rerouted to the physical and mental bodies. This indirect approach of dealing with emotions overtaxes these bodies. They are not designed to effectively handle emotions. The resulting stress can cause a myriad of illnesses and imbalances, from migraines to substance abuse. By strengthening the muscles of the emotional body, we decrease unnecessary stress to the other bodies.

The underdeveloped emotional body needs encouragement and support from us to begin to pick up its workload. We need to take the time to clear out the backlog of unresolved emotions. We need to practice skills that increase our awareness of our emotions and give us safe, responsible ways to release them.

Opening the Emotional Body

One of the first steps in learning to identify your emotional state is to check your current range of emotions. Write a list of the emotions which you are able to express with relative ease. Upon completing this list, notice which emotions are missing. Often people list anger as relatively accessible, while sadness does not show up at all. Conversely, some list sadness as a commonly felt emotion and anger as inaccessible to them.

Use the list of emotions below to answer the following two questions:

1. Which emotions do I commonly feel?

2. Which emotions do I rarely or never feel?

List of Emotions

abandoned	happy
accepted	hate, hated
accused	hopeless
angry	hurt
anxious	inadequate
appreciated	incapable
bored	joyful
blamed	left out
capable	love, loved
comfortable	miserable
confident	pleased
defeated	proud
desperate	put down
disappointed	rejected
discouraged	relieved
disrespected	respected
dominated	revengeful
doubtful	sad
embarrassed	satisfied
encouraged	stupid
enjoyment	unfairly treated
excited	unhappy
frightened	unloved
grateful	worried
	worthless

All Emotions Are Equal

Let's examine your judgments of emotions. In truth, all emotions are created equal. There are no good or bad emotions. Emotions are natural human reactions to situations. They are not logical or predictable. A chapter in a book makes one person cry, another laugh and leave another completely unaffected. The same chapter in the book makes you cry, laugh or feel unaffected, depending on your mood when you read the chapter.

It is not possible to do away with emotional responses to life. However, we can identify and clarify our feelings to allow healthy expression. Many of our current emotional responses are the result of a backlog of unexpressed feelings from the past. We suppress emotions that we judge or fear. Let's begin by looking at our biases and opinions of different emotions:

HOW TO BEGIN

1. Choose an emotion that is difficult for you to express. Write down your feelings and opinions of the emotion. For example: "Anger is dangerous." "Anger is unnecessary." "Anger is weak." "Anger is unladylike."

2. Consider your childhood and what you learned about the feeling. For example, you may have witnessed a parent who used anger excessively and destructively.

   Conversely, you may have had caregivers who did not express anger.

   Note any beliefs that prevent you from accessing the emotion.

3. The next step is to neutralize your prejudice or fear about a particular feeling.

Write the following affirmations as many times as needed to change your prejudice.

All emotions are equal.
There are no good or bad feelings.
All feelings are created equal.
It is safe and healthy to express all of my feelings.
I have a right to feel all of my feelings.

Finding Your True Feelings

A fundamental step toward free emotional expression is an honest, candid assessment of your feelings for your family. Your childhood experience may have been very different from that of your siblings, relatives and friends. Your unique role is valid, shaped by many factors, including your temperament and position in the family. It may be difficult at first to uncover your true feelings. Be patient with yourself during this process.

Let's look at an example. Mariah is an independent and capable woman with a shy, sensitive nature and a good sense of humor. She had been coming to me intermittently, along with her mother, to do grief work for her brother who died of AIDS several years before. However, this visit was not about her brother. One month earlier, her mother had died unexpectedly, leaving her without a family. Her father, also dead, was physically abusive in her childhood. We had been addressing her issues of trust ruptured by the childhood abuse. Our work included my witnessing some of her early traumas. She recounted one dramatic evening when she had stopped her father from striking her mother with a metal poker. Twenty-two at the time, she remembers hanging onto the metal rod with superhuman strength to protect her mother from the blow. Her tenaciousness was fueled by a terrifying memory when she was fourteen. She found her mother on the floor, her leg twisted in an abnormal way. In a fit of temper, her father had knocked her mother out and broken her leg. When she saw her mother lying unconscious on the floor, she thought she was dead. This terrifying memory gave her the strength to protect her mother from her father at any cost.

We talked about the rage and fear that comes from being put in this untenable situation. No child should have to think of protecting a parent, especially from her other parent. She had unreleased rage at both parents. She was articulate and clear about her rage at her father. It was still very difficult for Mariah to feel angry at her mother, who had been victimized with her. We had been in session for half an hour when I felt an urge to light the candle on the coffee table beside us. I continued listening as I lit the white candle. We were discussing her father's ashes which she kept in the garage. She explained that she did not want them in her house. Suddenly the power in the building went out. Except for the warm glow of the candle, we were plunged into darkness. We went to the window and looked at the bright lights of the neighboring buildings. We alone had lost power. We both felt a chill move through the room. I quickly asked Mariah if she felt comfortable continuing our session. She nodded, her eyes wide with intensity. I felt we had the opportunity to release some of her pent-up feelings. Her father's presence was strong. She was able to confront him, telling him things she had been unable to express years before because of his dangerous temper. Her inability to confront him directly had left her shy and reclusive. This evening she faced him with power and dignity. She gave him back his shame and abuse. At the end of the session, we walked down the darkened stairwell together. In our silence we shared the power of the experience. As I hugged her good-bye, I was struck by her courage and willingness to delve into these painful memories.

A sensitive child can sense and identify weaknesses and imbalances in others. If you are particularly sensitive, it is important that you honestly express your impressions of your parents' actions. Look at the content of your dreams as well as your gut instinct in order to help you know your true feelings and impressions. The following exercise will help you make an honest assessment of childhood feelings:

HOW TO BEGIN

This exercise will begin to open your cellular memory of your relationship with a parent or caregiver. Your cellular memory is the body memory. Your physical body remembers every experience, even the ones your conscious mind forgets. This physical ability to recall is amazingly accurate. Your cellular memory bank will remember the anniversary of a trauma, even if the event happened many, many years earlier. Your body memory and its accuracy can help you retrieve painful or scary memories about your childhood. Body memories that are not remembered and released can cause physical and emotional disease and imbalance. The suppression of the truth about your early life can cause you to live a life of secrets, lies and pain.

1. Take a sheet of paper and put your father's (or mother's) name at the top. Then begin writing your thoughts and impressions of him (or her). Do not worry about grammar or content. Write anything that comes to mind.

2. Notice how your body feels as you remember your father (or mother). The feelings may be pleasant or discomforting. Notice any areas of physical tension or discomfort. Note these areas of your body on the paper as well.

The most important ingredient in reworking your past is a willingness to remember. When you state your desire and intent to retrieve your truthful past, your body, psyche, emotions and soul will work together to aid you. Express your willingness to remember and you will. For further study see chapter 4.

Feeling Sadness

In general, sadness is more accessible to women than to men. In our society, men are discouraged from displaying sadness. It is judged as a feeling that reflects weakness and ineffectuality. Men have been conditioned to sublimate sadness at a high cost to their health and intimate relationships. It takes a tremendous amount of energy to suppress feelings. Emotions are designed to move through the body and mind. Men and women who wish to access their sadness more easily will benefit from the following practice:

HOW TO BEGIN

Find a quiet, safe place where you can lie down undisturbed for thirty minutes. Take a blanket and fold it in quarters. Then, roll up the blanket. You can also use a rolled bed pillow. Lie on your back over the roll, placing it crosswise directly under your shoulder blades. Place a small pillow or support under your head if you feel discomfort in your neck. You may also place a rolled pillow under your knees if you feel any discomfort in the lower back. This position will open the chest and allow oxygen to move into the upper lung area. Most of the day you spend leaning forward in a position that collapses the chest. This posture closes the emo-

tional center and depresses your ability to feel. You breathe more shal-
lowly and your cells receive less oxygen. Laying over the roll increases
your oxygen intake and helps release held emotions. If you like, put on
music that touches you and opens your heart.

Stay in the open-chest position for at least five minutes. You may feel
vulnerable and exposed at first. You may feel frightened or tearful. You
may not experience any particular emotions. Stay with any feelings that
may arise. Remember that feelings are transient. They move in and out
of the body like ocean waves. They are designed to cleanse and refresh
the psyche and then move back out to sea. When you are ready, roll to
your side and use your hands to help you sit up.

You may wish to write about what you discovered during this exercise. Notice how your body and your mind feel after the release. You
may note that you feel more relaxed or more energized. The resulting
openness may feel peaceful or frightening. There is no correct reaction.
Whatever you feel is the right response for you. This exercise is a very
powerful one to do before going to sleep and will stimulate dreams to
clear and heal your emotional body.

Another way to begin accessing your sadness is to watch movies. You
can rent a sad movie that will help you cry and release. Many men who
never cry will sometimes cry at a movie. Books and music also help
access hidden sadness. Conscious release of sadness brings you new
energy and vitality.

Expressing Anger

Contrary to sadness, anger is usually more accessible to men than
women. Our society has supported the male expression of anger as
strong and powerful, yet tends to label angry women as hysterical or
bitchy. Because of this societal conditioning, women may cry, become
depressed or overeat rather than express their anger. Depression, excessive guilt and shame are symptoms of suppressing angry feelings. Men,
on the other hand, may express anger irresponsibly by dumping their
rage on others. In either case, the responsible identification and release
of anger is a necessary step in clearing your physical and mental bodies.

For people who have a fear of expressing anger, it may be important
to have a witness during this exercise. If adults used anger excessively
and abusively in your childhood home, you may have stored fear on top
of your angry feelings. The projection of excessive anger can feel like
imminent death to a child. The child's survival instinct will suppress the
expression of anger to prevent increased abuse or even death. These
deep fears may arise as you begin to access your anger.

HOW TO BEGIN

Choose an incident, distant or more recent, during which you felt angry. It is fine to use a current situation. There are several ways to begin. You may want to take pen and paper and begin writing down your outrage. Write as fast and furiously as you want. Write large and bold. Use any profanity or forbidden words that come to mind. You may scribble with the pen, making slashes and illegible marks. Let the pen and paper receive the rage. Write for as long as you feel the anger. Write the same feelings over and over again if you wish. The purpose of this exercise is to get the rage out of your mind and body.

You can also use playdough to release pent-up anger. Squeeze the dough with your hands or make a figure and pound it. Make balls of dough and throw them. For further release, gather a large pile of used magazines. Sit on the floor in a private space. Close your eyes and focus on your anger. Feel your anger as you rip and tear the magazines. Use words or angry noises to help you get the feelings out of your body. Try to tear the magazines whole. The magazines' resistance can sometimes stimulate frustration and help you release. Do not worry about the mess and disorder. Let the child in you indulge in a tantrum without the thought of cleanup. If crying is an easy emotion for you and you begin to cry, take a few breaths and redirect your feeling to your rage. If sadness is difficult for you to feel and you begin to cry, then let yourself cry for as long as you can.

You can also use a soft, cushioned area for beating, using your fists or a rolled magazine. You may feel self-conscious and uncomfortable at first. You may not feel any anger when you first try the beating. Just keep going through the motions of releasing anger. Your physical body will appreciate the release.

When you are finished, let yourself feel the effects of the work. Feel the increased circulation in your arms and hands. You may feel lighter, more alive and more relaxed. Your chest may feel more open, and it may feel easier to breathe. If you feel fear, reassure the frightened inner child that it is safe to express anger. It feels good to release stored anger from the body.

Healing Shame

Shame: A painful emotion caused by a strong sense of guilt, embarrassment, unworthiness, or disgrace.

Diary Entry, Age 36

In shame, the soul burns slowly and deeply. I have not felt a sharper, more debilitating, and unrelenting pain. I cannot get away from

*it—even in my sleep shame directs my dreams. My hideaway from
shame is unpredictable—my cover can dissolve or crumble in an
instant and leave me exposed, raw and visible. Sunburned in the
desert. Shame is setting me on fire—any daily event, innocent com-
ment or chance meeting can spark the flame. And I am torn—
between nursing the flame of shame or rescuing myself from its
unbearable heat.*

In considering the definition of shame, I note the word, "disgrace."
This word means "without grace." By its very definition, shaming means
to take away the possibility of grace. Grace is the divine and enduring
quality of forgiveness and ease that accompanies every situation. There
are no exceptions to the presence of grace. Everyone in every situation
is automatically granted this gift. It is no wonder that a shamed child
grows into an adult afraid to face responsibility, risk and change. In a
world without grace, the stakes seem too high.

The expression "Shame on you!" is usually accompanied by a pointed
finger and a disapproving look. It may also be followed by physical or
emotional punishment. In the past, shaming was an accepted parental
response to any behavior that was deemed unacceptable or inappropriate. It was believed that shaming a child was an effective tool for changing the child's behavior. We have subsequently discovered that shaming a
child produces low self-esteem, embedded feelings of worthlessness, and
a fear of risk-taking and commitment in adult life. Shaming is not a beneficial parenting tool. It is important to give your child and others in your
life feedback about disrespectful or harmful practices, but this can be
done without shame and personal denigration.

Everyone, adults and children, makes mistakes. We forget rules, we
project our fears, we act from our egos. As we model appropriate behavior for our children and give them nonshaming feedback when they
make mistakes, they will discover an inner system of loving and responsible actions.

The Bucket Theory

There is good news in dealing with the healing of your shame. The
bucket theory states that there is a limited amount of stored shame from
your past. As you begin to release your feelings of shame, you may feel
that you are made of shame-filled cells. You may feel as if there is no end
to the shame. This is an illusion. There is a bottom to the bucket.
Through consistent and focused release, you can empty your body of
shame.

The Sponge Theory

The sponge theory states that a child acts as a sponge, soaking up other people's shame. If shaming was used in your childhood family, you acquired shame at an early age. You may have developed a sense of sexual shame long before you were developmentally capable of knowing your sexual self. You may be ashamed of your appearance based on your parents' prejudices and judgments. Soaking up the shame around you is a learned behavior and can be unlearned. You can rework the past to uncover the shame of others. Then you can consciously return the shame and consequently squeeze out the sponge of shameful feelings. Let's look at an example:

* * *

When I was about seven years old, I asked a young neighbor boy to come to our house to take a bath. He lived in a small house with no indoor plumbing. When I heard that he had never taken a bath in a tub with running water, I was excited to be able to share this wonderful experience with him. Taking baths was one of my greatest pleasures as a child. In my excitement I did not think to ask my mother's permission. I thought she would want this child to have this pleasurable experience.

I brought him into our house and ran a warm tub. We began to play. Five minutes into the bath my mother came into the bathroom. She became very upset and quickly got me out of the tub, swatting me on the bottom. The frightened neighbor boy hurriedly gathered his clothes and rushed out. I remember feeling shocked and ashamed. I felt bad for my friend, who was sent away in disgrace. All at once I felt a flood of shame for my nakedness and my desire to share joy with my friend. I cried for both of us. I felt I had done something very wrong.

In truth I had done something very loving and thoughtful. I had extended a gift to a friend. My mother's sexual discomfort was projected onto our innocence and sharing. I remember many times when innocent actions were interpreted as wrong and shameful by others. Unable to see the projection of shame, I took it on as my own. It has taken me years to sort out my shameful experiences. Now when I feel shame, I repeat the following statements:

I have done nothing wrong.

My intention is loving.

This person may feel shame and fear.

I have no reason to feel ashamed.

Healing Shame

Shame is healed by moving deeply into your feelings. Shame is painful to feel because it includes self-hate and self-judgment. Remove the self-hate and you discover a clearer feeling, such as anger, rejection, frustration or grief. Shame thrives on feelings of worthlessness. Since your worthiness is a constant, unchanging variable, shame is based on an illusory principle. Try going deeper into your feelings to find the emotion underneath the shame. It is most likely a feeling that is threatening to you. Underneath the shame and guilt, you often find fear, anger or grief.

Note: It is true that sometimes feelings of guilt and shame come from irresponsible or inappropriate behavior. In these cases, guilt and shame can help us realize that we have hurt another person and that we need to alter our behavior. The following exercise is specifically designed for feelings of guilt and shame that do not stem from behavior that hurts another:

HOW TO BEGIN

This exercise helps you identify and release feelings of shame. Have a pen and paper nearby so you can take notes. Find an incident in your life in which you felt shamed. It can be direct shaming by someone or an embarrassing situation. It is important that you allow yourself to feel some of the body symptoms of shame. You may feel flushed, hot or itchy. You may feel uncomfortable in your body and want to hide. As you remember and replay the shaming scene, try to remember the original feelings. If your memory is sketchy, imagine how you might have felt. Play the scene as if you were in a drama class.

Next, breathe into your feelings of shame. As you breathe, go deeper into the incident. Ask yourself what other feelings are present. Give yourself permission to feel the emotions underneath the shame. Do you feel hurt, sad, angry or confused? Do you feel misunderstood, trapped or put down? Use the "List of Emotions" on page 32 to help identify your feelings. Write down any feelings that arise. Let yourself experience them. Cry, rant or complain aloud or on paper. If appropriate, return any feelings directly to others involved in the incident. Use your statements to return the shame. (See chapter 4, "The Blame Stage.")

Let's look at the bath incident from my childhood. After the incident, I felt ashamed and embarrassed about my behavior and my actions. As I replay the scene, I feel anger at my mother for ruining my innocent, enjoyable time. The healthy feeling underneath my shame is rage at my mother for spoiling the bath. To heal the memory of the bath incident, I directed my rage and disappointment at my mother through writing, talking and beating a pillow. My writing and speaking included such statements as: "You were uncomfortable with the bath. We weren't!" "You felt shame, not us!" "You felt embarrassed, not us!" and "I give you your shame, to feel and heal. It's not mine!" As I released my internalized rage, I reclaimed the innocence of my experience.

Use this exercise to reclaim any memories bound in shame. You do not need to directly confront the person responsible for the shaming. A therapist or trusted friend can act as a witness. You deserve to clear the shame, to preserve your innocence and reclaim your peace of mind.

Take and Retake

Mistake: A misconception or misunderstanding.

Retake: A subsequent filming, photographing or recording undertaken to improve upon the first.

Many of us grew up in households where projected blame and shame were prevalent. A mistake, which is a natural outgrowth of any learning situation, became a negative and painful experience. Therefore, we learned to associate the word "mistake" with feelings of failure and shame. Now when we make a mistake, we may feel anxious and embarrassed. Since mistakes are a major part of any new learning experience, we may become reluctant to try new ventures for fear of shame. If so, then we are unable to initiate change in our lives.

In looking at the dictionary definition of the word, I realized that a mistake is not intentional, shameful or bad. I always felt I should have been able to prevent any mistakes, that I should have somehow known better in each case. However, in every learning situation there will be misinterpretations and misunderstandings. There will also be trial and error. So I have chosen a new word to describe a mistake: a retake.

In the movie industry, the filming of a new scene opens with the expression, "Take one, take two, etc." You have the same license to try a "scene of life," then replay the scene as many times as you like until you are satisfied with the outcome. If the word "mistake" is a loaded word for you, try to use the concept of retake. Give yourself permission to have retakes in your life.

The process of making a mistake means that you are trying new behaviors and taking risks in your life. It is easy to avoid mistakes if you are repeating familiar experiences and not challenging yourself in new situations. Every time you make a mistake, you can be proud of your courage and initiative to expand your scope of life experiences.

* * *

Your feelings are a crucial barometer for helping you discern life situations. Feelings are not logical or rational, but they are always honest. Take time to know and release your feelings. Your physical and mental bodies will appreciate the lightened load. Your emotional body is highly equipped to handle the most intense and complex of emotions. As you access your feelings, your capacity for joy and peace will naturally increase.

Chapter 3

The Body as Messenger

When the emotional body cannot freely express itself, the physical body incorporates the unresolved energy. It handles the misplaced emotional energy the best it can. Since the physical body is not designed to manage feelings, physical symptoms often develop. We can learn to interpret these symptoms in order to rediscover the original unresolved emotions.

Consider the physical symptom as a messenger who knocks on the door to deliver a message. The message identifies emotional energy that needs to be acknowledged and released. If we ignore the messenger, he will knock louder and louder until we answer. If necessary, he may knock down the door to get our attention.

Let's see how this relates to physical symptoms. If we get a headache or stomachache, we often take a pill to suppress the pain. We seldom take the time to uncover the unresolved emotion underlying the physical symptom. When we do not attend to the symptom, the messenger may increase the intensity and severity of the symptom to get our attention. For example, the headache may turn into a migraine or the stomachache into an ulcer. Often we use medication or surgery to suppress the symptom, once again missing the message. The messenger moves from one body part to another until the message is received. The messenger has one goal—to deliver the message. If we can consciously receive the message, the messenger/symptom can go away. Through learning to listen to the body, we can learn to decipher our own symptoms and develop a unique "body dictionary."

One of the best works in this area is Louise Hay's book, *Heal Your Body*. She has developed a detailed dictionary to help us understand and interpret our symptoms. I highly recommend this book for further study.

Let's look at some interpretations for specific body parts. Use the following ideas to help you go deeper into the symbolic representations of your physical symptoms. Add your own ideas to create a personal body dictionary.

Body Dictionary

Brain: Represents the seat of thought and beliefs. Problems may indicate confusion in your thoughts or belief system. Do your beliefs represent who you are? Were you fed truths or lies about yourself and your purpose? Does your life reflect your beliefs?

Ears: Represent listening and hearing. Problems with hearing may indicate resistance to hearing the sounds around you. Are you afraid to hear some news? Are the people around you yelling at you or putting you down?

Eyes: Represent "I"-dentity. The left eye can represent your feminine identity, and the right eye, your male. Eye infections can reflect hidden shame or guilt. Problems with visual acuity may indicate a fear of seeing a life situation clearly.

Sinus: Represents emotional expression and release. Blocked sinuses can be a result of blocked expression—creative or emotional. Indicates a need to cry or have a tantrum. May deal with issues of self-esteem and not feeling good enough. Sinus pressure may represent external pressure needing to be alleviated. Are you being pressured at work or in a relationship? Are you pressuring yourself unnecessarily?

Throat: Represents the avenue of verbal expression. Are you holding back words or feeling guilty about words spoken? Are you holding in your power? Problems may signify frustration in creative and emotional expression.

Neck: Represents your ability to see many sides of a problem—support for your belief system. Are you being rigid about a situation? Is your pride holding you hostage? Are you resisting seeing the whole picture? Are you in a situation that gives you a "pain in the neck?"

Shoulders: Represent responsibilities and duties. If tight and sore, are you carrying more than your fair share of responsibility at work or in a relationship? Can also represent needing protection from a fearful situation or person. Are you feeling scared, anxious, or defensive?

Back: Represents the main support of the body. Problems may indicate lack of support as a child. Lower back pain can be fear of lack of finances. Are you feeling abandoned and left out in the cold? Are you feeling unable to support yourself? How can you build more support into your present situation?

Breasts: Represent the tender, vulnerable parts of self, as well as the mothering instinct. Problems may indicate resentment or hurt from relationships. Do you need to actively release resentment from the past? Are you overnurturing others and neglecting yourself?

Arms: Represent your ability to give and receive as well as manipulate your environment. Are you overworked and underpaid? Is it difficult for you to give or receive? Do you feel frustrated in your present situation?

Hands: Represent creative expression and labor. Problems may show frustration in creative expression or overuse of hands for work and labor. Do your hands like what they do? Do your hands have time to play? Are you trying to control a situation that is out of your control?

Skin: Represents the outer boundary of the body—the largest sense organ. Rashes may signal unexpressed anger and irritation. Is someone getting "under your skin"? Blemishes can signal unresolved shame rising to the surface to be cleared. Hives and allergic reactions reveal the need to clear the body of old shame, anger and fear.

Stomach: Represents the center of power and manifestation in the world. Problems may indicate fear of expressing power in the world. Is it safe for you to powerfully express yourself in your current job or relationship? Are you overworked or being exploited in a situation? Are you having trouble digesting an idea?

Intestines: Represent assimilation of ideas and experiences. Problems indicate deep-seated fear and holding. Are you feeling worthy of being nurtured? Are you facing a fearful situation? Are you having difficulty digesting changes in your life? How can you encourage feelings of safety in your present life?

Bladder: Represents release of toxins. Problems may come from holding feelings inside, especially anger. Are you pissed off, and do you need to responsibly release your anger?

Hips: Represent the joints for moving forward in life. Problems may arise when you feel held back or afraid of change. Are you afraid to risk moving forward? Are you reluctant to leave old jobs or relationships that no longer fit? How can you build trust in yourself to support stepping out into the future?

Prostate: Represents support for male creative power. Problems may indicate frustrated or shut-down creative expression. Can you give yourself permission to explore and enjoy your creativity? Can you relax the drive to produce and allow your creative expression to flow?

Uterus: Represents the seat of female creative power. Problems may indicate difficulty manifesting powerfully in the physical world. Are you longing to express creativity in the world? How can you take steps to manifest your creativity in the physical world?

Legs: Represent self-sufficiency and support. Left leg can be feminine support, and the right leg, masculine support. Problems may arise from lack of childhood support. Do you feel overwhelmed by adult responsibilities? Can you allow others to help you get back on your own two feet?

Feet: Represent your understanding. Problems may indicate changes in your vision of yourself and your life. Are you feeling understood? Examine your connection with the earth—your groundedness. Are you feeling spacey and disconnected from the people and events around you?

Communication with Your Body

*The technique described below is not recommended to replace traditional or alternative medical advice and support. For best results, follow your usual medical routine while you are using this technique.

The body is our vehicle of mobility, communication and manifestation on the physical plane. When the physical body is symptomatic, it is asking for attention and support. We can learn to communicate with the physical body, to understand our symptoms and correct any imbalances. First, we must examine the symptom. Common everyday expressions such as "pain in the neck" and "thorn in my side" can hold clues about the message of the symptom. Next, we need to communicate with the symptomatic part of the body. Finally, we endeavor to fulfill the needs revealed by the analysis. Let's look at an example of one of my reoccurring symptoms:

* * *

In my thirties, I developed chronic bladder infections. I had a childhood history of bed-wetting and frequent urination. This childhood symptom later transformed into painful bladder infections. As a child, I learned to keep my anger inside. In my attempt to be a good girl, I repressed any expression of anger. The repressed anger was stored in my bladder. Because I was unable to express how pissed off I felt, my bladder was literally burning with anger. In my thirties, when I felt an infection setting in, I would communicate with my bladder through writing. Invariably, my bladder felt angry. I wrote pages and pages, cursing and blaming. I would release my anger by beating on the bed and ripping magazines. I threw glass into the recycling bin with angry words. I yelled, screamed and cried out my rage. As I released my anger, my bladder sometimes worsened temporarily. As if riding the wave of my anger release, my bladder would get hotter and hotter. After the release, the symptoms would begin to subside.

I combined the emotional release, with soothing drinks of lemon water or hot water with onion slices. I took cranberry capsules and sometimes an antibiotic if infection was evident. Weekly acupuncture and Chinese herbs helped strengthen the chi, or energy, of my bladder and kidneys. Through writing, I reassured my inner child that she had every right to be angry, and I encouraged her to get the anger out of the body. I did anger-release exercises regularly. (See chapters 2 and 4.) Over time I had fewer and fewer infections. Occasionally, I experienced the symptoms without coming down with an infection. Eventually the bladder symptoms stopped altogether. I now feel a subtle tightening or warming of my bladder whenever I need to release my anger. If I ignore my feelings, I will feel a painful twinge or strong pressure in my bladder.

When you take time to listen to your symptoms, they begin to speak more softly. It is wise to attend to minor symptoms as if they were serious. This practice can reduce the necessity of a severe physical symptom in the future. Remember, once the message is delivered, the messenger/symptom can leave.

Exploring the Symptom

1. Write down the symptom.

2. Note the part of the body involved.

3. Note the nature of the symptom. For example, is it a break, a fever or a rash?

4. Write down any thoughts that come to you about the body part and the nature of the symptom.

5. Do not censor your thoughts. Write down anything that comes into your mind. Your intuition knows how to heal the symptom. If reoccurring, write down the history of the symptom.

Let's look at the example of my bladder infections:

Listening to the Bladder

1. Bladder infection

2. Bladder, urinary tract

3. Infection, burning sensation, aching, pressure, constant urge
   to urinate.

4. Pissed off, losing control of bladder. Infection is hot and burning
   inside my body. No one can see how uncomfortable and angry I am.
   I can't sit still. I feel urgent, anxious and desperate. I feel I can't
   stand the pain any longer.

5. Anniversary of husband leaving me when I was eight months pregnant. Feeling the pressure of the baby on my bladder. Feeling helpless and powerless. Feeling I have to hold my anger to get through
   the birth. I feel as if I cannot hold the anger any longer. I need to
   get my anger out of my body. I'm tired of hurting inside and pre-
   tending everything is okay when it's not.

Use this example to gather information about a current physical
symptom. Each symptom tells a story. Follow these simple steps to
reveal the message of your symptom.

Dialoguing with Your Body

The symptom is a messenger. Once you are familiar with the symptom, you can dialogue with the body. Active communication signals the
physical body that you have received the message and the symptom can
subside. Let's go back to the example. After I write about the bladder
infection, I dialogue with my bladder.

> *Dear Bladder,*
>
> *I know that you are hot, swollen and in pain. I appreciate your
> holding rage and hurt for me. I know that you are not equipped
> to do this any longer. I want to express the anger and get it out
> of my body. I want to feel my feelings and give you a break.*
>
> *Thanks again for reminding me I had not finished this emotion-
> al piece. I was scared to release so much hurt and anger during
> my pregnancy and labor. I know it is time to release the feelings.
> I appreciate all you do to keep my body healthy and free of
> waste. You deserve to feel ease and comfort in your job.*
>
> *Is there anything else I need to know to help you get well?*
>
> *love, Susan*

After asking this question, I sit quietly and wait. I feel my bladder
tighten. I pick up my pen to write the words I hear: mad, mad, I hate
you, angry, angry. I write until the feelings subside. I feel my bladder
request regular anger-release work. I respond with the promise to regu-

larly release my anger through ripping magazines and beating on the bed. I feel how I unconsciously held my anger by tightening my bladder. I resolve to become more conscious of the holding and breathe relaxation into the bladder area. I thank my bladder for temporarily storing anger for me. I commit to the regular release of my anger.

Body Wisdom

Your body wants to communicate with you to heal physical symptoms. Allow yourself to take time to listen to the messages of your symptoms. Sit quietly and listen. Write down anything that comes to you. You may be surprised and amazed at the information you receive. Watch for dreams about your symptoms. Write them down and work with them. You may remember hurts and fears from the past. You may have insights about your future. Your body is trying to help you heal and grow through the symptoms. Communicate with your body, and you will find a wonderful resource of profound information about your true self.

Coming Home to the Physical Body

Disassociate: To remove from association; to separate.

The physical body houses your soul. It acts as a physical protector and shelter for your psyche. It also serves as a vehicle for moving you through the physical world. Just like your house and your car, it requires regular maintenance and attention. If you leave your car by the side of the road or your house unattended for long periods of time, they fall into disrepair. It is the same with your physical body. There are many reasons to disassociate from certain parts of the physical body. Injury, illness, impairments, shame, abuse and cultural taboos can discourage active communication with specific body parts. It can be painful and frightening to reassociate with alienated parts of your physical body.

This next technique will help you take an inventory of your physical body. You can become more aware of the parts of your body that need care and attention. I recommend using an anatomy book or other resource to help you visualize and connect with different organs and systems of the body. *The Anatomy Coloring Book* by Wynn Kapit and Lawrence M. Elson is designed to encourage a deeper understanding of the body. The more you associate with your physical body, the healthier you become.

HOW TO BEGIN

1. Take a pen and paper. Find a quiet space where you can feel safe and undisturbed. Take a few deep breaths and sighs to let go of your active mental thoughts. You are taking time to associate with your physical body.

2. Begin with your feet. Look at your feet and write down any feelings you may have about them. You can include your likes and dislikes. Note any injuries or problems with your feet and toes. Notice any difference in the right and left side. Acknowledge the work that your feet do for you—such as supporting your body weight and transporting you. Place your hands on or over your feet and breathe energy into them. Notice if you are drawn to any particular spots. Try asking your feet if they have any needs or requests. Write down anything that comes into your mind.

3. Continue this process as you move up your body, moving your attention to your ankles, calves, knees, etc. When you reach the pelvis and trunk, you can use the same method to connect with the organs and systems. You may wish to use an anatomy resource to help you locate the organs. Because the organs are hidden from view, it may take longer to make the connection. You may wish to explore the outer body first. Notice which organs and systems seem easier to access.

4. Make a commitment to spend time with your physical body, paying special attention to the discomforted or injured parts. Touching and holding the affected body parts will help them feel connected and loved. Mental messages of approval and support bring your consciousness into these parts of your body.

Moving the Energy

We are made up of systems of energy. When the energy is flowing, the systems run smoothly and efficiently. When the energy becomes blocked or stagnant, the systems suffer. Breathing and exercise help keep our energy flowing. Feeling and expressing emotions also encourage physical energy to move. Acupuncture and massage can stimulate the natural healing flow of energy within the body.

Disease and pain reflect energy that is stuck or resistant to movement. You can learn to move your energy in order to release the trapped energy. It is best to receive the message from the symptom before you move the energy. Remember that the symptom is a messenger to help you know yourself better.

Conventional surgery plays an important role in healing. However, if a diseased organ is removed or repaired without delivering its message, the messenger may try again. It is worth our while to examine and question our illnesses and pains to understand the hidden message.

Clearing the Cobwebs

Symptoms such as headaches, stomachaches, swelling and inflammation may indicate an excess of energy in a particular body system. Often when we are injured we push the painful part away from our minds. This tendency to divorce ourselves from the injured body part reduces communication with the healer within. The pushing away isolates the injured part. This is the opposite action necessary to communicate with and heal the injured part. Here is a simple technique to assist your body in releasing physical discomfort and promote healing:

HOW TO BEGIN

First, place your hand directly on or over the body part that is in discomfort. As you touch the part, begin to breathe gently and smoothly. If you have just sustained an injury, do not be concerned about the smoothness of your breath—just place a hand on or over the injured part. If possible, send reassuring thoughts to this part of your body. Imagine that your breath is traveling to the body part. Speak silently or aloud, addressing the body part by name. Look at the part of your body. Imagine the body part healthy and comfortable.

With your hand on or above the body part, begin to draw the excess energy out of the injured or painful area. Move the hands as if you are removing cobwebs from your body. Do this gesture for several minutes. There is a constant flow of energy in and out of your body. This energy flow facilitates health and well-being. Since the flow is dependent on your breath, continue to breathe deeply and evenly. It may take some time to feel the release. You can do this exercise as often as you like. Your attention to the area in discomfort will help it heal.

Your body is like a garden—the beds you tend blossom and grow, while the areas you neglect fall to ruin. Associate with your body as much as possible. The physical body is honest and loyal. If you treat your body with respect, it will naturally honor your need for health and ease.

Balancing the Four Bodies

We are composed of four bodies—physical, mental, emotional and spiritual. Each body houses specific qualities necessary for wholeness. The physical body deals with our physical health and well-being, including exercise, rest, nutrition, body therapies, hygiene, nurturing and play. The mental body encompasses communication and intellectual understanding, including study, finances, reading, writing, documents, planning and executing projects. The emotional body handles our feelings, including weeping, laughing, grieving, rejoicing, creating, releasing and loving.

The spiritual body addresses our relationship to a source greater than ourselves and encompasses prayer, nature, dreams, music, art, worship and fellowship.

Contemporary culture emphasizes the physical and mental bodies. The majority of the commercials on television deal with cars, sports, beauty products and communication services. On rare occasion we may see a commercial commenting on the importance of emotional health or spiritual practice. If we balanced our life according to the media, we would spend ninety-five percent of our waking time on the physical and mental bodies. It takes our conscious effort to make time for the emotional and spiritual bodies.

This next exercise identifies any imbalances in the four bodies. A quick checklist of the four bodies points out the neglected areas. Let's look at two examples:

Katherine's Checklist

Katherine is feeling out of sorts. She has a headache and general malaise. She feels out of balance, yet does not know what she is lacking. She takes out her journal and makes four columns. Under each heading she rates the attention she has given each of the four bodies during the week.

Physical	*Mental*	*Emotional*	*Spiritual*
swam 2x		cried at the movies	prayer group

Katherine looks over her lists. She notices that she has not attended to her mental body this week. She thinks about her list of things to do. Balancing her checkbook and paying bills is top on her mental list. As she thinks about her finances, her headache worsens. She has been worrying about her money, but not taking any steps to remedy the situation. She decides to attack the financial issue. She balances her checkbook and pays most of the bills. She then makes a few calls to set up partial payments. When she finishes, the tightness around her head lessens and she feels more energized. Now when she checks her four body checklist she sees balance. Let's look at another example:

Charlie's Checklist

Charlie feels detached and emotionally flat. His girlfriend complains that she cannot connect with him. This week Charlie spent extra time at work finishing a project. On Wednesday he met his friends for their weekly basketball game. He decides to do the checklist to see where he is out of balance.

Physical	*Mental*	*Emotional*	*Spiritual*
played basketball	completed project		

When Charlie looks over his list he sees the imbalance. He has been working mentally and physically while neglecting his emotional and spiritual bodies. He decides to watch Spielberg's film *Schindler's List* with his girlfriend. He knows the movie will open him emotionally. After the movie they can talk about the spiritual aspects of the film.

Food for the Four Bodies

Here are some ideas for feeding your four bodies:

Physical: Take a walk, dance, rub your feet, get a massage, go for a swim, floss your teeth, go outside, stretch your arms up, touch your toes, sew on a button, change your sheets, put your feet up, get a haircut, play with a ball, vacuum, eat a good meal, clean out the fridge, skip, rub your scalp, breathe, take a nap, clean out a closet, give clothes away, shine your shoes, buy something new.

Mental: Balance your checkbook, go through the mail, pay a bill, remember a birthday, send a card, take a course, organize piles, throw out old papers, plan and execute a trip, talk politics, read a book, write a poem, send a letter to the editor, listen to the news, give to a charity, answer a letter, solve a problem, discuss a movie, ask a question, give an opinion.

Emotional: Cry at a commercial, tell a joke, tickle someone, hug someone, pet a dog, hold a cat, smile, help a friend, help a stranger, remember something sad or happy, rejoice in life, get mad, paint a picture, let go of a resentment, love yourself, watch a scary movie, cry in the rain, tell your secret, keep someone else's secret, breathe.

Spiritual: Meditate, pray, go to a new church, watch the trees sway, look at the stars, read an inspiring work, write about your God, read a poem, listen to music, sing, remember a dream, fix someone dinner, hold a hand, smile at a stranger, share your fortune, compliment someone, thank life.

You can do this exercise daily, weekly or biweekly to check your balance. It is helpful when you are feeling off-center and are uncertain how to re-center. This simple checklist quickly identifies the neglected areas of your self. In time you will automatically know which body needs attention and remedy the imbalance.

Chapter 4

Time for the Child

A newborn baby is an emissary from the spiritual world. At birth, the soul moves into human form with a clear memory of its purity and innocence. We see this clarity and honesty in a child's eyes. As the caretakers of these children, it is our job to preserve the memory of wholeness.

Our children are our greatest teachers. Innately, they are experts in matters of the heart and soul. We are here to guide them in the workings of the physical world as they remind us of our spiritual nature. We are more knowledgeable about the physical plane and teach them safe boundaries and respectful actions. They, in turn, teach us about love, compassion and trust.

Many of us were not honored as children. Our innocence and honesty frightened our parents. Many of our parents thought their job was to bring us fully into the harsh reality of the physical world. Therefore, we suppressed and hid our memories of joy and completeness in order to find acceptance in our parents' eyes. Consequently, all of us, adults and children, have moved farther and farther from Spirit.

In this chapter we will work on reestablishing contact with our inner child, then turn our attention to the children in our care. We become more receptive and sensitive to the needs of the children in our care once we are able to contact the child within us. Whether we are the parents, guardians, caregivers, relatives, teacher or friends of these children, we will be better equipped to love and support them.

Contacting the Child Within

The child within is your most valuable resource. Without this vulnerable and innocent self, you would lack creativity, health, prosperity, passion, open-mindedness, honesty and playfulness. If any of these qualities are missing in your life, then your inner child is waiting for you to make contact. It is never too late to connect. You breathe together.

No matter how old you are, you have a child inside of you. This child still carries the memory of unconditional love and generosity of spirit. As an adult you automatically become the parent of your inner child. It becomes your job to re-parent her with awareness by honoring her true nature.

Child Meditation

This exercise is designed to help you contact the child within. You will need paper and a pen. You may want to have a photograph of yourself as a child and any memorabilia from your childhood—a teddy bear, doll, treasure box, baseball glove, etc. You will also need some quiet time reserved for your inner child work. You can spend as little as five minutes or as long as you like. A five minute touch-in is better than no contact at all. You will need more time in the beginning to connect and establish a level of trust. In time you can shorten the sessions.

Find a private space where you will not be disturbed. If you have a photograph, look into the eyes of the child in the photo. Hold the cherished keepsakes. If you are not using a photo, close your eyes and imagine yourself as a child. Say your childhood name three times. Keep your breath flowing. Open your heart to this sensitive and vulnerable part of yourself. Gently encourage her to come closer. Do not force a connection.

Do not be concerned if your childhood memories are vague or sketchy. In time you will remember more and more. Stay in touch with any feelings that arise. Breathe into the feelings and let them flow through you. Write down your impressions and sensations. Do not be discouraged if you do not sense the child. It may have been years since you last made contact. Regardless of your impressions, you have made the first contact. You are rebuilding trust in this important relationship. Be patient and understanding of yourself and your inner child. When you are ready to end the meditation, thank your child self for her time and attention.

Watch your dreams for several nights after this exercise. Your child within may feel more comfortable contacting you through a dream. You can use the exercises in chapter 8 to help you interpret the messages.

Contact Letter

The next contact will be through a letter to your inner child. The letter will become concrete evidence of your intent to prioritize the feelings and needs of your inner child. Let's look at a letter that I wrote to my inner child:

Dear little Suzy,

I am so sorry that I left you alone and scared for a long time. I am sorry that I was critical and mean. I am sorry that I starved you and made you run and swim when you were very tired. I don't blame you for hating me and not trusting me.

I want to hear your feelings and needs. I want you to come home with me when you are ready. I want to have you back in my life. I need you very much. Thank you for listening to me. I love you.

Susan

After you write your contact letter, sit and become open to receiving a response from your inner child. You may feel nothing. You may feel a shiver of recognition or a strong emotion. Use the exercises offered in chapter 2 to assist you in identifying and releasing feelings. Let your experience speak to you. Do not try to force contact. The letter is a beginning. Your inner child has heard you on some level. It takes time to feel the connection.

Writing to the Child Within

After writing a contact letter, you are now ready to listen to the feelings and needs of your inner child. To deepen the connection, you can dialogue with your inner child to discover her feelings and needs. Using two questions (see below) you can gather important data about the inner child's well-being.

In *The Power of Your Other Hand* and *Recovery of Your Inner Child*, Lucia Capacchione suggests using your nondominant hand to answer the questions. Both of these books are invaluable resources for healing the child within. According to Capacchione, the nondominant hand affords a more direct link to inner child consciousness. I have used this technique with powerful results. As the nondominant hand writes, it helps quiet the inner censor. Let's look at an example:

* * *

I begin by writing the question, "What are you feeling?" Since I am left-handed, I then switch my pen to my right hand to answer. I try to let my mind be receptive and open. My right hand, guided by my inner child, writes the following: "I hate you! You are mean and hurt me! Leave me alone!"

I then write the second question with my dominant hand: "What do you need?" I switch to my right hand, and my inner child writes: "I want some free time. I feel pushed—too many things to do! I'm tired of working and helping others. What about me?!"

I then answer my inner child with my dominant hand: "I hear you. You have a right to be mad at me. I am sorry I am pushing you so hard.

I will take time off tomorrow afternoon just for us. You can choose what we do."

My nondominant hand writes: "I want to go to a movie. A kid movie just for you and me. I want popcorn and a drink." I return my pen to my dominant hand and write to my child: "It's a deal. Thank you for telling me how you feel. I love you."

* * *

Remember to allow your inner child to express any and all of her feelings. There are no rules. Listen and express sympathy for her feelings. Listen to her needs as well. Be realistic and honest with your promises to the child within. You may need to delay her wishes and needs. Making fewer promises that you keep is better than betraying her with broken promises. Be honest with yourself about your limitations.

It is important to let the inner child express herself freely and without censure. Try to allow the words to flow. Since you are contacting an unknown part of yourself, you may be surprised by the content. The most important element is continued communication. Make time to write to her regularly.

Inner Child Cards

A useful tool for communicating with your inner child is your own personal deck of "inner child cards." These can be helpful whenever you feel unclear or pressed for time. I use my deck for a quick reminder to consider the feelings and needs of my child self.

You will need a pack of index cards and a pen. It is helpful to use any child writing that you have done in the past. (See above, "Writing to the Child Within.") You can use direct quotes from your inner child to create the text of the cards. Put one statement on each card. Here are some sample statements:

Help me.
Please hold me.
I am scared.
Slow down.
I want some free time.
I am tired.
I need to play.
Listen to me.
Take time out for me.

Stop hurting me.

I am having fun with you.

Pay attention to me.

To use the deck, close your eyes and take several deep breaths. Keeping your eyes closed, draw a card from the deck. See how the card you choose connects with your present circumstances. Try to tune into the feelings expressed in the card. Most important, attend to the card's request. If the card says, "Slow down," then take several breaths and see how you can put some space in your busy day. If you are not able to fulfill the request immediately, then reassure your child within that you will follow up as soon as possible. Be sure to keep your promise. If you break a promise to your inner child, apologize as soon as you realize it. Using the cards regularly will increase your ability to automatically sense the needs and feelings of your inner child.

When treated with respect and honesty, children are very forgiving. Taking time to communicate in the present can heal the separation of the past. The health and well-being of your inner child affects every aspect of your life—from your physical health to your prosperity.

What Is Mine and What Is Not

Knowing who we are, our strengths and weaknesses, is our primary work as human beings. When we know our limitations, we can begin to support and strengthen them. Likewise, when we know our talents, we can begin to nurture and express them. Depending on the family personalities and environment each of us experienced in the past, we have formed a view of ourselves that may or may not be accurate. In some cases, the self-image may reflect some of the unfinished work of other family members. When this unfinished work is combined with our own inner work, we can become confused about who we are and overwhelmed by the weight of the unresolved emotional work of others. We can feel depleted and unable to focus on our own inner work. In this discouraged and exhausted state, we may inflate our weaker areas and deflate our areas of talent.

One way to know if you are carrying the unfinished work of someone else, is to see if you have a deep feeling of hopelessness to change a part of yourself or your life. This feeling may also be present when facing difficult pieces of your own inner work. However, if you have spent years actively working to change with little or no results, you may be carrying someone else's work. Sensitive or empathetic people are especially prone to picking up the unfinished work of others. Through honest assessment you can begin to unravel the threads of your being that are not integral to your spiritual wholeness and to give them back to their rightful owners.

Sorting through the Pain

Taking responsibility for your own path and the work you have chosen to do in this lifetime is a vital step of individuation and maturation. However, if you are born or placed into a home where one or both parents have rejected integral parts of themselves and have chosen not to be responsible for their inner work, there is a strong likelihood you will adopt some of their work as your own. Children crave acceptance and a place where they feel needed and accepted. They will often do whatever is requested of them to avoid the devastation of rejection—even if this includes taking on pain and fear that is not their own. Let's look at an example:

* * *

Mary was born to an emotionally and physically absent father and a narcissistic, alcoholic mother. Her mother is needy and turns to Mary to fulfill her needs. Young Mary is yearning for a place to belong and finds that place in taking care of her mother, emotionally and even physically. The damage of this arrangement is twofold: Mary loses the nurturing, essential to a healthy childhood, and she feels responsible for her mother's overwhelming emotional pain. Mary's natural need to belong overrides any feelings of resentment she may have about her family role.

In later years, this pain and resentment will reemerge in her psyche to be expressed or repressed. By that time she will have difficulty distinguishing her pain from her mother's. She may continue to try to resolve her mother's pain with no results. She will attract people who need an emotional surrogate, thereby adding to her pain and confusion. Mary will feel increasingly powerless in her own life as she uses her available energy to try to change or rescue others. This process depletes valuable inner resources needed to develop and enhance her own life.

One way to return another's pain is to learn responsible blaming. Let's look at the developmental importance of the blame stage and the steps of responsible blaming.

The Blame Stage

Blame: To hold responsible, to accuse. To place responsibility for (something) on a person.

The developmental stage of blaming others is relatively short and intense. From the age of three to five, children begin to broaden their world to include more activities, adventures and relationships. However, their maturity is not yet developed enough to handle all of the complexities of their expanding world. Sometimes they wet their pants or spill their juice, or some other mishap occurs as they work to find their coordination and balance in a broadening environment. Children begin to risk more and to become more self-conscious.

There is also a sense of omnipotent power at this stage. In the blame stage, children become all-innocent and others are cast as the wrongdoers. If allowed to run its natural course, the blame stage moves children to accepting more and more responsibility. However, if their environment is neither secure nor supportive, children can become stuck in this stage.

* * *

Four-year-old Sophie has just been given an ice cream cone. She takes a lick and then notices a squirrel playing nearby at the base of a tree. Following her natural curiosity, she runs to get closer to the squirrel, and in her excitement her ice cream falls onto the ground. Disappointed and frustrated, she may cry out, "Look what you made me do!" You are standing ten feet away, obviously not a part of the minor disaster.

A healthy caregiver knows the child is upset and confused about the spoiled ice cream. The child, who may be embarrassed, is trying to divert attention from her clumsiness onto another party, namely you. A supportive response might be, "Oh, you dropped your ice cream. You were excited about the squirrel, weren't you? Let's see if we can get you some more." In this way you gently remind the child of what truly happened and find a nonshaming resolution.

* * *

Sometimes it is not possible to replace a child's lost or broken object. In that case, you can console her while letting her express her anger, again possibly through blaming. You may gently reassure the child that we all lose or drop things. It is not helpful to embarrass or punish the child for projecting blame. Gentle reassurance that we all make misjudgments and errors in life will help her gradually accept her mistakes. If allowed to take its course, it is an appropriate developmental stage that naturally shifts to personal responsibility.

Internalizing Blame

It is crucial for children to distinguish what is truly their responsibility from what is another's burden. This discernment is necessary for developing healthy boundaries. In the sitcom *The Andy Griffith Show*, Andy Taylor was an exemplary father in this respect. Several of the episodes dealt with his misunderstanding of a situation involving his young son, Opie. He would jump to a conclusion and begin to blame Opie for an incident. After Opie explained what truly happened, Andy would apologize with a hug, "I did it again, didn't I? You're really something, you know that! Son, I'm proud of you!"

In many dysfunctional families, parents do not own up to their mistakes, and ofttimes they put the blame on their children. For example, a frustrated parent who has lost his way driving in a new town and is heading the wrong way down a one-way street may tell the talkative kids in the back seat, "Look what you made me do! Now we're lost and it's your fault!" Such a projection stems from the parent's embarrassment and frustration at the situation. Random blaming by a caregiver can result in the loss of a child's ability to accurately perceive reality. It may also cause the child to constantly doubt and question herself. In every situation, no matter how innocent, there will be potential for self-blaming. If a father comes home from work angry, for example, his child may wonder, "Did I make Daddy angry by playing with my toys on the steps?" Likewise, she may see that her mother is upset and wonder, "Is Mommy crying because I was noisy when I ran into the room?"

* * *

Let's review the consequences of an uncompleted blame stage. If the developmental stage is not completed, the child may internalize the blame as her own. She may take responsibility for actions and behaviors that are not her fault. Conversely, she may get stuck in blaming others and continuously project blame for her failures and problems. In either case, the adult life is stunted and unsatisfying. It is helpful to note that people often blame themselves or others in an attempt to avoid the painful feelings of shame and failure. Blaming reflects a fear of the consequences of increasing responsibility in life, and indicates low self-esteem and a lack of maturity.

Note: The importance of the following exercise cannot be overemphasized. Even if you feel you have completed this stage, you may wish to work on it and watch the changes in your life.

Completing the Blame Stage

It is not possible to wholly mature without completing the blame stage. The key to completing the blame stage is found in the relationship between the supportive inner parent and the inner child. You can become the healthy, supportive parent who allows the child within to complete the blame stage.

First, it is important to face the reality of your childhood environment. It is crucial to acknowledge the lack of safety and support for your original blame stage. It is also vital to rework childhood events that were not your fault, but for which you were blamed. This is especially important for the adult who uses excessive self-blaming.

Here are some questions to help clarify your childhood situation:

1. Did I feel safe in blaming my parents?

2. Did I feel loved even when I made a mistake?

3. Could I verbally confront my parents without fear of physical punishment?

4. Could I confront my parents without fear or shaming or verbal abuse?

5. Do I remember my parents admitting that they had made a mistake?

6. Was I punished unjustly?

7. Was I punished too severely for minor offenses?

8. Did my parents tend to blame others for their problems?

9. Did my parents react punitively before knowing the facts of a situation?

10. If so, were they later able to listen to my side of the story?

Writing Your Internal Negative Script

Whether you are stuck in blaming yourself or others, the blame stage is incomplete. If you are predominantly a self-blamer, you may wish to start by writing out the negative script that runs through your head. The negative voice that berates and criticizes you is most destructive if it remains hidden in your head. It loses power when you write it out.

Take paper and pen. Begin by remembering a recent mistake that you made. Re-create the incident in your mind. Now begin writing the negative comments that you heard in your mind. If you get stuck, remember another event where you did not measure up to your standards. Here are some common lines from a negative script:

How could you have forgotten that appointment!
Now you are in big trouble!

> *You are always messing things up!*
>
> *You can't do anything right!*
>
> *You should be ashamed!*
>
> *I knew you couldn't do it right!*
>
> *This is all your fault!*
>
> *This is completely ruined!*
>
> *You are so stupid!*

As you reread your negative script, you will see how extreme and exaggerated the accusations seem. Read it aloud to yourself. Exaggerate your tone of voice when you read the script. You may wish to try reading your script aloud in front of a mirror. This step can help you see how unreasonable and extreme the negative voice is. You may wish to share the script with someone you trust. This trustworthy person can reassure you that the negative script is unreasonable and hurtful to you.

Responsible Blaming

To complete the blame stage you need to find a safe and responsible way to express blaming feelings. The constant blaming of self and others is a reflection of unreleased childhood blaming. This next exercise gives you the chance to release the blaming consciously and responsibly. In private, or with therapeutic support, you can give yourself the opportunity to complete this vital developmental stage. The end result is the dramatic reduction of blaming self and others.

HOW TO BEGIN

Get paper and pen. Choose a memory or a current situation where you felt someone else was to blame for your loss or pain. Write out your feelings in statements using "you" to help direct your blame to the other person. For example:

> *You are wrong!*
>
> *You embarrassed me!*
>
> *You messed up!*
>
> *You are at fault!*

It is fine to repeat the same statements of blame. You can use angry or profane language. This writing is about your personal feelings of outrage and injustice. This writing is reflecting the frustration and impotence of a child. Let yourself experience your fury as a child. Do not try to reason out the blame or responsibility for the event. You are practicing feeling a child's blaming in a responsible way (i.e., in private and on paper). You can also speak the blaming statements. Below are a list of expressions to get you started:

How dare you!

You are to blame!

You should be punished!

I hate you for this!

This is your fault!

You are bad!

You are completing a necessary stage of childhood development. It is fine to sound like an angry child. After practicing responsible blaming using the present, you may wish to try using an incident from your past. Do not be discouraged if your childhood memories are sketchy and fuzzy. This is very common in dysfunctional families. Keep encouraging your inner child to remember these difficult memories. Reassure her it is now safe to remember and feel the past. Remember, it can be frightening for a child to blame a punitive parent. The consequences of your blaming behavior as a child may have been severe punishment or shaming. Be patient with yourself. You may need to have a therapist witness your blaming for safety or validation.

Repeat this exercise until you notice a reduction in your self-blaming or other-blaming behavior. You have completed the blame stage when you can own the following statements with relative ease:

I can accept responsibility for my own mistakes and problems,
with relative ease.

I do not automatically assume I am to blame if a problem arises.

I am not driven to blame others for their mistakes.

I am not afraid to admit a mistake.

I do not shame myself or others for making a mistake.

Consciously practicing responsible blaming reduces your fear, increases your self-esteem and gives you the confidence to willingly accept more responsibility and power.

Circle of Support

A child's sense of worth is formed over many years by healthy, supportive interactions with others. A child depends on external feedback to build a positive self-image. Daily encounters with positive and loving adults assures a strong sense of self. When the external feedback in a child's environment is explosive, negative or shaming, the child's self-image becomes weak and impaired.

As adults, we have the power to rebuild damaged self-esteem. We can provide healthy support and encouragement. This next technique boosts self-worth and confidence. By reaffirming the unique qualities and talents of the inner child, we strengthen a positive self-image.

HOW TO BEGIN

Find a quiet place where you can relax undisturbed for thirty minutes. You may sit or lie down. Be certain that your spine is well supported. When you are comfortable, take several deep, full breaths. Bring your attention to your breath. Follow your inhalations and exhalations with your mind. You can calm the thoughts in your mind by saying silently, "Breathing in, breathing out." Allow your breath to relax your body and mind. Deep, slow breathing is a natural tranquilizer that calms and soothes all of the systems of the body.

When you are relaxed, imagine yourself as a young child. You can use an image from a photo. Do not be concerned if you cannot visualize easily. You can sense that the child is present. Imagine that the child feels safe and secure with you.

Next, imagine a circle of chairs or cushions around the child. These seats are for the different parts of yourself. The different parts of self represent the many talents, interests and roles you have in this lifetime. For example, you may be a gardener, a sport's fan, an artist, a teacher, a traveler, a scientist, a chef, a hiker, etc. In turn, each self will look deeply into the child's eyes and verbally affirm the inner child. You will begin by saying, "I love the way you..."

For example, the gardener may say, "I love the way you enjoy digging in the dirt and watching the seeds grow. I love the way you like to squish your bare toes in the mud after a rainstorm." As you are praising the child self, send loving, comforting thoughts.

Go around the circle giving each self time to give the child support and praise. Remember to look into the child's eyes and to send love. In the beginning, there may be only a few different selves. This circle will grow as you realize how many different areas of interest you possess. Let the child bask in the warmth and support. The more time you make to practice this technique, the stronger your self-worth grows. In time you may discover you are automatically giving your inner child praise and affirmation during the day.

Honoring and Listening to Our Children

In the Balinese culture, newborns are continually held for the first nine months. The extended family naturally shares in this constant contact. Nestled in cloth carriers, the babies stay in close physical contact with their caregivers. They believe that children come directly from the divine lap of Spirit and are too pure to touch the earth. While visiting Bali, I was struck by the contentedness of the children. In my three-week stay, I met many families with children. During this time I only witnessed two incidents of crying. The Balinese respect the rights of their children, and this respect is naturally returned to the parents and caregivers.

Children have natural intuition, innate wisdom and boundless compassion. They also have bouts of temper and discord. Some of these emotions are a normal part of human development. In infancy, children have a keen sense of the feelings and moods of the parents and others around them. As parents, it is imperative that we honestly and humbly listen to the messages of our children. As sensitive barometers of dysfunction, their symptoms and behaviors will signal us of problems within the family system. Let's look at an example:

* * *

When I was eight years old, I developed an insatiable desire for pomegranates. I would await their arrival each fall with eager anticipation. My father would bring them home to me. I craved the tart, sweet, crunchy seeds. The more I ate, the more I wanted. I ate so many that my hands were stained dark by the juice. I remember wearing rubber gloves to protect my hands from the embarrassing discoloration.

The fall was a very difficult season for me. I suffered from severe hay fever. My eyes itched and burned. I could never carry enough tissues for my nose. It was hard for me to concentrate in school. At night my inflamed genitals were red and swollen. I was also wetting the bed regularly. Ashamed of the bed-wetting, I awoke early to change my sheets. I developed other physical symptoms ranging from earaches to eye cysts. I also had reoccurring nightmares that would send me rushing into my parents' room in the middle of the night. I was terrified of the dark and imagined monsters in my room. These symptoms persisted into my teens.

As I look back on my childhood, I see how many distress signals I sent out. Food obsessions, severe allergies, physical symptoms, bed-wetting and reoccurring nightmares are direct messages of psychic stress and anxiety. My psyche and my body were trying to alert the grown-ups around me that I was in trouble. I often wonder how my life would be different now if my distress signals had been heard. As it turned out, I developed anorexia nervosa and bulimia in my sophomore year of college. Obsessed with my body's weight and size, I spent my days exercising and fasting. Fearful of relating and ashamed to be alive, I punished my body relentlessly.

While healing the eating disorder, I learned about the myth of Persephone. She is Demeter's daughter who is abducted by Pluto and taken to the Underworld. Her kidnapping so saddens her mother that she stops the growth of all vegetation on Earth. Thus Persephone's abduction signals the first fall and winter. In the Underworld, Persephone refuses to eat. She misses her mother and her life on the surface so much she swears to eat nothing until she is freed. Yet during her stay of six months, Persephone weakens and eats six pomegranate seeds. When Demeter finally finds her daughter and pleads for her release, those fated six seeds determine Persephone's destiny. Pluto agrees to free her only if she returns to him for six months each year—one month for each seed eaten.

The myth of Persephone is the motivating myth of anorexia nervosa. I did not consciously know the story of the young girl and the exotic fruit. Yet at eight, I was obsessively drawn to pomegranates. Like Persephone, I was prematurely introduced into the dark and unfamiliar world of sexuality. My father's unresolved sexual issues affected me strongly. As a sensitive child I could detect his unconscious sexual feelings and began to carry them in my own psyche. Overwhelmed and terrified by intense sexual feelings, Persephone and I were both driven to regain control by disassociation. Choosing to starve, we both desperately tried to free our bodies from the darkness of the Underworld. Unknowingly, we moved toward death to escape the fear and emotional pain.

My eight-year-old psyche used the symptoms to alert my parents. They were unable to heed the signals and find the help I needed. In working with children, I have found that they send out signals that reflect an accurate picture of their distress. You can find these signals in their physical symptoms, behaviors, dreams and obsessions. Take the time to become more sensitive to your children, and you can help them heal their issues with less pain and drama.

Emotional Legacy

To open to your children's messages, you must be willing to face your parenting mistakes. Making mistakes is a natural part of parenting. Any unresolved issues of the parents will be passed on to the child. It is common knowledge that family scripts are repeated unless they are consciously rewritten.

Family denial of a child's distress often comes from an unwillingness to face the family dysfunction. This unwillingness stems from fear of blame and shame. You must be willing to love and support yourself through the difficult task of examining your child's life. You must also be willing to reclaim and work through any unresolved issues and forgive yourself for unconsciously handing them to the child. A parent that takes this difficult step saves the child years of pain and trauma. A child is eager to heal. If you find that you have projected blame or shame onto your child, apologize immediately. A child's psyche will recognize the truthfulness of the apology and begin to heal immediately. Let's look at an example:

* * *

You have had a difficult day at the office. Having misplaced an important paper, you need to redo the work or receive a reprimand. You are anxious and distracted when you arrive to pick up six-year-old Sam. Sam senses your distance and begins to whine and plead to have dinner at his favorite fast-food restaurant. At the end of your rope, you snap, saying, "Can't you be quiet for one minute?! No, we can't go to Burger King. That's a crazy idea! Just be quiet and leave me alone!"

As Sam bursts into tears, you realize what happened. You have two choices. You can continue projecting your feelings, or you can explain and apologize. An apology may go as follows: "Sam, I'm sorry I snapped at you. It's not a crazy idea to go to Burger King. We just can't go tonight. I know you're disappointed. We'll find a time this week to go. I'm tired and fussy from work. It's not your fault."

Children understand projection and tantrums—after all, they exercise them daily! Children forgive easily, especially when they hear the truth. You do not have to give details that may be inappropriate. Simply tell them that you are having a hard time or working on some difficult issues. Reassure the child that your upset feelings are about you, not her.

The next exercise helps you assess your child's current emotional well-being. From this assessment you gain insight into your own unresolved issues and help remove them from the child's psyche.

Child Assessment

1. Begin by doing a current assessment of your child. Be as honest as possible. Your willingness to be honest about your child's emotional health speeds up the healing process.

2. List as many symptoms and behaviors as you can. Include physical illnesses, behavioral and social problems at school and at home,

learning difficulties, phobias, obsessions, etc. Write anything that comes into your mind, even if it seems trivial. Use your intuitive right brain to help you brainstorm. Use chapter 3 to understand the emotional cause of the symptom.

3. Ask your child to tell you her dreams. With her permission, keep a log of these dreams. You can use dream books, classes or a therapist who specializes in dream interpretation to analyze the dreams.

4. Make a comparison of your child's issues and your own at the same age. Take time to remember and write about your behavior and feelings at that age. Note any traumas or illnesses that you experienced. Be aware of any similarities. Often the child will unconsciously reenact a parent's history.

5. As you uncover any unresolved issues about your own past, make a promise to deal with these problems. I suggest that you psychically alert the child that you are taking responsibility for the unresolved issues. You can do this telepathically through a meditation or through a letter you write in your personal journal. (See "Letter to Your Child" below.) Do not give the child the letter at this time. The child will intuitively sense when you reclaim the issues. Remember that her symptoms may also be the result of an actual physical reenactment of your trauma. Be certain to carefully investigate any suspicious people or situations. Trust your intuition and gut reactions.

6. Take steps to find a therapist for your child. If this work resonates with you, find a therapist that is willing to work with dreams and symbols. Share your findings with the therapist. Depending on the age of the child, it may be appropriate at some point to share your relevant history with your child. Let a therapist help you decide on the timing.

* * *

Letter to Your Child

Dear Anna,

I am sorry that I put my addiction work on you. I know this has been very hard on you. I want to reclaim my unfinished work on my teenage drug and alcohol habits. I now see myself when I see you lying or disobeying. I need to remember and feel my teenage years. I want to take my work back to lighten your load. I am sorry that I didn't do this sooner.

I am committed to facing my past addiction through therapy, dreams, anger work and journaling.

I love you very much,

Mom

* * *

This step is a powerful contribution to your child's healing process. A child is a sensitive and accurate emotional barometer. Any unresolved and unclaimed psychological data will be unknowingly transferred to her open, receptive mind. As a parent, you can consciously choose to reclaim and resolve this data and remove the burden from the child. It is important to continue to attend to the child's present emotional and physical problems. After you are willing to hear the cries for help, you are better equipped to provide the appropriate healing program. I strongly recommend finding a skilled therapist to help you with this work.

The Key to Peace

War and violence are expressions of the anguish of lost innocence. They are misguided and desperate attempts to regain a sense of worth and power. The healthy child possesses a strong sense of worth and personal power. Each adult who takes the first step toward healing the inner child brings us closer to world peace. When we each know and love the inner child, we will not be capable of violence to ourselves or others. Renewing respect for all children, inner and outer, ensures a peaceful future for our planet.

Chapter 5
Redefining Relationships

Relationships give us the opportunity to know ourselves better. Each person we encounter brings us a piece of our own personal puzzle. Our reaction to each encounter alerts us to the nature of our spiritual lessons. By closely examining our relationships, we gain a profound understanding of our paths. Whether the relationship is familial, platonic, romantic or professional we can collect personal data.

Our first relationships are with the members of our original family. Therefore, subsequent associations reflect these early connections. The more we analyze and dissect our familial relationships, the quicker we move into satisfying, intimate affiliations. Let's look at a way to use present relationships to complete unfinished relationship work:

Understanding Reenactment

The human psyche has an uncanny way of replaying familial relationships. No matter how hard we try to pick a mate different from our father or mother or to find a boss more supportive than the last one, we find ourselves reading from the same script with the same cast of non-supporting actors.

The pattern of reenactment is a learning device of the psyche. It is not designed merely to frustrate and fatigue the human spirit. We are each born into particular family situations to teach us lessons that we need to learn. If we have not mastered the unique lessons of our family relationships, then we continue to attract people with similar characteristics. These stand-ins show us our unfinished relationship work. In this section we learn how to clarify the reenactment to uncover the unfinished personal work. We can then interrupt the reenactment cycle and attract more loving, supportive relationships.

The Original Cast

We automatically cast and recast our lives with characters similar to the family of origin. To become aware of reenactment, we must first become conscious of the makeup of the original cast of characters. Let's look at two examples of reenactment of unfinished family work:

Fred's Reenactment

Fred is frustrated and discouraged about his career. He feels over-worked, underpaid, and unappreciated. Each time he changes jobs he feels certain that he has chosen a more supportive and encouraging workplace. However, within months the old pattern returns and he finds himself reliving the past. Fred decides to delve into his childhood to discover the origin of his work problems.

Fred was born in 1951 to Harry and Sally Johnson. His father was intelligent, hardworking, critical and stern. His mother was creative, frustrated and prone to emotional outbursts. Fred was the first-born, followed by a sister, Gwendolyn, in 1954.

To begin clarifying the original cast, Fred looks at his relationship with his family. He lists three adjectives to describe each of the members. Fred writes "spoiled," "competitive," and "caring" to describe his sister, Gwen. He describes his mother as "emotional," "angry," and "scattered" and his father as "critical," "discounting," and "unsupportive." Next, Fred takes a brief work relationship history. He writes down the names of his last three employers. Beside each name he lists three adjectives to describe them:

1. James Allen—tough, pushy, bright

2. Tom Speight—exacting, nervous, tight

3. Barbara Cane—strong, domineering, perfectionistic

As he studies the names and the descriptions, he notices a pattern emerging. All three employers remind him of his dad. Each employer had similar stringent requirements for excellence just like his father. Fred shared his father's love of learning although he never felt he measured up to his father's high standards. Fred kept trying to impress his dad with excellent schoolwork but never seemed to do well enough. His father would continually edit Fred's work and find ways to improve it. Fred was in awe of his dad and his brilliant mind, but he never felt his father's approval or affection. In contrast, his dad continually praised and applauded the efforts of his younger sister. Fred tried in vain to capture the same attention from him. He also recalls that in each job there was another employee who received merit-pay increases or acknowledgment while he was overlooked. He remembers his childhood feelings of frustration and hopelessness in failing to win his father's approval. He reexperiences feelings of jealousy and resentment toward his sister. He felt similar feelings in each of the three jobs.

Fred is tired of feeling unappreciated and overworked in his professional life. Somewhere deep inside Fred knows that he is talented and
industrious. Using anger-release writing and beating, he releases his anger
at his father and his resentment toward his sister. (See chapter 2.) In
reclaiming and facing his unresolved feelings about his father and sister,
he is able to reduce the intensity of the present work reenactment. As
Fred continues to release the childhood emotions, he will eventually
attract a more supportive and appreciative employer.

Rachel's Reenactment

Rachel feels defeated about her relationships with men. Her two marriages ended in messy, high-drama divorces. Even though she is sober and
responsible, she has a penchant for attracting addictive, controlling men.
No matter how hard she tries to find a healthier man, she continues to
repeat her old pattern. Rachel wants to understand and resolve the family
issues that prevent her from attracting healthy relationships.

Rachel was born in 1963 to Susan and Gary Barnes. Her mother was
alcoholic and angry. Her father was gentle, passive and often absent. She
had two older brothers and a younger sister. She was married twice, once
at twenty-four and the second time at twenty-nine. Each marriage lasted
approximately four years and ended in divorce. Both husbands were verbally and physically abusive.

After the second painful divorce, Rachel is motivated to understand
how she found another man so much like her first husband. She thought
he was very different when they met and fell in love. She begins her
original cast analysis by looking at her relationship with her mother.

Susan Barnes was strong-willed and emotional. She was a physically
and verbally abusive alcoholic. Rachel remembered hiding in her room
when her mother would start to drink. Her mother would often vent her
anger on the young girl. Gary, her father, was traveling much of the time
and denied the intensity of the mother's abuse. He discounted the girl's
fear of her mother. One of her older brothers was also alcoholic. He
would vent his rage on Rachel. Her other brother was distant and preoc-
cupied, offering her no protection.

Rachel chose her high school steady and two ex-husbands for her "intimate relationship history." She saw a pattern emerging as she wrote the
three adjectives:

1. Larry Stone—heavy drinker, sexually demanding, possessive

2. Paul Mason—angry, workaholic, controlling

3. Daniel Worthington—heavy drinker, physically abusive, demanding

Rachel realizes that she consistently chooses partners like her mother and brother. She recognizes the same feelings of fear and anger she felt as a child. As a defenseless child, she was too frightened to confront her mother and brother. Therefore, hiding and suppressing her feelings had been her only recourse. She resolves to remember and release her rage for her mother and brother to consciously take the reenactment off her choice of partners. She remembers and records nightmares that express the suppressed childhood trauma. With the help of her therapist, she feels safe enough to actively express her hurt and anger. (See chapter 2.) She also decides to use the exercise of the three adjectives after the first date rather than after the divorce.

HOW TO BEGIN

1. List your nuclear family members. You may include aunts, uncles, cousins, etc., if you feel they played important roles in your childhood.

2. Take each name from the list. Describe the person using at least three adjectives. Add any memories of the person. Give yourself permission to write whatever you want. Be honest with your feelings. Notice any physical reactions such as tightening of the jaw, stomachache, headache, etc.

3. Identify a main problem in each relationship. For example, Fred wrote, "My work is never good enough. I try and try and my father never gives me credit." Patricia wrote, "I am afraid and unsafe in my own home. My mother and brother dump their anger on me."

4. Now choose a problematic relationship in your present life. You may choose a work relationship, an intimate relationship, a friend relationship, etc. Write a brief history of this area of your life. Use the three adjectives to describe each character in the original drama.

5. Label your role in the present relationship. For example, Fred wrote, "My bosses are too demanding and hard on me. I am overworked and unappreciated." Patricia wrote, "My partners use me to vent their anger. I reach out to love and I get hurt and frightened."

6. Now go back to the original cast. Look at the three adjectives of each family member. Find the family member that most resembles the person in the present relationship. Compare your original role with the role you play in the present situation. Compare your feelings within the familial and present relationships. Do not discriminate by gender. A male boss can remind you of your mother, and your wife can remind you of your father.

7. Now you have an idea of the origin of your reenactment. You may use chapters 2 and 4 to help clear the pain. The more you concentrate on the original pain, the less you will draw reenactment relationships and situations to you.

Reenactment Release Contract

This practice is designed to decrease the drama in a present relationship by recognizing and owning the emotional work of the original affiliation. We each play a significant part in all reenactments. Unconsciously, we ask others to play the members of the original cast so that we can restimulate the suppressed experiences and emotions of the past. After we consciously see our part in the play, we can deliberately release the stand-ins from their roles. We can agree to take responsibility for our past and heal the emotional pain without the external drama. The release contract is for personal use and is not to be sent to the stand-in.

Fred's Reenactment Release Contract

With the realization that his current employer is playing the role of his father, Fred writes out a "release contract" to help reduce the intensity of his current work situation.

Dear Barbara Cane,

I am aware that I have asked you to play the part of my exacting and controlling father. You have played that part very well. I am now ready to take the role from you and put it back on my father. You are now released from that role. I am now ready to deal with my anger and jealousy issues through therapy and anger release work.

Signed: Fred Johnson

Rachel's Reenactment Release Contract

Rachel sees how she transferred her mother and brother issues onto her marriage partners. As her ex-husband Daniel Worthington continues to pursue and harass her, she decides to try writing out a release contract to reduce the level of drama he brings into her present life.

Dear Daniel,

I admit that I have asked you to play the part of my abusive and alcoholic mother and my tormenting brother. You have played these parts with expertise and endurance. I understand that I have unfinished emotional work that I am now willing to face without your help. I now release you from the roles I have

asked you to play. I am going to do this work through therapy,
journaling, dream work and anger release.

Signed: Rachel Barnes

By taking responsibility for their parts in the reenactments, Fred and Rachel regain a sense of empowerment and control. They are no longer passive victims of abusive situations. Both Fred and Rachel follow up by asking their therapists to witness the release contracts and help support them in actively tackling the unfinished family work.

Reenactment is a learning device designed to raise spiritual consciousness. No matter how conscious you become, there will always be a degree of reenactment. The goal of this exercise is to bring awareness to relating so the dysfunction and drama can decrease. When you are in a frustrating interaction, use the three adjectives to identify the original cast member and the unfinished work. Write a contract to release the person from the reenactment and take action to clear the original relationship. Through awareness you deepen and redefine your relationships with yourself and others.

The Velcro Theory

The old expression "It takes two to tango" is an accurate maxim for describing relationships. Every encounter is shaped by the energy and behavior of each participant. It is necessary to have mutual agendas to create a power struggle or a yelling match. Therefore, it is possible for one individual to change the outcome of an encounter. Let's examine the relationship phenomenon called the velcro theory:

Velcro is an effective fastener made up of two distinct systems of hooks and loops. It is the interplay between the hooks and loops that makes velcro work. Each side depends on the other to cause the strong, sticking action. If one side is missing, then the fastener is useless.

In some encounters, we unconsciously agree to play a match to another person's particular velcro. In other words, we bring a set of hooks to match their loops. When we get close to each other, we fasten together and get stuck. When stuck together it becomes difficult to maintain centeredness and clarity. Often each participant will stubbornly stick to her guns—or, in this case, her part of the velcro! The ensuing power struggle can continue for years. Only when one of the participants decides to go deeper into understanding her individual hooks or loops can the pattern begin to change. Let's look at an example:

* * *

Samantha and Austin have been dating for several years. They are both strong-spirited and opinionated. At first they enjoyed their frequent, lively debates. Presently they are growing increasingly frustrated and irritated with each other. Samantha needs Austin to agree with her, while Austin wants Sam to side with his views. They are constantly bickering about minor details. In these discussions they both seem to exclaim, "I am right! You are wrong!" Since neither person is willing to give in, they both remain locked in a continuous struggle.

Finally Sam is so sick of this pattern she decides to go deeper. She examines her childhood family dynamics. Her father was very authoritative and dictatorial. She never recalled his admitting that he was wrong. As a child she was intimidated by his sternness and afraid to stand up to him. He monopolized the right position, while the rest of the family fell into the position of being wrong.

Sam realizes that she is replaying this relationship with Austin. He is opinionated enough to remind her of her father. She now feels strong enough to express her opinion and stand up for her views. However, she is also acting out the part of her father by demanding to always be right. Samantha realizes how hard it is for her to admit that she is wrong. She played this role so often with her father that she adamantly refuses it in her present relationship. In her mind she is constantly looking for someone else to be wrong so that she can be right. She is reenacting her father's pattern. She can improve her relationship with Austin by releasing her constant need to be right.

She decides to practice alone. She finds a private place to focus on her breathing and clear her mind. Next, she recalls a recent argument with Austin. She remembers how hard she argued her point. She reminds herself to breathe deeply as she replays the scene in her mind. Next, she begins to alter her role in the scene. She imagines listening while Austin states his viewpoint. She feels uncomfortable at first and wants to interrupt. She tries silently repeating, "You are right. I am right." At first this is very hard for Sam to do. She can feel the outrage in her body. Her child self screams, "I am right! You are wrong!" Sam knows this is her frustrated child who had to keep quiet so many times in her conversations with her father.

She stops the visualization to let her inner child write out the frustration. Using a large piece of paper and crayons, she writes in large letters: DADDY, YOU ARE WRONG! YOU ARE WRONG! YOU ARE WRONG! I AM RIGHT! I AM RIGHT! I AM RIGHT! I AM RIGHT! She writes and writes and writes. When her hand is tired and sore, she goes back to the imaginary scene with Austin. Again she listens as he states his opinion. This time Sam is able to see that no one needs to be wrong. She checks her attachment to being the right one by silently chanting, "You are right. I am right." It is easier to say after venting her rage at her father. By dealing directly with her anger at her father, she removes the velcro causing the constant bickering with Austin.

In the weeks that follow, Sam continues to let her inner child regularly release anger through writing. As a result, she feels more calm and centered. She is now a better listener and does not interrupt Austin as often. It is easier for Austin to hear her opinion when she states it nondefensively. When she feels the old pattern reemerging, she silently recites her new mantra, "You are right. I am right." Their conversations now end with both of them feeling more supported and heard. They agree to disagree. The old velcro of right or wrong is unable to stick when Samantha removes her part.

* * *

Most of our velcro patterns are old and ingrained. Many were developed from a need to belong, cope or survive. Therefore, it is important to be patient when removing a velcro pattern. It is vital to examine the original motivation in developing the pattern. The following steps will help you trace the origin of the velcro. Remember that only one person needs to become conscious of the velcro pattern to stop it. It is satisfying to see the habitual patterns drop away, clearing the way for healthier interactions.

1. Look honestly at the current problem. State your role and the role of the other person(s). It is possible for a group of people to play the role of the opposite side of the velcro.

2. Examine more closely your part of the velcro. See if you are reminded of any childhood family patterns. Go deeper into these original velcro encounters. Describe your memories in writing.

3. Feel the emotions that arise during the present encounters. Write down your feelings. Compare these feelings with the childhood memories. If you do not remember how you felt, imagine how a child might feel in the same situation. Write your feelings honestly and without censure. Remember that the reenactment is created to help identify and release stuck emotions. Take time to vent the feelings—cry and grieve, rant and rave, complain and whine, scream and yell. You have a right to these feelings. It is powerful to own and responsibly vent your feelings.

4. Explore your options for a new role in the relationship. Be certain that you guard your rights and boundaries. Ending a power struggle does not mean giving up your power. See if you can find a new way to react to the situation while maintaining your integrity. Seek professional help if the problem seems too difficult. Practice your new way of relating in visualization or with a trusted friend or therapist.

5. Try the new pattern in the relationship. Be gentle with yourself if you slip back into the old pattern. Ask to take a break if you find yourself caught in the old behavior. Keep practicing and you will have gratifying results.

Try using the velcro theory the next time you are stuck in an unsatisfying interaction. You do not need to wait for anyone else to change. You can choose to develcro and change the dynamics of any relationship now. It may take two to tango, but it only takes one to unstick the velcro.

The Altitude Theory or "Why Do I Always Pick the Wrong One?"

Imagine that you are an airplane pilot. You are experienced and seasoned. Your favorite flying altitude is 35,000 feet. From this vantage point you feel confident and comfortable. You are familiar with other pilots who fly at the same altitude. Many of them are your friends. You think of these other pilots as being in your "squadron." You signal to them when you pass and you speak to them on the radio about interesting sights and observations. Since you fly at the same altitude, you can share your thoughts and ideas with them easily and effortlessly. You have friends in this group but no romantic involvements. You are single and ready to be in an intimate relationship. You feel restless and eager to be involved. You do not currently see any available partners in your squadron. So you decide to fly a little lower to see what you can find. For the next week you fly at 25,000 feet. It's fun to be around different pilots. You signal them and make a few radio contacts. None of them seem quite right from your vantage point. You feel restless and decide to dip down a little lower.

At 15,000 feet everything seems new and exciting. You meet a whole new group of pilots, and one catches your eye. A relationship is set into motion. For several months it feels stimulating to be in this new territory. However, before long you start to develop some symptoms—fatigue, irritation, frustration and a feeling of emptiness. You feel a longing to fly at an altitude that suits you better. You suggest flying higher, but your new friend does not seem at all interested. You let it go for a while and spend more time with his squadron. Again you suggest that you two spend some time with your group of friends at your altitude. Again, he dismisses the idea. Soon the symptoms begin to increase. The fatigue turns to exhaustion, and the irritation blossoms into anger. You are frustrated and perplexed. What went wrong?

Keep the Nose of Your Plane Up!

In my own work and in helping others, I have noticed a curious relationship pattern. We often have different criteria for our friends and our mates. For example, we demand that a friend be trustworthy, on time and emotionally accessible. Yet we mate with someone who is dishonest, late and emotionally closed. We put up with behavior in a mate that would never be tolerated in a friend. This is even more curious when we realize that we are much more physically and financially involved with a mate than with a friend. We are risking more with someone we trust less.

HOW TO BEGIN

Bringing this behavior to your awareness is the first step in choosing to stay at your right mating altitude. Here are some other steps to help you choose a mate from your true squadron.

1. Make a list of your requirements for a friend.

2. Check this list when you are thinking of becoming involved in a new intimate relationship.

3. Be honest with yourself in noting the excuses that you make for the new mate. For example: "He had a really hard childhood. He just needs a little time."

4. Remind yourself how many times you have dipped down into lower altitudes and how the relationships have turned out. Ask yourself if you deserve better.

5. Face your fear that there are no men or women at your right altitude. This is not true. There are plenty of potential mates available in your squadron. The reason for not seeing them lies in your unfinished business with family and past relationships.

6. Commit to staying at your right altitude. Continue to balance your own life. From this balanced stance you will experience a sense of completeness that enables you to attract a partner of equal integrity. Let's look at an example of unfinished family business continuing to negatively affect one woman's choice of partners:

Mabel, a slight, dark-haired woman, walked into my office for her first reading. She settled comfortably in her seat, and I took her hands and closed my eyes. Immediately I could sense a block in her lower energy centers in the belly and pelvis. I decided to do psychic surgery, a technique for removing blocks from the energy centers.

Fully clothed, she lay down and I spoke to her softly, taking her into a light hypnotic state. Her tension began to dissolve as I reminded her to relax her muscles and sink into the futon. I began to scan her body by placing my hands several inches over her.

When my hands hovered over her right side, I felt the presence of a surgical scar. I saw a six-year-old, frightened and alone, undergoing a serious operation. I asked Mabel if she understood my impressions. She burst into tears as she explained that she had an emergency appendectomy at six. She had been rushed to the hospital, separated from her parents. She was not told what was happening and felt that she was going to die. Since she was so frightened and alone she was emotionally paralyzed, unable to ask for help or share her feelings. This pattern of an inability to express deep feelings had continued into her adulthood, restricting the depth of her intimate relationships. She complained of issues with trust and of reoccurring abandonment, continually attracting partners who were not there for her. The distant, abandoning men were safe since they did not ask her to go into her deeper feelings. She contributed to the problem by keeping her resentment and hurt inside.

This trauma was stuck in her psyche and needed to be cleared. Together, in our minds, we went back to the hospital. We replayed the events of the day of the surgery. We stayed with the little girl throughout the administration of the anesthesia. We explained to her that she was sick but the doctors were going to help her feel better soon. We held her hands and reassured her. We were with her through the surgery and waiting for her to awaken in the recovery room. The client cried throughout the process. I could feel sharp pain coming from the scar and shooting into my hand. I drew out the pain and released it into the air.

There would still be much work for the young woman to do to heal her relationship issues. She would need time and support to begin sharing her feelings in her intimate relationships. However, the reworking of the childhood memory would help her clarify her issues and become more conscious of her old patterns.

Healthy Relating

A healthy relationship supports your quest to be whole and complete. Your quest to become whole is enhanced by the other's wholeness. You do not need the other to feel complete. You choose the relationship to support the mutual unfolding of your wholeness. You each work to claim your unfinished family business. You both claim the affirmation "I am whole and complete as I am." With or without a partner, you enjoy the fullness of your life.

Chapter 6

How to Be Your Own Psychic

Psychic: Of or pertaining to extraordinary, especially extrasensory and nonphysical, mental processes, such as extrasensory perception and mental telepathy.

Everyone has the potential to develop and employ psychic abilities. These so-called paranormal skills are innate and natural. Since our society has not chosen to honor and encourage these talents, we have neglected them. The millennial acceleration ushers in an opportune time to amplify natural psychic abilities. The two most important factors in the successful development of your psychic abilities are motivation and practice. Interest and desire act as magnets in drawing out intuition. The more we practice these developmental techniques, the stronger our intuition grows.

Emotions and Intuition

There is a strong link between emotions and intuition. The two energies travel down the same pipeline. It is more difficult to access clear intuition if the emotional body is stuck or shut down. This is also true for the connection with the inner child. Since the child within is naturally emotional and intuitive, a healthy inner child relationship improves psychic expression.

I strongly suggest first completing the courses in chapters 2 and 4. Your intuitive skills will greatly benefit from the preliminary clearing of your emotional pipeline.

The Importance of Grounding

Grounding is the term used to describe a solid, firm connection with the earth. A grounded person is able to stay aware of physical surroundings and make informed, intelligent decisions. Since intuitive right-brain activity often involves nonphysical arenas, it can be more challenging for right-brain people to stay in touch with the physical plane. All of us know people who seem spacey. They may seem to be somewhere off in space, tuned into a different channel. These people may have strong right-brain connections and have to work harder to keep their groundedness. As we develop our right-brain capabilities, it becomes more important to increase our ability to become grounded. We are like lightning rods—reaching up higher and higher to receive electromagnetic waves of information about the past, present and future. Like a lightning rod, we must have a strong and deep ground wire to help absorb the energy we receive. The more time and energy we spend grounding ourselves, the more psychic we can become.

Tips for Grounding

One key to grounding is healthy, open feet. The feet are the foundation for the body and the psyche. The more firmly we are planted on our feet, the further we can reach out into alternative realities. Any activity that gives the feet room to breathe and move increases grounding.

The first grounding technique is to take off your shoes and let your feet have room to stretch. Walking barefoot is an effective grounding exercise. For additional opening, try walking on different surfaces— grass, sand, rocks or mud. The varying textures will increase your sensitivity and awareness. Wiggling and stretching the toes and rotating the ankles are also beneficial. Pampering the feet with a massage increases openness in the soles of the feet.

A simple grounding tool is a one-inch dowel. You can also use a broom handle. Place the dowel lengthwise on the floor and stand on it with your bare feet. Find the sensitive and sore places on the soles of the feet. Stand for a few minutes, taking deep and full breaths to encourage the feet to relax and open. It is normal for the feet to be tender. Try putting one foot on the dowel at a time to control the amount of pressure on the foot. Roll the feet back and forth over the dowel. Gently encourage the feet to relax and open. The pressure points on the soles of the feet will be stimulated and positively affect the health and well-being of the whole body.

After using the dowel, stand and notice any differences in your body. Do you feel lighter? Do you see more clearly? Does your mind feel sharper? Do you feel more relaxed? Do you feel more energized?

Grounding Visualization

This is a guided meditation to help you improve your connection with the earth. As you improve your system of roots, you allow your wings to lift you higher. The meditation is most beneficial done standing with your bare feet firmly planted on the floor or ground. If seated, place both feet flat on the ground. Massage the feet or use the dowel exercise before doing the visualization. You may wish to tape the meditation so you can close your eyes and listen.

HOW TO BEGIN

Find a quiet place where you can spend thirty minutes undisturbed. Find a firm, level surface indoors or outdoors to stand with bare feet. You can stand against a wall for support and balance. Take a few minutes to adjust your stance until you feel comfortable.

Close your eyes. Take several deep, full breaths. As you exhale, let go of the activities of the day. Let your mind empty and relax. Follow your breath in and out to help your mind center and focus. Take a few audible sighs to release any tension.

Now bring your attention to your feet. Rock back and forth a few times to help the feet open. Bring your body back to the center and stand firmly on two feet. Notice if you tend to stand more on the heels or toes, or put more weight on one foot. Adjust your weight so it is evenly distributed over the soles of both feet. Spread the toes as much as you can. Imagine spreading the toes forward and the heels backward.

Now bring your awareness to your legs. Imagine lines of energy running through your legs. You can picture these lines of energy as roots of a tree. These roots move down the legs and through the soles of the feet. You can imagine the soles of the feet made of soft, rich soil. Visualize and feel the roots breaking through the soles of the feet to penetrate the earth. Imagine the roots growing deeper and deeper into the earth or floor beneath you. Feel the anchoring and stabilizing effect. You can send the roots as deeply as you wish.

As the roots penetrate the ground, your heart and mind can begin to lift higher and higher. Feel the spine lengthening and growing upward, out of the rooted feet. Feel the heart gently lifting upward. Relaxing your jaw and eyes, feel the body grow out of the rooted feet. Continue to breath and release any tension. Enjoy the sensations in your body and mind. Try using this exercise daily or weekly to improve mental focus and increase feelings of security and well-being.

The Importance of the Right Brain

Our society emphasizes the learning style of the logical left brain. The left brain is linear and sequential. Our current educational system favors students with left-brain strength. People with dominant left-brain styles of learning are naturally applauded, while right-brain dominant people may feel unsupported. The future educational system will include more courses to encourage and support the talents of the intuitive student. In the meantime, it is up to each individual to train and exercise right-brain capabilities.

Let's look at the difference between left and right brain communication. Imagine a large ship on the ocean. The ship is expansive, with many decks and sophisticated equipment. The ship will represent your left brain. The left brain houses a wealth of information, and every fragment is stored in a specific location—as every article of equipment has its place on a well-organized ship. When you learn the layout of the ship, you can easily find the equipment each time you need it. It is the same with the information of the left brain. Every fragment of information has a specified and logical placement. You can call up this information by remembering where you found it the last time you looked for it.

Now let's look at the ocean as the symbol representing the right brain. The tides and currents of this vast body of water constantly change the placement and even the form of its contents. An object you saw in the surf in the morning can be far away at sea by midday. It may even be inside a fish or broken into tiny pieces. The fluidity, vastness and unpredictability of the ocean makes it impossible to catalog its contents. This is also true for the right brain. Your right brain does not have the same concrete, consistent filing system as the left brain. There is a wider scope of possibilities and potentials. There is no defined system of linear time. In the ocean of the right brain, you can receive a message in a bottle days before it is sent. Conversely, messages reach the ship's left-brain communication center as they are transmitted.

Each hemisphere has its own specific method of recall and memory. It is important to use techniques that enhance these individualistic capabilities. The following exercise is designed to access the information of the intuitive brain:

Automatic Writing

A common tool for practicing right-brain communication is automatic writing. It is the process of allowing your right brain to communicate without being censored by the left brain. It is akin to stream-of-consciousness writing—allowing the hand to write whatever comes into the mind. Writing with the left brain includes the logical ordering and sequencing of thoughts. The left brain is trained to organize and clarify the incoming thoughts. Right-brain writing thrives on random and seemingly disconnected ideas. The less you impose order and sequence onto right-brain thoughts, the clearer and more accurate they become.

When you practice automatic writing, you are dipping into an immense sea of information. Rather than looking for linear and logical sequencing, you are open to whatever happens to be swimming by at the moment. You are not looking for logical patterns, just enjoying and relishing the variety and spontaneity of the information you receive.

Later you will be able to decipher the messages. Some messages will not be relevant for weeks, months or even years. I have received information in automatic writing that did not become manifest until years later. It is important to keep your writing dated and to check it periodically for pre-cognitive information.

HOW TO BEGIN

1. Find a quiet space. Interruptions may disrupt the flow of energy, so unplug the phone and inform housemates that you will be unavailable.

2. Find a comfortable seated position. Have a pen and paper by your side or on your lap. Write the date at the top of the page. Relax your hands, turning the palms face up, and close your eyes.

3. Use a meditative tape, music or your own meditative process to quiet your mind. The high gear of the left brain often overrides the more subtle voice of the right brain.

4. Take ten deep, slow breaths. Follow your inhalations and exhalations with your mind. You can repeat silently: "Breathing in, breathing out."

5. With each breath, feel your physical body relaxing and releasing its tension. Feel your shoulders release downward and your jaw loosen and release.

6. Now invite your intuition to come forward. Say silently: "I am now willing to listen to my intuition. I now hear my intuition clearly and easily."

7. Keep breathing slowly and deeply. Allow yourself to sigh audibly several times.

8. Gently pick up your pen and write the opening statement: "I am now open to learning from my intuition." You can also write a specific question to be answered.

9. After you have written the question, allow your mind to wander and stay relaxed. Let go of your expectations. Try saying silently: "My mind is clear and open."

10. Write down anything that comes into your mind. Resist the temptation to judge or censor what you write. It may feel like the information is coming from outside of you. It may feel like you are imagining or making up the data. If you have impressions of sights, sounds, smells or physical symptoms, note these in your writing.

11. Work toward keeping your pen moving. If you get stuck, try repeating the affirmation: "I am now open to learning from my intuition."

12. Stop writing whenever you wish. Read over what you have written. Take notes about your feelings during this exercise. Remember to reread your automatic writing from time to time to check for precognitive hits.

Weekly Predictions

This is an easy and fun psychic exercise that I learned from Patricia Hayes at Delphi University. Designed to build confidence in your ability to know future events, it can be done every week or whenever you choose. It is fun to do when you are traveling and can be practiced by adults and children. Often my daughter and I will do this exercise while we wait in an airport or start on a road trip.

1. Take a piece of paper and put your name and the date at the top of the page. You may want to note your location if you are traveling. Then add seven days to the date to note the end date of the predictions. For example: April 3-10.

2. Now you are ready to prepare to write your list. You can record the following relaxation instructions for playback or use your own relaxation technique. Close your eyes and take five or six deep, full breaths. As you exhale, feel your shoulders relaxing and dropping. Feel your jaw loosen and relax. Feel your eyes floating gently in the sockets. Let your tongue rest on the bottom of your mouth. Allow your mind to clear. Recite: "There is no wrong answer. Whatever I see or feel is right for me."

3. As your mind clears and opens, ideas, images or sensations will come to you. Write down whatever you see, feel or sense. Do not judge your impressions. If the impression is an image, make a sketch of it. Continue until you have ten to twelve items.

4. If you get stuck, go back to the relaxation. Check and see if you have tightened your jaw or shoulders. Breathe and relax. Try sighing a few times. Recite: "My mind is clear and open."

5. When you are finished, read your predictions and put the paper in a safe place. As your week unfolds, look at your predictions and see if you have any hits. Remember that your right brain is symbolic. You may need to interpret some of the items using dream interpretation resources.

This exercise builds your confidence in your psychic ability. Even though the predictions may seem trivial, you will have concrete evidence of your natural ability to know future events. Your increased confidence brings access to more pertinent future knowledge.

One of my most striking weekly predictions occurred while on vacation. It is normally a time when you disengage your left brain and are more open to psychic revelations.

Rocket in the Round

Leaving my young daughter with her dad, I went on retreat to New Mexico. I was excited to be getting off by myself for an adventure. This was my first visit to Santa Fe and Taos. I felt a strong spiritual sense that I would love this area of Native American mysticism and ritual. As I flew across the country from the East Coast, I wrote some predictions in my notebook. I made a list of ten things:

- *bandage*
- *turbans*
- *dragonfly*
- *hose*
- *rocket in the round*
- *flying bird*
- *sweet pastry with crème*
- *weather—stormy*
- *footwear*
- *architectural blueprints—aerial view*

As I reread my predictions, I felt skeptical. The items seemed so disconnected and bizarre. I was particularly puzzled by "rocket in the round." I folded up the paper and continued to read my novel. Four hours later the plane landed and I disembarked.

One of the first people I saw in the Albuquerque airport was a woman with an ace bandage covering most of her right arm. I smiled, thinking of my first prediction. And then to my surprise, I saw two men wearing turbans directly behind her, smiling and talking animatedly. It was fun to get out my paper and see the predictions written in black and white.

The week unfolded as I explored New Mexico. After I arrived, I discovered a UFO museum. Eager to explore the extraterrestrial museum, I walked onto the grounds. I saw two buildings, one low and rectangular-shaped, the other tall, round and painted to look just like a rocket. There was my "rocket in the round."

At the end of the week, I flew back home. I arrived home several hours before the time I was scheduled to meet my daughter. I felt like taking a shower and putting my feet up. On my way to the bathroom, I felt a sudden urge to turn on the television. It was 4:00 P.M., not a normal viewing time for me. Following the impulse, I turned on the television. It was tuned to the public station, and *Mr. Roger's Neighborhood* was airing. At that moment he was showing his young audience some architectural blueprints and a wooden model of a house with no roof, revealing the rooms from an aerial view. I remembered my last prediction of "architectural blueprints—aerial view." This is a good example of the importance of following your spontaneous hunches and illogical thoughts. If I had resisted my urge to turn on the television at that moment, I would have missed the validation of my final prediction.

An Iguana in Copenhagen

It is important to remember that your rational brain does not have enough information to judge or discount your weekly predictions. Your left brain will tell you that this exercise is silly and useless. Your logical mind may tell you not to write down an especially odd prediction. You must remember that the rules of the intuitive brain are not rational or predictable. Here is an example using one of my daughter's predictions:

* * *

We were on our way to Denmark, and we wrote our predictions in the airport before takeoff. My daughter, Sarah, who was nine years old at the time, had a favorite pet iguana. So when the second item on her list was "iguana," I smiled to myself. I thought that she was probably thinking of her pet and had put that thought in her predictions. However, one of the very first public buildings we entered after arriving in Copenhagen had a huge carved iguana over its entrance. We both saw it at the same moment and laughed aloud. In this country of cold wind and ice, it seemed unlikely to us that the iguana would be an architectural totem.

It is very crucial to suspend your judgment and to trust whatever comes to your mind. You will be glad you did not censor, when your weekly predictions come true. It may take more time than allotted for your predictions to be revealed. Take out old predictions periodically to check for matches. Keep practicing, and you will be rewarded.

Seeing with Your Hands

Psychic talent can be expressed in a variety of ways. Some people are gifted visually and see images with their mind's eye. Some have a kinesthetic gift of feeling and use their body to intuit information, while still others have the ability to hear information.

HOW TO BEGIN

This exercise is designed to help identify your areas of strength. You will need a pen and paper, several 81/2" x 11" manila envelopes, and some magazines. You may ask a friend to help you by selecting several pages from the magazines. It is best to choose pages with prominent pictures. You can do it yourself by blindly selecting several pages from a magazine. If you are choosing blindly, then choose magazines that have pictures on every page. Ask your friend to place one page in an 81/2" x 11" manila envelope. Number the envelopes 1, 2, 3, etc. If you are doing it yourself, close your eyes and blindly select one page to place in each envelope. You now have several closed and numbered envelopes with a mystery page inside each one.

1. Select an envelope. Write the number of the envelope on the top of a clean sheet of paper. Sit and follow your breath. Take several deep breaths. As you exhale, relax your shoulders, hips and jaw. Breathe deeply and slowly to allow your mind to become quiet and calm.

2. Thank your left brain for all its help and allow it to relax and defocus. Allow your thoughts to float and drift. Keep your attention on your breath as you inhale and exhale.

3. Invite your right brain to open and expand, allowing it to come into focus. Your right brain will be doing this exercise for you. Repeat the statement: "I am now open to learning from my intuition."

4. After you feel your mind releasing and opening, focus on the envelope. You may hold the envelope to your head or heart area. You may hold your hand, palm down, several inches from the envelope to practice sensing the images. Remember that any images that come into your mind are welcomed.

5. Write down everything that comes into your mind. Note any visual images or impressions. Write down any words or sounds you hear with your inner ears. Write down any physical sensations you feel in your body. For example, if you have a strong sensation in your head, you may be holding an image of a head or an ad for a

headache powder. Do not judge what you sense. You will be glad that you wrote down all of your impressions.

6. Now you are ready to open the envelope. Examine the pictures on the page. Look carefully for symbolic connections with your description. Look for words in the written text that may match your writing. Remember to check both sides of the page. Do not be discouraged if you do not have any hits. With practice you will develop your abilities. Let's look at an example of a man discovering the style of his psychic gift:

One of my clients tried this exercise to test his right-brain strength. His work is in the field of chemistry, and he has a predominantly logical view of the world. However, his curiosity led him to explore this unknown portion of his brain. One of the exercises we tried was seeing with his hands. During the exercise, he relaxed, held the envelope and began to describe his impressions. He saw letters and began to spell a word: D_U_C_K. When we opened the envelope, the predominant image on the page was a large mallard duck. Holding the next envelope, he saw the color red, and we found a page of striking red images upon opening the envelope. He was surprised at these evidential results.

There are many ways to develop and explore your psychic energy. Play with these exercises to find your strengths. The more you explore and practice, the more your psychic energy expands.

Learning from Material Loss

We are spiritual beings operating in a material world. Our task is to integrate the material ego self with the transcendent spiritual self. Since our metaphysical classroom exists in a concrete world, many of our lessons involve material objects. We can use our attachment to these material possessions to help us understand our spiritual lessons.

In this section we will look at techniques to help us recover or release lost or stolen items. Invariably, we all experience the loss of valuable items—from jewelry to important papers. We all know how frustrating it is to search endlessly without success. Many of us have also experienced the pain of loss through theft. At times it is possible to relocate these items, and at other times they are not retrievable. In either case, we can access valuable information about our spiritual paths by analyzing these losses. Our attachment to the valuable items can motivate us to search more deeply into the psyche, in the hopes of either finding the lost items or reconciling ourselves to their disappearance. Whether we relocate them or not, we will have gained important insight into the psyche.

The Universal Draft

When we are motivated, we can accomplish amazing feats. When we are resistant, we can ignore important aspects of our lives with fixed passivity. Life has a way of bringing us the lessons we need rather than the ones we want. I call this phenomenon the "universal draft." The draft is compulsory conscription into service such as the military. In the case of the universal draft, we are compelled to face and work through a spiritual lesson. Occasionally it is possible to volunteer to do a spiritual lesson. However, more often we tend to avoid the more difficult and painful lessons. Since the human ego seeks the least threatening route, it often seems against our nature to volunteer for a difficult spiritual mission. Just as in the military, the draft forces us into the situation, and we are faced with dealing with the lesson.

Since our world is a classroom, we can sometimes be guilty of truancy. Some of the most rewarding classes for our spiritual growth are also the hardest and most intimidating for us to begin. We find many distractions from the lesson at hand. Facing loss can serve as the impetus to begin work that may be long overdue. Because of our emotional attachment to our possessions, we feel motivated to recover them. We will often extend ourselves emotionally, and take emotional risks when motivated to find a cherished belonging. In this way, we can take advantage of the ego's attachment to the material world. The possibility of recovering the lost item can act as the carrot that moves us forward into unexplored and fertile spiritual terrain.

The universal draft moves us into more difficult lessons. All of us have experienced the altering state of consciousness that comes with a crisis. Trivial annoyances and worries seem to fade and dissolve. We develop a sharp, single-minded focus. Daily routine activities lose importance and attention. Facing adversity, we are brought directly into contact with our most important essence. It is often during these times that our spiritual growth accelerates. We can observe this phenomenon when we face a physical or material loss. Let's look at an example:

* * *

A young woman, married with three young children, was preparing to have her jewelry cleaned. She put three rings and a charm bracelet in a cloth bag and placed the bag in her car to be delivered. The next time she remembered the cloth bag, she could not find it. She searched to no avail. Months later she came to me for help.

First, we made a list of the lost items—her engagement ring, her wedding ring, a clatter ring and a charm bracelet with charms of her three children. All of these items were emotionally important to her. The jewelry was symbolic of her roles as a wife and mother. By misplacing the jewelry, she had lost the outward symbols of being a wife and a mother. I was interested in exploring how she currently felt in her life. Lost items can be unconscious messages to the psyche concerning an imbalance. I asked her how she was feeling about herself. She said she loved her family, but admitted to feeling disconnected and self-conscious. She felt out of touch with her ability to play and have fun. The duties and responsibilities of her roles as wife and mother were overpowering her connection with herself.

When she made the appointment, I asked her to watch her dreams during the week before her appointment. She had three significant dreams. Two involved her seeing her lost jewelry around her. The third dream dealt directly with her need for more fun in her life. Her psyche was ready and willing to give her information about the life lesson connected to the lost jewelry.

We discussed ways she could start to find more fun and play in her life. She loved being a wife and mother but needed to regain a fulfilling sense of self. We made a plan for her to prioritize herself and begin to reconnect with her own needs. She needed to reestablish her identity outside of her roles as mother and wife.

* * *

This is a good example of universal draft at work. Normally it is difficult for the young woman to take time for herself. However, when faced with the loss of her jewelry, she found the time. She was motivated to spend money and energy to retrieve her lost items, and in the process she went deeper into her feelings. She used the lost items to delve into her psyche and regain new balance.

Fulfilling the metaphysical lesson that is offered through a loss often allows for the lost item to be recovered. In some cases, the item may be destroyed or irretrievable. In that case, the release of the item is part of the lesson. The person is practicing letting go of the physical attachment to the item. In either case, the person comes out the winner. The gaining of personal insight and spiritual growth can bring comfort and awareness that allow a person to understand and accept a loss. Let's look at another example:

* * *

One day I received a phone call from a young woman in the framing business. She is a careful and conscientious worker and was very distraught to find she had misplaced a client's artwork. As I tuned into her situation, I felt that her lesson involved her fear of disapproval and of being shamed for wrongdoing.

The client had brought the framer an original print by her deceased aunt. The aunt was very revered and loved by her niece. Of German descent, the artist had survived the Nazi occupation and bequeathed much of her artwork to her niece. I could feel the intense emotional attachment they shared. The original piece of art was a direct and vibrant connection between the two women.

Since the artwork was irreplaceable, the framer was pushed into feelings of inadequacy and shame. Shamed often by a critical father, she relived the feelings of her childhood. We discussed the importance of her telling the client of the missing artwork. For her own personal work, she needed to face her fear directly by telling the client that she could not find the artwork. She faced her past and found the inner strength to face her feelings of inadequacy. She called her client and set up a meeting for the next day. She found the print that night. She knew she needed to follow through with her plan to tell the client of the temporary loss even though she had found the print. This experience launched her into an intensive and committed spiritual training that continues as I share her story. She used the lost item as a springboard into a ten-year program of weekly sessions of spiritual healing and evolution.

The Spiritual Detective

Finding lost items involves detective work. It is your job to gather all of the information available to you to solve the mystery. You can also use your dream life to bring you valuable clues. You can combine all the available information to help you understand the spiritual lesson.

HOW TO BEGIN

1. Look at the symbolic meaning of each lost item. What area of your life is symbolically represented by the item? For example: wedding ring, marriage; work document, professional; check or money, financial; family heirloom, childhood.

2. When did you lose it? Was the timing connected with any important anniversaries or dates? Were there any other noteworthy events at the same time?

3. What was the emotional climate in your life at the time? Assess your level of stress. Note any health, work or relationship difficulties.

4. What emotions were triggered by the loss? For example: wedding ring, sadness; work document, fear of being fired; check or money, fear of lack.

5. Is it difficult or frightening for you to feel and express these emotions? Use chapters 2 and 4 to access and clear the feelings.

6. Were you reminded of any past events that evoked similar feelings? If so, elaborate. The lost item may be alerting you that it is time to clear these old feelings. You can get help from a therapist if the feelings are overwhelming or frightening.

After you have gathered all the information available, you may wish to use the following exercise to clear away the frustration of futilely searching for a lost item. You may do this exercise alone or with others. Group psychic energy can be potent in locating missing items.

Relax and Let Go

It can be very frustrating to search for a missing item. Often you search through the same piles and the same drawers as your tension mounts. The more you frantically search, the more you separate yourself from your intuition. Your logical mind tells you where to look and pushes you compulsively. This exercise is designed to break the compulsion and activate your right brain. This technique allows your intuition to bring you valuable information.

1. Stop searching for the item. Set aside fifteen minutes of quiet time for yourself. Find a comfortable sitting position. If you are in a group, ask everyone to sit and hold hands. This combines the energy of the group and strengthens the outcome. Close your eyes and take several deep breaths.

2. Next, state your intention to temporarily stop the search. For these fifteen minutes, agree to let go of the search. Each participant can state aloud, "I am no longer looking for _____." Keep breathing through the process. You are allowing the item to find you.

3. Continue to breathe and allow your mind to relax. Let go of expectations and desires. Breathe and be aware of any impressions. Remember, there are no wrong answers. When you are ready, open your eyes and write down what you received. If you are in a group, share your impressions. Moving slowly and calmly, follow any of the impressions. It can be helpful to hold a "connecting item" in your hand as you look, such as a key to help you find a lost key or a

checkbook to find a lost check. The connecting item will help direct your right brain to the correct file in your mind. The connecting item acts as an energetic magnet to attract the item to you. If you are unable to find the item, stop the search. Turn your attention to other activities. After a break, repeat the above exercise.

Psychic Communication

Right brain communication is available to each of us in any given moment. Each person carries a cloud of information around their physical body. As you learn to decipher the cloud you can receive unspoken messages from those around you. You can use this ability to sidestep difficult or even dangerous encounters and to enhance your ability to tune into yourself, your children and your friends.

When I was a child, I experimented with different ways to send and receive information. I spent hours on the beach enamored with collecting shells, starfish and shark's teeth. I developed a simple technique for finding the rare shark tooth among the broken shells. I would walk slowly down the beach strand with my eyes closed, breathing deeply until I felt a slight shiver move through my body. I would then squat down and gently move my open palm face down over the expanse of shells. When I felt an electrical impulse in the palm of my hand I had found a shark's tooth.

In later years, I used this same method to help me in the Graduate Record Exam (GRE) for entering graduate school. I was nervous about taking the exam, since I had been out of college for several years traveling abroad and working. My inner guidance was very clear, telling me to try and enjoy the experience. I decided to skip the usual cramming and go to a movie the night before. I meditated the next morning before the test and used my yoga breathing all through the test. I kept reminding myself to smile and think of humorous thoughts. I used the palm scan for difficult multiple choice questions. Normally I score significantly higher in language skills, so I was pleasantly surprised to see my math score was nearly comparable to the verbal. The combination of knowledge, relaxation, humor and a little help from psychic impulses helped me through.

Later, still in my psychic practice, I used a similar method to dowse for wells. Instead of using dowsing sticks, I noted the sensations I felt in my body. I would walk the land until I felt a strong tingling in my legs and hips. The tingling grew stronger when I stood over a wealth of water. I was able to help several homeowners locate wells with a good, strong water supply.

To follow your intuitive radar you must be willing to risk following hunches even if you do not know where you are headed. Your intuition may tell you to walk up to a stranger or drive a different route to your job. If you stop to ask why or allow your left brain to talk you out of the hunch, you may miss a rewarding adventure.

Hands Off

One afternoon, I was in a gift store browsing through cards and books with a friend. Across the store I overheard a man mention St. Louis as he was checking out. I was inexplicably drawn to stand near him as he described his home city. I asked him to tell me more about the city. He seemed a little surprised by my interest but was willing to describe the city. I was particularly drawn to his description of the city's arch. He explained that the arch symbolized the gateway to the West. After several minutes I thanked him, and my friend and I left the store. She looked at me quizzically and I shrugged. I did not know why I was suddenly so interested in St. Louis.

That afternoon at my office I was clearing some items off my desk. I accidentally knocked my ceramic wizard on the floor. In the fall both of his hands snapped off at the wrists and I clearly heard the words "Hands off! You have no control of this one!" Without understanding the signifi-cance, I knew the message was important. I wrote it down and dated the paper. I took the hands and wrapped them in a tissue and continued with my clients.

Two days later, I was with a client who was practicing her psychic exercises during her session. I had taken her into a light trance state, and she was receiving information. Sitting across from her, I took the oppor-tunity to tune into my own state of mind. I heard the phone machine click quietly with an incoming call. Simultaneously, I felt a strong chill and a wave of nausea. I often heard the subtle click during sessions, so I was surprised by my reaction. I wrote automatically on the page in front of me—"Numb, scared—I've never done it. I feel little and insignificant." I then returned my attention to my client and finished the hour.

I moved quickly to my answering machine as soon as she left. In a shaky and subdued voice, my oldest sister had left a cryptic message to call her as soon as possible. With trembling hands I dialed her number. She told me that our dad had died unexpectedly at the St. Louis airport. I knew that my parents were traveling from North Carolina to Hawaii to retrace the steps of their first meeting and subsequent marriage and hon-eymoon. I did not know their journey took them through St. Louis.

All the events of the past three days flooded into my consciousness. I had sensed a hidden connection with St. Louis. Interestingly, in spiritual terminology, the Gateway to the West is the entrance to the land of the dead. Although I had not known the extent of the "hands-off" situation, I felt better equipped to deal with it. The cryptic events and messages were preparing me for an event that "I've never done before." My father's death was the first death of a family member or friend.

There was another synchronistic event several years later involving a second ceramic wizard. This smaller wizard was given to me by my mother and played "When I Wish Upon a Star." It was sitting on a table where it had stood for several years. Three days before another unexpected death, I knocked it off the table and the hair broke off. The owl riding on the shoulder fell to the floor beside the hair. Nervously I picked up the hair and the owl. My thoughts turned to the death of my father. Three days later, my hairdresser and good friend Tony died. I thought of the many deep conversations Tony and I shared during my haircuts. How appropriate that the wizard donated his hair to relay the message. I buried the ceramic hair and owl on Tony's property in a private memorial service.

The key to psychic communication is being as clear and open a channel as possible. The success rate is directly related to the clarity and power of the sender and the receiver. The clearer your emotional body is, the stronger your energy will travel and be received by others. The more receptive you are to yourself and those around you, the more information you will be able to pick up. At times we may unintentionally pick up information from a strong sender. One such encounter happened to my daughter and me on a trip to Jackson Hole, Wyoming.

After a full day of skiing, we arrived early to have dinner at a favorite spot, The Cadillac Grille. As we walked into the empty restaurant I was already tasting oysters and Caesar salad, a menu that reminds me of my father. A marine biologist by profession, he brought us seafood as often as possible and oysters were his favorite.

Our waiter arrived and took our order. Sarah and I nibbled on the freshly baked bread as we stretched our sore leg muscles. The young waiter arrived with our salads and turned to me asking, "Would you like some fresh ground pepper on your salad, Susan?" I paused and looked at Sarah. Her fork was arrested in midair and her eyes were large and surprised. I knew by her expression that she had heard him clearly say my name. We knew we had not given our names as we entered, nor does my daughter call me by my first name so we were surprised he knew it.

"Do you know my name?" I asked him as he stood poised with the pepper grinder. He looked surprised and said. "No." "Well, you just said it!" I told him. He had not remembered saying my name, although we had both clearly heard it spoken. I told him I was interested in this kind of phenomenon because of my line of work. I asked his name. "Sean," he said. It is an Irish name, the same derivative as John, my father's first name. The waiter was Irish and French Canadian. My father was one-half French Canadian and had adopted Ireland as his second home, spending summers in a cottage on a lake in Ireland. I told the young waiter that I was not surprised that my father had found a way to get a message to me. And I thanked him by giving him a brief reading on a current relationship.

Communication with Comatose Patients

It is common knowledge that people in a comatose state are aware of their surroundings. Loved ones of a comatose patient are encouraged to talk or read to them as if they were conscious. This practice keeps the lines of communication open and vital. The comatose state, commonly known as "being unconscious," is actually a very conscious state of mind. We label this state as "unconscious" because we lack the skills to speak the language of the comatose.

As in the dream state, the ego of a comatose patient is partially submerged, and the subconscious is more alert and active. The right brain of the comatose person stands open and receptive. The comatose patient may be actively trying to send messages to loved ones. The last stages of dying reflect a similar state of being. Often the dying person is trying to complete relationships or give last minute instructions or messages from this distant state of consciousness. By using a right-brain approach we can receive clear communication from those who are comatose or near death. As we become more attuned to telepathic communication we can help the comatose and the dying to communicate their needs and wishes.

Relieving the Pressure

I picked up my messages one afternoon and heard the voice of Sally, a client and friend. Her voice was heavy with concern and fatigue. Beth, her life partner, was in critical condition after being crushed by 2,000 pounds of drywall. When paramedics arrived on the scene, she had been without oxygen to the brain for seven minutes. With a collapsed right lung, fractured spleen and broken ribs, she was rushed to the hospital, intubated and given pain medication.

Two days after the accident, the doctors were eager to remove the tube from Beth's throat. It is imperative for the patient to have a certain level of consciousness and cooperation to remove the tube. When the doctors had tried earlier, Beth became semiconscious and combative. It was necessary to sedate and restrain her to prevent her from injuring herself. Sally was very concerned, and she turned to me to see if I could help in any way.

I told Sally to call me from the intensive care unit on her next visit and we would try to get some reassuring messages to Beth. As I tuned in, I could tell that Beth was frightened and disoriented, not knowing where she was, what had happened, and not recognizing her partner, Sally. Sally listened in as I talked softly to Beth through the phone.

I could sense that Beth was caught in the past, feeling small and helpless and afraid of the people around her. She telepathically spoke of some difficult issues with her parents. I reassured her that we could discuss these in length and I would help her release the uncomfortable feelings. I could feel the pressure in my own chest as she talked of feeling "smothered by her parents." She had felt pressure since her childhood to put her parents' needs before her own. A long-standing pattern of taking care of others at her own expense had preceded the accident. I spoke to her about taking care of herself and letting go of the need to take care of her parents and Sally. I told her that everyone in the hospital was there to help her get well. I reminded her that Sally was a dear friend and helper. The confused and frightened part of Beth was very young. I spoke to her gently, hoping to give her a comforting and reassuring anchor in the pain and confusion of the hospital.

She also complained of being very tired. She said repeatedly, "It's hard to come back." I knew that she was referring to coming back into her body. I reassured her that she could take her time coming out of the coma. I reminded her that her only job was to rest and be taken care of, not an easy task for an independent and caretaking woman.

I suggested that Sally stay with her for the next four hours repeating these messages to her. She had been nonresponsive for hours, yet when we began to talk, her heart rate changed. As I spoke to her about her close relationship with Sally, she turned her head toward her. I felt reassured that Beth would be able to cooperate with the tube removal the next day. I also reminded Sally that it may take longer than expected because of Beth's need to rest and take her time reentering her body.

By the following evening Beth was lucid. The tube was removed without incident and she was able to speak to Sally. After eight days in the hospital she came home to rest and heal. She came for several sessions to work on the issues of boundaries with her family as soon as she was physically able. Her recovery has been steady and strong. From her near death experience, Beth has been given a unique perspective of her world. It will take both Sally and Beth time to integrate the experiences the accident precipitated. They have both used this frightening and painful event to dive deeper into their issues and build a stronger and more intimate bond. Sally was wise to follow her intuition and seek help in communicating with Beth in her altered comatose state.

The two following stories recount examples of communication with mothers in the last stages of dying and their very conscious attempt to let their children know the extent of their love for them:

Alberta's Boys

Charlie telephoned to tell me that his mother, Alberta, was comatose in a local hospital. I had seen both of them as clients some years before. I remembered how I enjoyed my time with this feisty Italian woman. The next day I met him and his brother Paul at the intensive care unit. Alberta had been on the threshold of death for several weeks, unable to communicate or breathe on her own. We gathered around the bedside, and I tuned into her thoughts. Although she lay still and pale, I could feel the aliveness and agitation of her right brain. She passionately wanted to complete some unfinished business with her sons before she died. She was worried about their relationship and wanted to know that they would work on it. She had very specific messages for each son. Acting as the interpreter, I was able to allow her to communicate these last wishes to her sons. When each son received and verbally answered her messages, her heart monitor reading leapt in recognition. The grown boys were able to communicate their love and last messages to their mother through me.

The intensive care nurse came in and told us that Alberta needed to rest. We encircled her bed, touching her lovingly and telling her to go whenever she wished. I kissed her gently on the forehead, hugged her sons and went to my car. She died ten minutes after I left the hospital. She had said good-bye and now could rest.

Several days later Charlie, his girlfriend Lori and Paul left for the beach to scatter Alberta's ashes. They called to tell me they were leaving, and I told them I would be with them in spirit. Several hours after they left for the coast I received a very strong telepathic message. A voice said, "Tell them to wait for the dolphins. They want to join in the ceremony. They must not start until the dolphins come." I hurriedly called the cell phone number, hoping I would reach them. Paul answered and I told him the news. "No matter how long it takes, wait for the dolphins," I told them emphatically.

When the three arrived at the water's edge, they patiently waited with their mother's ashes beside them. The day was unremarkable, the sky a dull gray. Two hours after they arrived, they were astounded to see a pod of thirty dolphins leaping and frolicking right in front of them. They were so glad that they waited for their arrival. Simultaneously the clouds parted to reveal a brilliant blue, the sun shone in rays upon the sand. They wished Alberta well as they tossed the ashes into the sea.

Frederica's Ascent

My friend Gwynn and I were carefully following the last days of our friend Frederica. Diagnosed with cancer six months earlier, she was on a fast track, having anywhere from a few months to a year to her death. We watched her move rapidly through the stages—physical, emotional, mental and spiritual—changing unpredictably like the weather on an island—sometimes calm, sometimes wild, always Frederica. Her grown children and Gwynn were always present during these months, caring for her physical needs and supporting her spirit.

As we made plans to have our weekly get-together, we intuitively knew that our dinner would be flanked with visits to Frederica at the Hospice In-Care Facility. We arrived to find two of her children, Kathy and Tony, weary and concerned. Gwynn and I could see from Frederica's appearance and breathing that her passing was imminent. Yet, we could also feel her restlessness and unease. She seemed caught and held, and her children sensed that something was wrong but did not know how to help her.

Often a dying person has a need to communicate unexpressed feelings or unspoken words before passing over. An awareness of this unfinished business may not crystallize until very near death. Too weak to speak, the eyes of the dying may reflect the need to deliver these last-minute messages. Wanting to speak but too weak to utter the words the breath or the body struggles to communicate to loved ones. As in labor, the breath is key to an easy and peaceful transition.

As we entered the room, Frederica lay on her side, one hand curled under her chin like a child. Her eyes, clear and deep, were unblinking, and her brow was slightly furrowed. As soon as my eyes met hers, we locked gazes. Immediately she began to pour thoughts into my mind. "Do they know how much I love them?" her mind kept asking mine over and over again. "Yes. I know they do." I reassured her, remembering the loving, concerned faces of her grown children. "You must tell them," she insisted telepathically. "I will tell them. I promise," I vowed. Her children had been reassuring their mother that they loved her, repeating it over and over again. Yet her concern was that they know of the depth of her love for them. As I promised to deliver the message, the quality of her breath shifted. I could feel the wave of death trying to lift and carry her, and, like a surfer, she was positioning herself to best catch and ride it to the shore.

I saw a flicker of fear in her eyes. "You are safe. Ride the wave," I told her gently. I then felt a circle of dolphins moving into the room, their liquid eyes filled with compassion and joy. They were there to accompany her, escorting her home. "Can you see the dolphins? Ride the waves with them." Her eyes sparkled, signaling recognition of the gentle presence of the dolphins. I felt the wave lift us both. "I'll stay with you as long as you wish." Again her breath shifted, deepened and smoothed.

As she relaxed, her brow smoothed and her heart opened further. I gasped as my mind was filled with beautiful images of sunsets, snowfalls and sleeping babies—all the beauty Frederica had collected in her life. Frederica is a passionate and vibrant artist full of reverence for all aspects of life, as seen in her vivid, expressive paintings. These scenes of beauty blended with colors and faces, and all the paintings she had envisioned were merging to form a wondrous home for her. I was witnessing the construction of her personal heaven; like a mother bird feathering her nest, she prepared her new home. I wept with joy for the beauty of her heaven.

After delivering Frederica's message to her children, Gwynn and I went to eat dinner. Kathy and Tony went into their mother's room to share memories and continue supporting her passage out of her physical form. We received the call from Hospice as we were paying the check. We rushed to her bedside minutes after she took her last breath. With a grown child holding each of her hands, she had let go. Her face was smooth and glowing. Her lids slightly closed, her eyes lifted upward, her mouth in a hint of a smile. She reminded me of a portrait of St. Theresa in the moment of her ecstasy, her face reflecting a glimpse of God and heaven. Her body was vibrating and energized. Fascinated by the combination of wisdom and innocence reflected in her face, we watched subtle changes in her expression. Stroking her and holding her, we celebrated her new life. The vibration in her body gently ebbed and flowed. Suddenly I felt her spirit return, seeming to animate her face once again. "I'm not dead!" I heard her cry. "I know," I told her with tears running down my cheeks. We stayed with her for hours as entranced as new parents with their newborn infant.

How to Explore Right-Brain Communication

1. Take several deep breaths. Let out a sigh.

2. Clear your mind of thoughts.

3. Silently or aloud, talk to the person exactly as you would if they were conscious. Pause and listen.

4. You are listening with your inner ear. You have a complete telephone system inside your head—the speaker and the receiver. At first you may distrust what you hear, imagine, sense, feel or see in your mind's eye. Write down any messages even if you are not sure of their clarity. Trust your intuition.

5. Offer words of explanation or comfort to the person if their thoughts seem disoriented. Often the person will not understand where they are or what has happened to them. Tell them simply what happened and that they are safe and being cared for.

6. The communication is similar to talking to a child. You may need to repeat yourself. Tell them it is fine to keep asking the same questions. Often comfort and reassurance are the most vital messages to relay to them. In time, as you practice, you may be able to receive more specific questions and relay the answers to them.

Psychic communication brings a new depth and breadth to relating. It enables us to contact others during difficult times such as illness or the last stages of dying. It is liberating to know we can keep the lines of communication open despite physical limitations. The deathbed becomes a sanctuary for completion of this human existence and the gateway to new life.

Animals and Telepathy

Telepathy is a natural form of communication in the animal world. Many species of animals use instinct as well as sound and gestures to send and receive information. Telepathy protects animals by helping them sense the mood and intentions of the creatures around them. Animals' lack of ego allows them to be more versed in telepathy by not censoring the incoming data. Telepathy is a language common to man and animal. Our strong ego may be a stumbling block to easy access to our telepathic skills. We project ignorance onto animals because of our own inability to speak their language effectively. As humans get more in touch with their instinctual selves, the possibility of widespread telepathic communication will increase.

When you are involved with an animal encounter, it is important to keep your energy as clear and calm as possible. If you are frightened or agitated, you will induce similar feelings in the animal. When you meet an animal face to face, in a dream or a real-life situation, remember to take a deep breath. Animals are strongly telepathic and you can send a clear message to them if you can manage to keep your mind open. Fear tends to shut down the pathways that send and receive psychic energy. The first message to relay is that they are safe with you. Keep sending this message to the creature as you breathe and try to relax. If you are able, ask the animal for its message to you. If the animal is large or threatening, you may be too distracted or frightened to ask for a message. In that case, continue sending love and gentleness to reduce its fear and your own. Here are several examples of animal communing to illustrate the technique:

The Hummingbird

Several years ago I attended a yoga workshop held in an old schoolhouse. The high ceiling, wooden floors and large windows were a perfect venue for asanas and meditation. I loved the energy in the old building, so full of the memory of chattering children and lessons learned. I particularly enjoyed my teacher, Esther, and her gentle and wise teaching approach. It was a summer afternoon and we came back from the lunch break to resume our class. We had just settled onto our mats when a hummingbird darted in an open window. It was agitated as it flew higher and higher trying to find an exit route.

The room began to buzz as the group moved to help the bird. One man tried to open a nearby window but it was stuck tight to the windowsill. The bird was feeling the agitation and began beating its wings on the glass more frantically, moving further from the open window. I had an idea and quietly asked everyone to sit on their mats and breathe. I suggested we all visualize the hummingbird finding its way calmly to the open window. Immediately the forty students began to breathe with eyes closed, concentrating on the visualization. The frantic beating of wings stopped immediately, and without a sound the diminutive bird floated down and out the open window. It felt as if the bird had been carried out of the room on the breath and support of forty yoga students.

Several times, a bird has come down the chimney of my woodstove and become trapped in the belly. I would become agitated and nervous trying to direct the bird out by using a broom or a box. After a hectic game of chase, the bird would find its way out. I ended up feeling shaken and concerned for the bird. Soon after the hummingbird encounter I had an opportunity to try a different approach.

One morning I awoke to a strange scratching noise downstairs. I followed the noise to the woodstove and recognized the sound of a captive bird. I sat quietly down in front of the stove and breathed deeply. When I was calm, I began to telepathically talk to the bird. I told her she was safe and that I would not hurt her. I told her there was an open door near the stove entrance and when I opened the stove door she would easily find her way outside. I visualized this happening several times in my mind. While I was meditating, the fluttering of her wings against the stovepipe had stopped as if she were listening intently. I continued to send her love and gentle greetings. After several minutes, I calmly walked to the stove door, opened it and slowly sank back onto the floor. The bird hopped quickly to the sill of the stove door and without hesitation looked directly at the open door and flew out. I smiled at the ease of the encounter and felt grateful that I had a new way to help a captive bird find the open sky.

In the next two stories I unwittingly communicate with two animals. By staying open to their needs I was able to give them both their freedom.

The Great Escape

While working on the book, I often let Ig, my daughter's pet iguana, sun on the screened porch. In the summer we had thought he would enjoy exploring a larger area. He is two feet long, including a lengthy tail, and resides in a spacious 4 x 5-foot "condo" complete with a tree and hammock. Although he is usually tame and easy to hold, we had been noticing a feistier attitude as he matured.

The night before, I had dreamt of Ig. In my dream he was enormous—as big as a large alligator. He was angrily resisting our attempts to get him into a very small, Plexiglass cage, the size of a terrarium. A young girl was beating him. I yelled at her not to hurt him, pleading with her to no avail. Suddenly Ig turned into a cat and escaped. I then tried to call the police. There was no light in the house, and I could not see the numbers on the phone. I even tried to use the light inside the fridge but it was too dim.

In the next scene I am with my daughter. She is going to go up an aluminum ladder to the roof and try to catch Ig. I am worried about her climbing so high and I ask her, "Will you be okay?" A little tentatively she tells me, "Yes." We both know we have to try and get Ig from the roof because he will quickly travel from the roof to the trees and escape. I remember wondering how Ig got so big so fast and how surprised I am that he is so angry and unruly.

The next morning as I was writing down the dream, I remarked again to myself how angry Ig seemed. Sarah was in Michigan visiting her grandparents. When I called her that morning, I forgot to mention my dream. I went about my day and came home early afternoon to write. I settled Ig on the porch and went to the computer for several hours. When I came downstairs for a break, I checked on him. I saw that he had moved from his perch, and I stepped into the porch to find him. As I looked around I saw the screen in one corner had been pushed out leaving a small opening. I became frantic looking under the furniture to be sure he was not hiding. My anxiety grew as I realized he had escaped, just like in the dream.

My first reaction was one of panic and dread. I felt like a mother who had neglected to keep her child safe. I felt sadness and grief, knowing Sarah's deep bond with her iguana. I looked all around the porch for several hours. I looked under the house and scanned the trees. I even called a neighbor to help me go up a ladder to the roof. I wondered if the dream was trying to tell me to check the roof. Nervously I climbed up the ladder and onto the roof while the neighbor held it steady. I saw no sign of Ig. Looking for a bright green iguana in a summer woods is harder than looking for a needle in a haystack. He could be under a fallen log or in the tallest tree. Knowing how he loved to climb, I suspected he had climbed up a tree to bask in the sun, to feel the breezes and to listen to the sounds of nature.

With a sinking heart, I called my daughter in Michigan. Sarah was quiet for a moment and then said firmly to me, "It's not your fault. Ig has been acting restless. This must be what he needed." I told her I would look a while longer and then send Ig a telepathic message. Together we decided to tell him that we bless his journey to freedom and we welcome him back if he chooses. When the weather turns cold he will need warm shelter or he may die. We promised him that if he returns we will give him his freedom willingly next summer. We will house him in the winter and turn him loose to roam and explore in the summer. We also blessed his decision to choose to live in the trees, living as long as he could on his own.

I felt so many different emotions during this time. I felt angry at myself for not listening more carefully to my dream. I could have kept him in his condo for the day and then he would still be "safe." I then realized that maybe I had listened to the message of the dream. The dream was telling me that Ig was unhappy, that he felt trapped and angry. He chose to leave, and I gave him "the room to do it in." I saw how we sometimes try to keep someone in a relationship or a situation when they know that they need to leave. Ig taught me about letting go and allowing him to choose his destiny.

The Mouse

I arrived at my office building early one morning and headed up the stairs. A downstairs tenant stopped me and told me that a mouse had been sighted in several of the ground floor offices in the past month. He was ready to set a trap and was letting me know about it. I answered a vague reply and continued upstairs. I knew we needed to clear the mouse out, but I had strong feelings against the plan to trap it.

The mouse came into my mind several times that day. I felt anxious about the tenant's plan to trap and kill the mouse. I wanted to find a way to catch the mouse by using a live trap and hoped I could persuade the tenant to cooperate. The next day I was juggling a sick child with a full client schedule and the mouse slipped my mind.

Two days later, I unlocked my office door and turned on the lights. I had a phone session so I unwrapped a cassette for taping and dropped the ball of cellophane into the waste basket just as the client called. Five minutes into the session I heard the crinkle of the cellophane as it uncurled. I focused back on the client, and then heard the rustling of the plastic again. Intrigued by the length of time the cellophane was taking to unfurl, I leaned over and peeked into the trash can. To my surprise, I stared into the tiny black eyes of a small, gray mouse. I gave a startled cry and asked my client to hold a few minutes. As I was taking the mouse outside to free her, I thought of her deliberate journey up two flights of stairs and past two other suite doors to squeeze under my door and find her way into the wastebasket, making it easy for me to free her. She had devised her own version of a "live trap." Once outside, I told her to steer clear of the office building as I tipped the wastebasket onto the grass. She paused for a moment and then skittered quickly toward a shade tree. For more animal encounters, see chapter 7.

Be Your Own Psychic

You are your own psychic. Enjoy the myriad of daily opportunities to practice your telepathy and intuition. Motivation and practice are the keys to your success. You have a right to claim this invaluable tool to help you survive and thrive on the planet Earth. Believe in your abilities, and they will flourish.

Chapter 7
Encountering Synchronicity

Synchronicity: The phenomena of coincidence; to occupy the same position simultaneously.

Synchronicity is the phenomena of coinciding events that appear related. Most everyone has experienced synchronicity—thinking of an old friend and receiving an unexpected letter, learning a new fact and seeing reference to it, or humming a tune and suddenly hearing the same tune on the radio.

Synchronicity affirms the connectedness of all beings and the existence of a plan outside our view. Awareness of synchronistic happenings puts us in touch with cosmic timing—a sense of perfect unfolding that operates outside of the ego's realm. Coincidental events are happening constantly. They seem to come in waves—ebbing and flowing throughout our lives. There may be a rash of synchronized happenings and then a quiet period.

As a psychic, I am trained to be conscious of synchronicity. Since I am on the lookout for them, I notice that there is a steady flow of synchronistic events. Following the trail of synchronicity sensitizes us to the constant flow of divine relationship around us. Reading accounts of synchronistic encounters will increase the phenomenon in your life. Let's look at three synchronistic birthday surprises.

Matching Presents

My oldest sister and I were born three years and three days apart. Both being Cancerian women, we share a love of children, home, tradition, food and worry. Birthday celebrations are important to us both, and we can always trust each other to come through with thoughtful, fun birthday gifts. One year was especially notable.

Several years ago, I gathered a variety of gifts to send to my sister— silver earrings, lace wrapping paper, a humorous notepad and a funny card. When wrapping her presents, I had difficulty choosing a box for the earrings. I finally selected an octagonal-shaped box. I wrapped the gifts, added the card and packaged them to mail. I deliberated for several days about whether to use UPS or the U.S. Postal Service. I finally decided on UPS and sent the package the day before her birthday. I hoped it would arrive on time.

The next day, I received a package from my sister via UPS. It arrived at 3:00 on her birthday. I put the package aside to await my birthday and called to wish her a happy birthday. My package had just arrived at her house—at exactly 3:00. My delay in sending her gifts enabled the packages to arrive simultaneously. She had just opened the card and presents. Without explaining why, she said I needed to open my card and presents right away.

Upon opening the cards, we discovered we had sent each other the same birthday card. The synchronicity grew as I opened her gifts. She had sent me silver dangle earrings in an unusually shaped box, lace napkins, and a humorous notepad. I recalled laboring over the right box for the earrings—following the hunch to do something unusual had paid off in the synchronicity. My logical left brain could never have orchestrated such a birthday surprise.

A Pair of Susans

I was invited to a potluck gathering to celebrate a friend's fortieth birthday. I planned to take my usual offering—artichoke dip. I set the cans of artichoke on the counter to prepare for the party. At the last minute, I elected to take a fruit salad and made a hurried stop at the grocery store on the way to the party. I washed and cut the fruit at my friend's house and placed the salad with the other dishes. I was surprised to see an identical fruit salad—watermelon, blueberries, and plums. I smiled and thought that I would like to meet the person that brought the identical dish.

Before eating, we gathered in a circle to meet one another. Our hostess suggested that we share our names and birth dates. Across from me sat a woman who introduced herself as Susan, born on July 2. I spoke up and told her that my name was also Susan and that I was born on July 2. We proceeded to find out that we were born the same year and were both in the healing profession. Suddenly I knew that she had brought the twin fruit salad. She added that she planned to bring marinated artichoke hearts but had changed her mind at the last minute and brought the fruit salad instead.

This synchronistic happening is another example of following hunches without logical cause. By overriding any protests from your left brain, you can be rewarded with a synchronistic encounter.

Triplets in Hawaii

The third synchronistic birthday story occurred at a yoga workshop in Hawaii. I arrived and found I was rooming with two women—one from Canada and the other from California. As we settled in, we shared some of our past travels. I discovered that one roommate was the sister of a former teacher. Through her sister, I had known about her three years before meeting her. We were smiling at this coincidence when I asked her birth date. She said she was born on July 2. I laughed and told her that that was my birthday as well. We ran to tell our third roommate our discovery. She shared our delight, asking us the date of our twin birthday. We told her, and she look amazed as she told us that she also was born on July 2.

We went on to discover that we had each raised one child as a single parent. We marveled at the fact that of the 18 participants in the workshop, we three were randomly assigned to room together. My yoga vacation was enhanced by this unexpected reunion of the July 2 triplets.

Encouraging Synchronicity

1. Pay more attention to messages on license plates, billboards, buildings and vehicles. See if there is a message for you.

2. Follow your hunches to reconfirm plans that you feel may not occur as planned. There may be miscommunication that you can straighten out to avoid mishap and frustration.

3. Notice what you are saying when you hear an emergency vehicle siren or car alarm. Take notice when a light flickers or flashes. Pay particular attention to what is being thought or discussed at the time.

4. Draw doodles and save them. You may be drawing or writing some pertinent design or information.

5. Write down and date odd, out-of-the-blue thoughts that come to you. There may be significant information in these so-called random ideas.

6. Walk into a bookstore and let yourself wander aimlessly. Let your intuition take you to a particular aisle and pick out a book. Note the title and subject.

7. Take notice of repetitive chance encounters with friends or strangers. Note the feelings or memories that accompany these encounters.

8. Pick up a book or magazine and open it randomly. See how the contents of the page connect with a current situation.

9. Allow yourself to do unexpected or unreasonable things—there may be a synchronicity waiting to happen.

10. Write and recite the affirmations "I live in a synchronistic universe."

"I deserve the joy and wonder of synchronicity in my life now."

Letting Your Right Brain Lead

Most of us live our lives through habit and duty. We make most of our decisions based on what we should do rather than on what we feel. For some parts of our lives this is a responsible and practical way to be. We follow traffic laws, pay our bills on time and meet necessary obligations. However, if we allow habit and duty to rule every aspect of our lives, we miss the joy of spontaneity and the delight of surprise.

This next exercise allows you to tap into the decision-making power of the intuitive right brain. These right-brain decisions do not follow logical or habitual patterns. It takes time to trust this unorthodox manner of moving through the day. Start with decisions that have low impact—for example, where to have lunch, what present to buy or which movie to rent. Try this exercise the next time the universe cancels your plans unexpectedly. Familiarize yourself with this technique before using it to make major decisions. Observe the interesting and enriching encounters that flow from this method of moving in the world.

Let's look at an example of allowing the right brain to take the lead:

The Wizard's Attic

My daughter and I were all set to board our afternoon flight out of Key West when we heard the announcement. Thunderstorms and rain had temporarily closed the Miami airport. We had spent an adventurous week swimming with wild dolphins and exploring the town by bicycle. We were not upset to have our departure delayed. We could not return to our original lodging, so we needed to find a place for the night.

I recalled the name of a local bed and breakfast, and they were able to take us for the night. We took a taxi and checked in. We then tried to call some friends who were not leaving until the next day. We were unable to reach them, so we left them a message about our dinner plans. We knew exactly where we wanted to eat. That afternoon on the way to the airport our taxi driver had told us about a unique restaurant. We were disappointed to have missed it during our stay. We had told the driver that we would definitely dine there on our next visit to Key West.

My daughter Sarah and I enjoyed a leisurely dinner at Blue Heaven. It is an outdoor restaurant with picnic tables placed on a dirt floor with chickens and cats running underfoot. The food is delicious, and guests are invited to use the rope swing attached to a giant tree. Sarah immediately made some friends, and we both tried the rope swing. It was after 8:30 by the time we finished eating and swinging. We supposed that our friends Hannah and Doris had other plans for the evening and were not able to join us.

As we were riding in our cab to the center of town, I remembered a store I wanted to explore. I had spotted The Wizard's Attic, a New Age shop, as we were leaving town. I was eager to find a power totem to take home with me. I knew the store was probably closed for the evening, but I felt a strong desire to go. The cab left us at the corner, and we walked to The Wizard's Attic.

The shop appeared closed for the night. As I continued up the walk to peek in the window, I noticed the door was open. A heavy curtain was pulled across the threshold, and a friendly woman reached out to me as I hesitated at the opening. She said, "Come in! We have been waiting for you. We are just about ready to start." Seeing my confusion, she explained that they were having a full moon celebration. A local healer was leading a meditation and ritual. I told her my logical left brain had not known about the meeting but that my right brain had gotten us there just on time. We smiled at the synchronicity.

After a healing meditation and honoring of the full moon, the celebration ended. I was eager to find the owner of the store and tell her how I had stumbled upon the full moon gathering. I also wanted a symbol from her shop. I asked her to psychically choose an item that I needed at this time. She left and returned quickly with a small bag, and I handed her some money. I let my right brain decide the amount. Her mate, a psychic healer, was friendly and interested in our dolphin experiences. I told him about a recent injury, and he asked if he could remove some pain from the area. I welcomed the sensitivity and power of his touch. My daughter and I left the shop in a daze. Outside the shop I looked in the bag. I found a small rose quartz bear symbolizing the right use of power—a perfect totem for me at that time. The whole evening had been planned by the universe.

We awoke early the next morning in order to be at the airport by 5:30 A.M. I was anxious, and hurried to get all of our bags out on the sidewalk. I then locked our keys in the room and realized I had forgotten to call a taxi! It was too early for the hotel office to be open, and all of the houses around us were dark and silent. I panicked, not knowing where to find a phone at that hour. Sarah, grounded and calm, told me to take a deep breath. I looked up at the pregnant moon and asked for help.

Suddenly we saw headlights on our street. I decided to flag the driver down to see if he could help us. A large van pulled up, and I explained our problem to the driver. He smiled and said he was on his way to pick up some clients headed to the airport for the same flight.

He said he had room for us. I was very relieved, and we loaded the bags. He commented that he did not usually drive down this particular street to get to his destination. He had decided at the last minute to get some coffee, and that stop had put him on our street. On impulse, I asked him the name of his fare. He told us it was a mother and daughter, and we knew immediately that we had inadvertently hitched a ride to the airport with our friends. When we pulled up at the bed and breakfast, we saw the surprised faces of Doris and Hannah. They had never received our dinner invitation and thought we had flown home the day before.

From the plane we watched the sunrise over Key West. We had been offered an unexpected fifteen-hour adventure. We could never have planned it so beautifully ourselves. This experience inspired me to purposefully leave several unplanned days during my next travels.

Hawaiian Adventure

I was signed up for a yoga retreat in Maui and had decided to add several days onto my trip to explore the island of Kauai. I intuitively felt that I was going to meet a man on the retreat and form a platonic relationship. I sensed that he would also have planned a trip to Kauai after the retreat and that we would spend some time together.

I met Jim the first day of the workshop. Dark-haired and sensitive, he was personable and friendly. At dinner I overheard him talking about his plans to explore Kauai after the retreat. Later that evening, I told him about my premonition. We decided to fly together and each rent a car, giving us the freedom to see each other and explore the island on our own.

Upon our arrival, we found that only one rental car was available. This interesting turn of events made sense to us. We would save some money and have fun traveling together. We rented the car and drove to a small town. We arrived just in time to check in with the tourist bureau and discovered there were very few rooms left to rent. We finally found separate quarters in questionable boardinghouses. My room was high and airy but felt exposed and unsafe. Jim's was dark and low to the ground and came with a noisy parrot. We both slept fitfully and were glad to see each other the next morning. The next day while having breakfast, Jim spotted a notice on a bulletin board and found us a charming jungle bungalow, complete with a meditation tree house in a huge banyan tree overlooking a pristine river. We spent our time snorkeling, eating, doing yoga and relaxing. We were both glad that we had stayed open to the unplanned adventure.

Exploring the Enneagram

The same year, I signed up for a yoga retreat in Italy. I decided to take the opportunity to spend a few days in London. As I tried to make plans for London I felt a strong message to leave the time completely open. I felt uncomfortable not having any plans, yet followed the directive. The night before I left I called my friends in London to let them know I was arriving and would call them the next day from my hotel. In the airplane on the way to London I felt excited to see what would unfold.

I arrived at eight A.M. and found my way to my hotel. At 9:30 I called my friends, and Katherine answered the phone. "Susan, I don't know what you have planned but my old roommate is teaching a ennea-gram workshop for a Sufi group at a church near your hotel. She has room for you if you are interested." I had been intrigued by the ennea-gram—an ancient system of self-study that employs a personality typing system for understanding yourself and others. I was excited about spending the day learning more about the subject. I took a bus directly to the church and entered a small, round door that led to a winding, spi-ral staircase. At the top of the stairs I found myself in a circular stone room. I met Katherine's roommate Liz, the teacher, and settled in my seat.

The workshop proved to be very informative. Liz was an enthusiastic and compassionate teacher, using anecdotal stories to explain the ennea-gram system. The enneagram delineates the strengths and weaknesses of all types of people. My type, number 4 was appropriately called the Author. Deep in the editing process of this book I resonated with the characteristics of the number 4. It was interesting to hear others talk about their lives and figure out their type. At the lunch break, four of us ended up sharing a table. Coincidentally we discovered we all shared the same type—number 4. I made some good friends that day as we explored the complexities of the enneagram.

I left the workshop at 4:00 P.M. feeling tired yet fulfilled. I had been up all night making the transcontinental flight, yet I felt it was too early to head to bed. I decided to go to Harrod's for some oysters. As I was eating and reading my novel I noticed a couple sitting to my right. They were chatting with the waiter and enjoying their dinner of crab legs. I had noticed the crab legs because one of my psychic predictions for the London trip had been crab legs. The woman caught my eye and I smiled at her. Without preamble, the woman asked me, "Are you famous?" Taken aback, I laughed and told her no. She then asked me what I did for a liv-ing. I told her I was a psychic and she was overjoyed. She had been try-ing to arrange a psychic reading for some time and wanted to know if I would give her a session. I agreed and we found a pub where we could sit with some privacy. She had many dramatic challenges and decisions pending in her life. We spent an emotionally intense hour in a discreet corner of the smoky pub. After the reading, she and her partner drove me to my hotel and I collapsed into bed. I sighed in pleasure as I slid between the crisp, white sheets. I was very gratified with my day.

Opening to Right-Brain Adventures

This technique can be used anytime you feel ready to break old routines and explore new options. You can also use it when the universe throws you a curve and your usual lunch spot is closed or your date cancels at the last minute.

1. Take several deep breaths to clear your mind. Invite your logical left brain to rest and relax.

2. Thank your left brain for all its help and good advice. Use your breath to help your body release any tension.

3. Feel your mind opening and expanding. Ask your right brain to guide the next decision.

4. Allow your mind to float and drift. Recite silently: "I am now opening to my intuition. My mind is open. My mind is clear."

5. Notice any thoughts or images that come into your mind. Validate all thoughts no matter how illogical or irrational.

6. Look for any qualifying physical symptoms, such as a feeling of lightness, goose bumps or a shiver up your spine.

7. Follow the impulse that feels the strongest and clearest to you. Watch the synchronicity and fun unfold.

Animal Messengers

The animal kingdom lives closely attuned to life's natural rhythms. Since animals do not possess egos, they do not resist or judge the inevitable cycles of life and death. They do not create and enforce their own laws to override natural laws. Since animals have not ruptured this inbred connection to their surroundings, they are excellent teachers and guides for us. Once examined and understood, the presence of wild and domesticated animals can enrich our lives. By healing our instinctual nature, we can in turn offer the animal kingdom the honor and respect they deserve.

Animals communicate in many different ways. They use sounds, signals, body gestures and telepathy. Telepathic communication requires a keen awareness. Animals constantly sense and feel their surroundings. Survival depends on their ability to receive and interpret information. We have ignored our telepathic senses. We have developed technological devices to sense for us, and therefore our natural abilities have become dull and inactive. Animals teach us the importance of utilizing our instinctive abilities.

In observing animal presences, be aware of any behavior that goes against the animal's nature. Normally shy animals may seem bold or unafraid, and nocturnal animals may appear in broad daylight. Listen to their cries and note their behavior to help you receive the message.

The Garden of Eden

One of my first animal encounters came when I was newly immersed in spiritual study. I was actively learning and practicing meditation and yoga. I was reading any spiritual material I could find. At the time, I was reading *Jaguar Woman* by Lynn V. Andrews. On this summer afternoon, I was home reading in my hammock. Suddenly I felt a strong, urgent message to leave the book, take a green apple and go to a park twenty-five minutes by car from my house. I felt compelled to follow the insistent message.

I got the apple and drove to the park. I pocketed the apple and walked the trails. I felt strong energy around me. The trees seemed to be speaking, and the air felt charged with electricity. I sat with closed eyes, breathing deeply, and listened to the plants around me. After sitting for awhile, I felt the urge to walk again. I suddenly felt hungry and thought about eating the apple. As soon as I had that thought, I heard the directive to walk ten steps and put the apple on the ground. I counted my steps, placed the apple in the center of the trail and stepped back. Several minutes later a small green snake, the same bright green of the apple, came out of the brush. It curled itself around the apple and was still. Surprised, I blinked my eyes to be certain I had not imagined the snake. I felt a little dizzy and disoriented. I squatted down to watch the snake on the apple.

I tried to breathe in and listen to the message of the snake. I immediately thought of Eve and the Garden of Eden. The symbolism clearly pointed to issues about my femininity, sexuality and guilt. After all, the snake came when I thought about eating the apple. The message fit perfectly with the personal work I was doing. I was healing the shame that accompanies anorexia nervosa and bulimia. After several minutes, the snake slithered off the apple and disappeared into the brush. I thanked the snake and left the apple as an offering.

The encounter with the snake increased my interest in my spiritual studies. My dreams became more vivid and lucid. I trusted my hunches more often, with rewarding results. I noticed chance encounters with people and animals and took time to interpret the intrinsic spiritual messages.

The Red Fox

I taught a class entitled "Empowerment." Designed to help people express their spiritual and emotional power, the class included an exercise on choosing an animal as a helper or ally. Using the *Medicine Cards* by Jamie Sams and David Carson, each participant selected a card to designate their animal companion for the week. I drew the card of the fox. My family name is similar to the word "little fox" in Dutch. I had always felt an affinity with the fox and its ways. The card of the fox describes a person's use of camouflage, adaptability, and swiftness of thought and action. As I ended the class, I told everyone to be aware of any synchronistic encounters with their chosen animal. I reminded them that the encounters could be with the actual animal or through pictures or replicas.

The following afternoon, I was driving home from my office. As I passed a house in a country neighborhood, I noticed a large animal in the back yard. I slowed down to see it better, and to my astonishment I found myself face to face with a large red fox! It stood very still as I pulled my car off the road. The fox and I stared at each other for a long time. I tried to feel or sense any additional messages I might have missed from the Medicine card's interpretation. I kept my eyes glued to the fox for fear it would disappear. I thought how strange it was for this normally shy, covert animal to be so visible and bold during daylight.

The following day I had more insight into the strengths and weaknesses of fox energy. I saw clearly how I yearned for invisibility and secrecy in fearful situations. The nocturnal fox met me in broad daylight in a neighborhood setting. If the fox could risk visibility to meet me, then I could be more forthright and direct in my relationships. The next two stories continue the theme of setting boundaries in relationships.

Guard Your Territory

On a hot summer afternoon about two weeks before my thirty-ninth birthday, I heard a strange noise in the backyard. I followed the sound and found a large owl perched on a dead tree near my bathroom window. I was struck by the nocturnal bird's presence at midday. I stood and listened to the odd call. It was a long sustained whistle followed by a hiss. I called my nine-year-old daughter to see the owl and listen to the call. After hearing the owl, she said confidently, "The owl is marking his territory." After twenty minutes of emitting the strange cry, the owl flew into the woods. The following afternoon, I arrived home around 3:00, and soon after I heard the sound again. The owl sat perched in the same tree. The owl came for three days in a row.

The owl has been a special totem for me since early childhood. I was nicknamed Suzy Owl and had over 200 different owl statues in my childhood bedroom. The owl is the totem of truth and wisdom. Owls are noted for their ability to see the truth and speak about it boldly.

I was preparing for a spontaneous birthday trip to London. The owl's visitation occurred three days before my departure. I arrived in England, on my birthday, for a week with a good friend. The trip quickly turned into an exercise in patience and understanding when I found my friend in a difficult emotional state. Short-tempered and uncommunicative, she directed her anger onto me. I found myself unexpectedly needing a whole new set of boundaries to maintain any sense of peace. I remembered the owl and its warning to me. My daughter's intuition was right—the owl was preparing me for a lesson in protection and shielding.

During our visit, I stayed as clear and centered as possible. I was able to label my friend's projection and avoid counterattacking. The owl's warning seemed to comfort my hurt feelings, and I had the courage to leave my friend and complete the trip on my own. Later, my friend wrote an apology explaining that she was having a personal crisis at the time of our trip.

Six years have passed since the owl's message, and the owl has not returned to the tree. Periodically I hear owls hooting in the woods nearby, but I have not heard the territory call repeated.

Roll Over and Play Dead

Several years ago, I was called by a journalist who wished to have a psychic reading and to write an article about the experience. We set the date, and I met with her. The reading went very well. I was able to give her some clear information about several difficult relationships. There were several psychic hits, including some childhood experiences and names of people close to her. After the reading, she wrote me a personal letter to thank me for the reading and to say she had started to heal using some of the suggested techniques. I felt relaxed and positive about the upcoming article.

I was excited the day the paper came out. I found an early copy and quickly read the article. I was very shocked and upset to find the description of the reading to be negative and patronizing. There were several statements that completely contradicted my impression of the reading and her subsequent letter to me. She spoke disparagingly about the psychic profession and indicated she believed it fraudulent and unhelpful. I felt betrayed, confused, angry, hurt, embarrassed and publicly shamed. I thought of many different ways to react—from an angry phone call to publishing her personal letter to show her disparate views. I needed to feel my emotions, and I let my imagination run wild with ideas and plans of revenge. I was especially aware of my feelings of having been publicly shamed and exposed.

I was reminded of an episode of *The Andy Griffith Show* in which Andy's young son, Opie, publishes embarrassing gossip in his newspaper. Andy frantically tries to recall all the copies in print before the townspeople read them. I, too, felt the urge to empty all of the newspaper holders. I slept fitfully that night and awakened with the article on my mind. As I was getting ready for work, I felt a strong urge to pick a bouquet of pansies for the kitchen. This was not a common occurrence, especially on a busy work morning.

I followed the urge and brought the vase into the kitchen. It was 10:00 A.M. on a bright, sunny day. As I placed the vase on the counter, I happened to glance out the kitchen window. I saw a large, gray opossum walking across my backyard directly in my line of vision. I had never seen this nocturnal animal in my yard, night or day. Yet the opossum strolled by in full view in the midmorning. I already knew the particular significance of this odd visitation. In the *Medicine Cards*, Sams and Carson state in the text for opossum: "Rely upon your instincts for the best way out of a tight corner. If you have to pretend to be apathetic or unafraid, do it! Oftentimes if you refuse to struggle or show that hurtful words bother you, your taunter will see no further fun in the game. Warriors have used opossum medicine for centuries, playing dead when the enemy nears and outnumbers them."

It certainly addressed exactly how I was feeling—attacked and outnumbered. I took the advice to heart and breathed out my fear and anger. My fear of public ridicule did not become manifest. Several new clients called after reading the article. Everyone seemed to have the same impression about the article. They agreed that the author seemed unclear and confused. Months later, I ran into the author and told her my feelings. She explained that she had been frightened by the accuracy of the reading and had needed to appear skeptical even though her experience had convinced her otherwise. I was reassured that her fear had directed the writing of the article. I was glad that I had not let my fear direct my response.

Communing with Animals

Animals survive by using their instinctual nature. As domesticated beings, we have lost touch with our natural urges and built-in radar. Our intellect has overshadowed the natural gifts of the instinctual nature. By communing with animals, we can regain some of our lost instincts. We can restore our ability to sense danger, find our way when we are lost and heal our wounds when injured.

Animal encounters occur naturally as a result of exploring the instinctual body. Animals sense instinctual openness. The more you nurture and explore your instincts, the more naturally animals will relate to you.

I have had many healing encounters with animals. Due to my childhood connection with dolphins, I was drawn to swim with wild dolphins in the Florida Keys. One of the most profound healings I experienced came through an adventure with three dolphins and a barracuda.

Barracuda Shaman

My daughter and I went to the Florida Keys to swim with wild dolphins. We went with a wife-and-husband team who had befriended a pod of wild dolphins off the coast of Key West. They would take small groups out into the ocean to spend time with the dolphins. The groups motored out to an area frequented by the wild dolphins and swam among them.

We were very excited the first day out. I had dreamt of dolphins for years and had close encounters on the beach in my youth. We arrived at one of the meeting places and waited quietly in the boat. Soon we saw the familiar dorsal fins swimming toward us. After a signal from one of our guides, we slipped into the water and began to swim alongside the dolphins. It was challenging to keep up with their powerful pace. Immediately three large dolphins encircled me. I later found out they were three male dolphins, Ruffles, Spur and Hatchet—so named for the unique shapes of their dorsal fins. I told them telepathically how honored I was to be with them. I could feel their good-natured, calm spirits. Their benevolent, wise eyes made me feel protected and supported. After swimming vigorously, I began to tire and I slowed my pace to rest. They synchronistically slowed down and waited for me to regain my speed. I swam as if in a trance. Finally I knew I needed to check my bearings. There were spotters on the boat following us but I wanted to make sure my daughter was nearby. I came to the surface and saw my daughter near the boat several hundred yards away. Suddenly I felt a tremendous blow to my right side. My first thought was that I was hit by one of the dolphins. As soon as I thought this, I knew instinctively that I was wrong. With their superb radar and gentle spirit, they would not strike me. I then thought of a shark. I have read that a shark will strike its victim with its blunt nose and then swim back to strike again. I became amazingly calm and serene. There was nowhere to go. I was too far from the boat to reach it. And so I waited. A second blow did not follow.

Suddenly I felt light-headed and dizzy and I began to swim to the guide. She came to meet me and I told her I had been hit by something. She went underwater to examine the wound. I was bleeding and needed to quickly get to the boat. We then looked under the surface and saw a dazed two-and-a-half-foot barracuda. He looked as stunned and confused as I.

Back in the boat, I lay and tried to catch my breath. I felt a sharp pain when I tried to breath deeply. My ribcage ached and I wondered if I had broken a rib. I calmed myself by tuning into the significance of this event. I knew this was not an attack. I had shocked the barracuda as much as he had surprised me. I had confused him by first swimming like a dolphin and then suddenly appearing upright and blocking his path. I knew instinctively that he had given me the equivalent of a shaman's blow. The place and power of the blow had been etheric surgery for me. Then I remembered the massage that I had the day before I left for my trip.

Starting face up on the table I told my masseur, Allen, I was feeling tight and anxious in my stomach. My fear level had been very high for several days, and I was uncertain as to the cause. I was looking forward to my upcoming trip to the Keys. He began to work on my stomach region using circular strokes to relax the tight muscles. I used deep breathing to help the process. As he was working on my right rib cage he stopped in surprise. He had been my regular masseur for ten years, so he knew my body well. He described the area as "cartilage-like." He spent the rest of the hour-and-a-half session on that area gently working it to release the hardness and the tension. My fear level was much lower by morning when we took our flight.

The barracuda's blow was in the exact same spot on my right rib cage. It seemed that Allen had been drawn to prepare that area for the shamanic surgery. Over the next few days I nursed the area. The bleeding stopped that evening and Advil helped ease the pain. I thought of the poor barracuda and hoped he was not suffering from the impact of our encounter. Surprisingly, the area never developed a bruise or discoloration.

The next day I went back into the water ready to see the dolphins again. Within moments a large barracuda swam near me. The guide was there and she slipped her hand into mine as if to say, "Relax. It's okay. There is no danger." I took a deep breath and watched the barracuda swim by. I became even clearer about the message of the barracuda. Like the shaman's blow designed to alter consciousness, the barracuda had dislodged fear that was hiding in the right rib cage. The rest of the trip I felt safe and comfortable in the water.

The first day after the blow, the same three male dolphins encircled me and seemed even more attentive and protective. It was as if they knew of my oceanic initiation with the barracuda and were lending me support. I had five swims with the pod, each time bonding more with these gentle and deeply spiritual mammals. It is easy to communicate telepathically with these intelligent and conscious mammals. The last day I remember wondering what it would be like to touch the dolphins. We had been asked by the guides to honor their boundaries and not touch them during the swim. As with any new acquaintances, you wait to be invited to cross physical boundaries. As this thought crossed my mind, I intuitively heard the dolphin next to me invite me to touch his side. He turned on his side and looked at me lovingly. I then felt an overwhelming sense of gratitude as I realized I already felt so connected that I did not need physical touch to validate it. Why would I need to touch his skin when I felt so deeply connected with his soul?

I dreamt of the three male dolphins for several days after returning home. Each dream I relived the joy of their company. One week later, I became violently ill, with a high fever and severe cramps. I felt it was wise to check with a physician. I went through a battery of tests to see if I had contracted an infection from the wound. The tests were negative. The fever lifted but the cramping and diarrhea persisted. For months, I felt a high level of anxiety and had difficulty controlling my bowels. It was as if I were "scared shitless." I wondered if I was experiencing post-traumatic stress. I went into a deep meditation and asked the spirit of the barracuda to help me understand the syndrome I was calling "barracuda fever." I was told that I had carried a pocket of fear under my right rib cage since childhood. The circumstances of the barracuda encounter were symbolic for me. As I swam with the three male dolphins I felt connected, supported and alive. As I came to the surface to share my joy and openness with the other swimmers, I was slammed in the side. I had a deep childhood fear of openly expressing my exuberance for deep relating. My father would frighten me when I was excited or exuberant by saying that I would die young if I didn't calm down. Since my disastrous marriage, I had been afraid to get back into "the swim of things" and risk my heart in a passionate, committed relationship.

The barracuda blow dislodged the fear and I began to release it, emotionally and physically. I had a series of flashbacks and nightmares of sexual abuse. I worked with the fear, writing my dreams and journaling to understand it more deeply. I dove deeper into my fear of intimacy, my fear of my father's sexual advances and my fear of visibility and power. It took eighteen months and the serotonin medication Buspar to resolve the intestinal symptoms. I knew that I needed to be patient with the process. The fear had been waiting years for the opportunity to be released. My surprise rendezvous with the barracuda shaman gave me the push that I needed.

Animal encounters are highly rewarding and intriguing. We can enhance our limited view of the earth by opening to the lessons of our wise and instinctual animal companions.

HOW TO BEGIN

1. Choose an animal to study and observe. Gather pictures or models of the animal. Study its characteristics. Note any personal feelings about the animal.

2. Visualize spending time with the animal in its natural habitat. The more you imagine swimming with dolphins, flying with birds or snuggling with wolves, the more you draw animal encounters to you.

3. Imitate the movements and sounds of animals. Stretch like a dog and caw like a crow. As you imitate the animal, feel your heightened sensitivity to your surroundings. Pay attention to any ideas or information that comes into your mind as you explore the animal.

4. Ask for dream meetings in which you can spend time with the animal. (See chapter 8.) Your willingness to learn interspecies communication can pay off by attracting animal teachers. I regularly spent dreamtime with a pod of dolphins. When I recently swam with wild dolphins in Key West, I already had developed an ability to communicate telepathically with them. From my meditations and dreams, I had cultivated my dolphin-speak.

5. Take time to sit outside. Close your eyes, feel the air and listen with your instinctual ears. The next time you are confronted by a noisy bee or buzzing fly, listen to the sound. Go beyond your automatic reaction and listen for a message. Is the bee gathering anger from your aura? Is the fly reminding you to focus and stop moving randomly about?

6. Write down your desire to have synchronistic encounters with animals. Try repeating the following affirmation: "I am now open to attracting animal encounters."

As you fine-tune your animal senses, you stimulate your instinctual brain to remember your homing device, your danger radar, your boundary meter and your weather barometer. By balancing your instinct with your intellect, you gain the exceptional perception of the animal kingdom.

Loop-de-Loop

I had an increase of animal encounters while writing this chapter. One such encounter helped me resolve some unfinished financial work with my ex-husband.

Late one evening after writing, I went into the bathroom to wash up for bed. I noticed some movement outside the second-story bathroom window. As I looked out, I saw a bat flying back and forth in front of the window. I had never sighted a bat flying so close to the house. I usually caught a glimpse of a bat as it darted overhead on my way home from work. The bat kept swooping in a repetitive pattern. I waited for it to fly out of sight, but it continued to fly quite close to the window. I took out the screen so I could see and sense the bat more clearly. I stood at the window, watching and feeling. Since I had been working on the animal section of this book, I was especially eager to get any messages.

Traditionally, bats symbolize transformation—death and rebirth of parts of ourselves and our psyches. Seeing a bat is a very positive and powerful omen for me. Earlier that evening, I had noted some unresolved feelings around money and my ex-husband. I had shelved it for later analysis so that I could work on the book. Upon seeing the bat, I began to focus on the money issue.

I looked back to my relationship with my dad and his use of money. He was generous with his money yet controlling and sexually inappropriate. I stated aloud some of my unresolved feelings about money and men. The bat continued to fly in its repetitive flight pattern. When I recited one particular idea, the bat suddenly broke its flight pattern to perform a double loop-de-loop in front of the window. I felt a shiver run through my body. I repeated the idea again. I realized that I had equated a financially generous man with a sexually controlling one. I continually attracted more tight-fisted or less abundant men for my partners. Unconsciously I felt that a generous man would also be sexually inappropriate. I knew from experience that this was not true. As I realized my erroneous belief, the bat swooped in the loop-de-loop pattern once again. At the two emotional peaks of my inner searching, the bat broke its pattern. It was time to become more conscious of this pattern.

The bat continued to fly to and fro. I thanked the bat and went to get the *Medicine Cards* to reread the chapter about the bat. I read seated under the window, and when I finished, the bat was gone. I continued to work on clarifying my issues of men and money.

The Crow

In the course of compiling this book I uncovered many difficult memories and deep layers of pain. This story contains a profound healing for me as well as the discovery of the title of the book.

I arrived in New Orleans with several hours to spare before heading to the yoga retreat held in a nearby monastery. I met my friend Elise, and we went strolling through the French Quarter. I was looking for a special amulet or token to take with me. While browsing in a New Age shop, I found an arrowhead. A local Indian tribe had blessed and empowered it in a special ceremony. It carried an aura of power and protection for the bearer.

When I arrived at the retreat center, I was greeted by the organizer, Sharon. We have a strong bond due to our mutual love of rituals, astrology, synchronicity and nature. She has a special love of rivers and explores the waters near her Louisiana home. I found her in the kitchen creating an offering for the crows at the monastery. I joined in, happy to share my love of crows with a like-minded friend. I have a strong connection with crows, always coming to spiritual attention when I hear their caws.

In ancient times, crows were the official mascot of monasteries. In old engravings, monks are often pictured with crows. the *Medicine Cards* defines crow medicine as an omen of change. The crow is a shape shifter and "sees simultaneously the three fates—past, present and future." When the crow card is reversed we need to be aware of holding on to old habits that do not suit our energy. Crow energy "weeds out the past beliefs or ideas to bring you into the present moment."

We talked as we rolled the crow treats into balls to prepare for cooking. I showed her the arrowhead I found in the city. She exclaimed that she had also brought an arrowhead with her. We noted that crows, monasteries and metal arrowheads were all traditionally associated with Saturn, planet of limits and form. When we finished molding the crow balls, we left them to cook through the night in a warm oven. They would be ready by the next day, Saturn-day.

The next morning we collected the treats and walked the meadows surrounding the monastery scattering the goodies and keeping a look-out for the black birds. I was awakened by their raucous caws early that morning. Yet as we walked midmorning, there were none in sight. Finally we found a single crow high in a tree. We placed some treats for him on the roof of a nearby shed.

I was in charge of several events during the week of the retreat. I planned to facilitate a manifesting ritual early in the week. In the ritual, each person would select a dream or desire they would like to mani-fest in their life. The group would take thirty seconds to imagine the person in this new state of being. I had also prepared a mask ritual for the end of the week. The ritual included selecting an old part of our personality that no longer suited us. We would design a mask to por-tray the outmoded part we were ready to release. The last night we would throw the masks in the bonfire as a symbol of letting go. I had chosen to release the mask of the single woman. The single woman mask seemed to be tightly glued to my face since my divorce fourteen years prior, and I felt it was time to shed it. I drew my mask and wrote "single" in large letters across the forehead.

Early one afternoon midweek, Sharon, Elise and I walked to the river. As we approached the shore a blue heron swooped close by our heads. We waded into the clear, cool water watching the light filtering through the leaves and playing on the moving water. A young turtle floated by, carried by the current. We gathered orange blossoms that fell from a tall tree.

On the way back I suggested we collect deadwood, another Saturnian symbol, for the bonfire on the last night. Suddenly I stopped dead in my tracks. My arms laden with dead branches, I looked upward. Several owls were hooting and hollering across the treetops. I had not heard these particular calls before, so I listened intently. Knowing the owl comes into my life as a warning of a betrayal or encouragement to see through an illusion, I closed my eyes and lis-tened with my third ear. "What are you trying to tell me? What do you want me to know?" I asked silently. I knew it was an auspicious sign—but of what?

That evening, I went to hear an organ recital at the chapel. My friend Lou and I sat in the front row. After the concert, a red-haired man was leaving the altar area and lost his footing on the stone steps. He began to fall backward off the raised platform. I leapt up and caught his head in my hands several inches from the stone floor.

Embarrassed, he scrambled to his feet and hurried out of the chapel. I remember thinking it was odd. I joked to Lou about "men falling at our feet." We had been discussing our singleness and a readiness to be open to relationships with men.

The next day was the farewell celebration and ritual bonfire. In class, we worked on balancing poses. Near the end of class we practiced one of my favorite poses, aptly named "the crow." While balancing on the hands with elbows bent, the knees perch on the upper arms and the eyes gaze forward. When I found my balance in this pose I had the impression of soaring above the earth. When I first began practicing this challenging pose I always placed a landing pad for my head in case I fell forward. I felt steady and focused in the pose. Patricia, the teacher, showed us how to go from the crow pose to headstand and back to crow. I had tried this more difficult variation only once and wanted to try it again. I asked Lou, my organ concert buddy, to spot me while I experimented. I came easily into the crow. However, on my way to the headstand I lost my balance and came crashing down on my forehead. Since my hands were firmly planted I had no time to catch myself and I had neglected to place a blanket as a landing pad. The full force of my weight landed squarely on my forehead as I struck the stone floor.

I immediately felt a flash in my head. Instantly I felt the vulnerability of a child. I fell as an infant falls, trusting and expecting strong hands to catch me. I felt familiar feelings of fear and hypervigilance. I began to cry, not from pain but from the realization of the early loss of my innocence and trust in the world. After the fall, I was suddenly surrounded by my classmates who are loving, like-minded women. I asked them to hold and comfort me. I was scared to open my eyes, worried that my vision would be blurred or distorted. I kept my eyes closed while Veronica, a skilled acupuncturist, placed needles for shock and head trauma. Glen, the chef and nutritionist healer, brought herbs to calm me and facilitate healing. After several minutes I opened my eyes and they checked to see that my pupils dilated normally. I lay and felt waves of shock and clarity ripple through my body and mind.

The most important realization was my desire to recognize and accept my own innocence. Often in dysfunctional families the children carry the unresolved work of the parents. As a child, I was too frightened to see the truth about my family. I had so many symptoms of severe emotional distress—prolonged bedwetting, chronic allergies, anorexia nervosa and bulimia, self-mutilation, severe anxiety and compulsions. As my forehead struck the cold floor I had a flash of knowing, "The evidence is clear. You can now see the truth about your childhood."

I felt disoriented and clear at the same time. It seemed as if I could see 360 degrees. I smiled to myself as I remembered what I had asked for in the manifesting ritual—telepathic communication with all animate and inanimate beings. My third eye, located in the center of the forehead, had been catapulted open to help fulfill that wish.

I rested in my room all afternoon with a soothing slab of river clay covering my throbbing third eye. I could not stand for more than a minute or two due to extreme dizziness. Lou came by my room to visit me. We recounted the synchronicities leading up to the falling crow pose. I showed her my mask, ready for the bonfire, with "single" across the forehead. The fall symbolically cracked open my stuck single status. We noted the synchronous accident in the chapel when the man's head nearly hit the stone floor and my unexpected rush to catch his head before it met the hard surface. We then remembered another interesting event. Lou and I had shopped several days before, and I bought a rug and she found two pillows. We laughed to think that we had both unconsciously felt the need for padding and softening—a rug to soften the floor and pillows to cushion the head. So many clues had tried to prepare me for this shamanic surgery.

The night of the bonfire was clear and cold. The moon shone brightly on us as we placed our masks into the transformative fire. After the ritual, Patricia suggested the women form a healing circle around me. Wrapped warmly in blankets, I lay in the center. One by one, the women came to my side to place healing hands on my head. Tears streaming down my face, I breathed deeply, taking in the love and support.

After a fitful night, I did not feel well enough to attend the last morning yoga class. Instead, I walked slowly through the meadow to the graveyard. I saw a troupe of wild turkeys strutting among the tombstones surrounded by wisps of fog. I ended my walk at the chapel and arrived just as morning mass was ending. I walked in and sat in the front row of the empty church. A robed monk appeared and placed a large Bible on the podium. He opened it to a particular page and carefully placed the ribbon marker. He left the church on silent feet. After several moments I walked to the altar to read the passage. "At the same time came the disciples unto Jesus, saying, Who is the greatest in the kingdom of heaven? And Jesus called a little child unto him, and set him in the midst of them. And said, Verily I say unto you, Except ye…become as little children, ye shall not enter into the kingdom of heaven. Whosoever therefore shall humble himself as this little child, the same is greatest in the kingdom of heaven." I was struck by the appropriateness of the text. I was grappling with my right to reclaim my innocence and release my shame and guilt.

In the yoga fall, I was responsible for neglecting to place a soft landing pad down for my head. I always have in the past when trying the crow-to-headstand pose. I regressed into a child role by expecting my spotter to take full responsibility for my head's safety. I reenacted a child's role, and Lou graciously played the absent mother. Ironically, the day before I had jumped up in time to save the man's head from the stone floor but later left my own head unprotected. The man, like my father, was red-headed and Catholic. I protected my mother and father and their denial of their neglect and abuse. I see this reoccurring pattern in my relationships. I protect the man and abandon myself. I am learning to take responsibility for my safety and protection and finding the courage to speak the truth.

At the end of the trip, I made my way to my car parked in the airport lot. I smiled to see two jet-black crow feathers on the front seat. I remembered I found them the day before I left on my trip. One appeared on the walkway to my car and the other in the trunk when I removed my luggage to check in at the airport.

It took me days to recover my sense of balance and clarity. Fortunately I had no neurological damage. My vision seemed clearer than before the fall and my peripheral vision widened. When I returned, I quizzed my mother on any falls I had sustained as a child. She remembered that I had fallen out of a parked car at eleven months old. My mother emphasized that I fell onto the asphalt, taking the full weight of the fall on my forehead. At the time of our conversation I had not yet told her about the New Orleans incident.

I also fell from a moving car when I was seven. I remember this incident vividly. On our way home from shopping, I told my mother that my door was only partially closed. She told me to move away from the door until she stopped the car to reclose it. She forgot my request, and a half hour later while reading my book I also forgot and leaned against the door. When we rounded a bend near our house I tumbled out of the car, landing in the middle of the road. Shaken and scraped, I felt disoriented and confused. I had asked my mother to keep me safe, and I was hurt by her neglect.

My massage therapist, Allen, had a dream for me when I saw him a few days after the fall. He dreamt that we were riding on a bus together and I gave him my valuables to keep. When he awoke from the dream, he knew the dream would have significance for me. The dream reflected the old pattern of entrusting my power to a man rather than taking full responsibility for myself. I can share many parts of myself, but I must keep my power. The yoga fall was a wake-up call. The lessons were clear to me—"Open your eyes and see clearly the events of the past. Quit taking blame for events that are not your responsibility. Claim responsibility for your own power and safety in the world."

During the yoga retreat I was still searching for a title for my book. For weeks I had been writing down entries, but so far I had no winner. It took me several days after returning home to realize that I had literally "fallen upon" the title. The fall had opened my third eye, a psychic's most important tool. Several days after I decided upon *Third Eye Open* as the title, I was riding in the car with my daughter. We were listening to her favorite radio station and I heard the lyrics of a song. "That's a good idea. Break a promise to your mother." These lyrics struck me personally. I knew the revelations in this book would be difficult for my mother. The family of denial has an unspoken agreement to keep the abuse a secret. I was breaking this promise of secrecy by publishing my book.

I listened to the refrain once more and then asked Sarah the name of the band. She answered, "Third Eye Blind." I smiled at the synchronicity. No longer willing to be blind to the truth, my third eye was open.

Increasing Synchronicity

Synchronicity is a natural occurrence. You have a right to enjoy the unexpected and informative nature of synchronicity in your life. Look for a message or lesson in the synchronicity. Analyze the experience as if it were a dream. Ask yourself, "What can I learn from this encounter? What part of my life needs my attention?" Honor each example of synchronicity with your awareness.

The universe wants to help you grow and awaken—from hearing the just-right song on the radio to chance encounters with humans and animals. From the book that falls from the shelf into your hands to the message on the license plate of the car ahead, synchronicity awaits our recognition and honoring. The more you take notice, the more it happens.

Chapter 8

Psychic Dreaming

One of the most powerful tools of self-knowledge is free of charge and readily accessible with a minimal degree of effort. Every night, the subconscious offers the conscious mind an in-depth and comprehensive look at the workings of the deepest part of the human psyche. While your conscious mind sleeps, you are given a private showing of several elaborate and clever movies—each one written, directed, produced by and starring you. The script is complete with humor, puns and imaginative casting. Upon awakening, you can record these original movies and gain invaluable insight into your life. The more you pay attention to your dream-movie life, the richer and more rewarding it grows.

Dreams are designed to bring the unconscious to consciousness. As human beings we are endowed with a spiritual self and an ego self. The desire of the spiritual self is to reemerge with God-consciousness by remembering the soul. The goal of the ego is to remain separate and uniquely human. Often, these two selves seem to work at cross-purposes. Dreams offer a compromise—an arena where the spirit and the ego can collaborate to create a message to the whole self. Through dreams, the spiritual mind can introduce concepts and ideas that are normally censored by the ego mind. The dream movie places the new concepts in a setting that is acceptable to the ego.

The recipe for recalling dreams is very simple. The most important component is persistence. Writing your intention to remember and record your dreams stimulates dream recall. Try writing the following statement at bedtime:

I now remember and write down my dreams.

Write this statement at least five times to help your unconscious absorb the concept. You can also be more specific and ask to dream about a particular person or topic.

I now remember and write down one dream about _____.

As you become more adept you can increase the number of dreams you order.

I now remember and write down three dreams about

_____.

It takes time to activate and develop your ability to recall dreams. Continue ordering dreams until you are successful.

Understanding Your Dream Characters

Often, you dream about people in your everyday life. Your subconscious chooses these people with care and attention. This next exercise helps you decipher the reason you dream about your third-grade teacher or the man who gets on the bus at your stop. Each dream character, no matter how small the part, has significant meaning in your life.

Choose a dream that contains a person. Write the name of the person or a description—for example, the man at the bus stop. Write down three adjectives describing the dream character. Write down the first three adjectives that come to your mind. After you have written the adjectives, read them back to yourself aloud. Then ask yourself, "How am I like this person? What part of me does he/she represent?" Let's look at an example:

* * *

I had the following dream while I was considering becoming more public about my beliefs through the publication of this book. In the dream, I am in a church listening to a sermon by a preacher—a tall man in his forties. His sermon is about life and love. A little child is sitting near him in a special seat. He begins by saying he wants to tell a story. I look up with interest. He quotes a Bible verse and then proceeds to elaborate using a story about basketball. I smile while thinking that this is a good way to modernize the old parables and bring them into the present day, especially in a university town.

Within a few minutes, a large portion of the congregation gets up to leave. Obviously upset and disapproving, they scoop up the little child sitting near the minister and leave the church. The dissenters seem to be led by a dark-haired woman. I am very moved by this scene and feel tears coming to my eyes. The preacher stands still, shocked and hurt. I start to cry as I feel the power and meaning of this event. In the dream, I know that the preacher's innovative teaching style is alienating some of the congregation.

I reach over to touch my best friend on her hand in a gesture of comfort and connection. I immediately feel self-conscious about touching her. I feel afraid I will be judged and shamed for expressing my love for her. I feel sad that I am self-conscious and scared of a mild display of affection. As I draw my hand away from my friend, I notice that some people remain in their seats, listening to the sermon. I decide that I will give the preacher a hug after the service to let him know I support his teaching.

Interpreting the Dream

To begin my dream analysis, I select three adjectives to describe each dream character. I start with the preacher.

Preacher

1. visible

2. vulnerable

3. outspoken

After describing the character using the three adjectives, I begin to explore my connection with the preacher. I ask myself two questions:

1. How am I like this person?

2. What part of me does he represent?

In writing this book I am visible, vulnerable and outspoken, like the preacher. I am afraid of being judged, humiliated and rejected. I am afraid that my community will shun me and that I will be alone. In this dream, I watch the preacher stand up and express his unique teaching style. I also witness the congregation rejecting him. This dream is helping me face my fear of moving ahead with my book project. I want to feel powerful enough to be visible and outspoken. Through my desire to hug him at the end, I am embracing the part of me that must accept the risk of ridicule and rejection.

Next, I decide to explore the little child and the dark-haired lady.

Child	*Lady*
1. special	1. judging
2. innocent	2. impatient
3. taken away	3. strong

1. How am I like each person?

2. What part of me does she represent?

The child seems to represent my inner child. She is close to the preacher in a special seat. She is comfortable and contented in her seat. The dissenters whisk her away from the scene. They seem to feel she will be hurt by the basketball Bible lesson. This character depicts another of my fears. I am afraid that I will lose touch with an innocent and special part of myself by becoming more powerful and outspoken.

The lady is playing the judging part of myself. She can also be called the inner critical parent. She represents a strong leader. She leads the group out of the church. She represents the part of me that is afraid to try new things and to be open to change. She is seen as a strong part of my personality, and I feel intimidated by her. By recognizing this part of myself, I can consciously work on owning my strong and critical leader. I can endeavor to lead with more tolerance and patience. By facing the judge inside, I can face my fear of change and innovation.

* * *

Use the three adjectives to decipher the meaning of the characters in your dream life. Taking time to comprehend your casting of characters in your dream life enriches your self-knowledge. For further dream study I highly recommend Robert A. Johnson's book entitled *Inner Work.*

Dreaming the Future

Dreams bring hidden knowledge into knowing. Dreams are often clairvoyant and can easily bring you information about your future. Since dreams come through the ephemeral right brain, it is important to write them down as soon as you awaken. It is very easy to lose a dream—it will slip back into your unconscious mind as a pebble slips from your hand back into a lake. It is easier to verify precognitive dreams if you document your dreams in a journal.

In psychic dreaming, you may dream about a person before meeting that person. By understanding the dream and the character, you gain valuable information about the future encounter. Reread your dream journal regularly to verify precognitive dreams of people in your life. I make it a practice to reread my dream journal each month. I often find a forgotten dream that displays striking clairvoyance about an area of my life.

Precognitive dreams bring a preview of coming attractions of life events. Let's look at an example of precognitive dreaming:

The Seal Crossing

I had one of my most striking precognitive dreams during a very diffi-cult time in my life. Married for two years, I was expecting my first child when I discovered my husband was having an affair. Eight months preg-nant, I was very vulnerable and hurt. I made it through the delivery with the help of a competent and supportive midwife and my best friend, Martha. The first challenging months of new motherhood were mixed with the drama of dealing with the crumbling marriage. I spent much of my time releasing feelings of shame, rejection and anger. The woman having the affair with my husband was aggressive and harassing. My husband was distant and uncommunicative. The drama of their relationship lasted for several years. I had the following dream when my daughter, Sarah, was seventeen months old.

I dreamt that I was at the main crosswalk of our town. I saw a large seal, wounded in the neck, crossing the street. I was struck by this scene and immediately went to call the police. The call went through, and a man said to me, "Check your meter." He repeated this two times. I was confused and said to him, "I called you to tell you about a wounded seal downtown. I'm afraid it will hurt someone. Please send an officer to get it." Then I hung up the phone.

When I awoke, I interpreted the dream. I knew that the wounded seal represented the broken promise or seal of the vows of marriage. I felt empowered that I had asked the authorities to take care of the wounded seal. In other words, I was stating that I was not responsible for the broken promise. It was my husband's broken vow, not mine, that ended the marriage. At the time I analyzed the dream, I did not understand the part about the meter.

Three days later, I went downtown to have breakfast with a good friend. We went to a restaurant that I frequented while I was a student at the university. I had not eaten there for many years. After leaving the restaurant, I wheeled my daughter in her stroller across the same crosswalk in the dream. Exactly midway we passed the woman having the affair with my husband—the symbol of the broken marriage vow. Our paths had rarely crossed in the eighteen months of the affair. She acknowledged my daughter and pointedly ignored me. I remember my shock and surprise at seeing my dream unfolding in front of me. It was very painful for me to see this woman in public, yet I felt comforted by having dreamt of the encounter before it happened.

I had told my friend about the dream during breakfast, and we were excitedly commenting on the synchronicity when we arrived at my parked car. There, sitting in his small cart, was a policeman writing out a parking ticket. My meter had expired. Now I understood the meaning of the dream policeman saying, "Check your meter." I was grinning broadly by this time, and the policeman looked annoyed. He said, "I have already given you one ticket and I can give you another." His words reminded me that the policeman in the dream had told me to check my meter two times. Excited to see the unfolding of my dream, I said, "That's fine!" He was so taken aback that he hurriedly drove away.

This day was a turning point in my grieving. I decided to go and buy a wading pool for some summer fun. I felt encouraged and connected rather than devastated and shamed. I had been given the gift of a psychic dream to ease a difficult encounter. By being prepared, I was able to see the event as a powerful rite of passage, rather than a humiliating chance encounter.

Sometimes a psychic dream happens weeks, months or even years before the event. It is important to reread your dream journals regularly to discover your precognitive dreaming ability. It is easy to forget a dream and its predictive content due to the illusive nature of dreams. I record my dreams regularly and am still surprised by forgotten dreams scribbled in my old journals. Let's look at an example.

Do You Dance?

I was rereading my old dream journals several weeks after returning from a yoga retreat in Hawaii. I started with the journal from two months earlier. This dream startled me with its accuracy: I am approached by a man of medium height with sandy colored hair. He says to me, "Do you dance?" I tell him that I performed dance some years before and that I am impassioned with yoga. He comments on my voice and says he has a recording studio. He asks me if I am willing to be recorded. I agree, and the dream ends.

My thoughts immediately turned to my new friend Bill, whom I met in Hawaii. We partnered during one yoga class and each recognized a kindred spirit. There was no doubt in my mind that I dreamt of Bill before I met him. He was of medium build with sandy-colored hair. He was a skilled musician with a recording studio. He had brought recording equipment with him as well as his ukulele. I taught the group a hula I learned in my childhood, and Bill accompanied us on the ukulele. He set up his recording equipment so we could enjoy an instant replay. He also surreptitiously recorded our afternoon at a waterfall, capturing the rush of the falling water along with our quips and squeals. The real-life experience included dance, recording and yoga just as in the dream. I did not recall this dream until I reread my journal. I would have missed this wonderful opportunity to celebrate the psychic power of dreams.

In this same journal, I rediscovered a dream about Patricia, one of my yoga teachers who lives in Boston. She was in Paris during the dream. I saw her going up an escalator and buying a pair of shoes. I noted the dream and shared it with her when she came to North Carolina several months later to teach a workshop. She smiled in surprise and told me that she had been in Paris the week that I dreamt of her. She had decided on the spur of the moment to attend a conference and she had bought a pair of shoes in a large department store with an escalator.

The Rewind Button

I awoke from this dream to find I had overslept. I rushed to get ready for work while I mentally reviewed my unique dream experience. I was swimming laps beside a man at the local YMCA. He was larger than life and as handsome as Adonis. I stopped at the end of my lane to watch him swim. To my surprise, when he did his flip turn, I saw that he was not wearing a swimsuit. I found a dream-rewind button to replay the flip turn. I replayed the scene several times, watching his bare, muscular form change direction. I wrote this dream in my journal, excited that I had found a rewind option in my dream life. I recorded another dream the same night that took place in the English countryside. I noted that several of my recent dreams had taken place in England.

About six weeks later I was doing household chores while listening to the *Phil Donahue Show*. The show featured guests who had overcome disabilities to become entertainers and inspirational speakers. I stopped my chores to watch more closely. The next guest rolled himself out in a wheelchair. He was a broad-shouldered, handsome man with long, flowing hair in his early thirties. He talked of the motorcycle accident that left him quadriplegic at eighteen years old. He was currently on a speaking tour visiting high schools and colleges lecturing on ways to overcome obstacles and manifest dreams.

I was moved by his optimism and independence. I could see that he was more self-sufficient with his disability than some of my ablebodied acquaintances. He then shared an incident that had happened to him at the local swimming pool. He was doing his regular lap swim when he noticed that some folks on the sidelines were cheering and clapping. "How nice," he thought to himself. "They are cheering me on." However, as the cheering grew more pronounced he became curious. He then realized that during his swim he had lost his swimsuit. Since he has no feeling in his hips and legs he had not noticed that he had been giving them a flash of bare skin with every flip turn. I knew that I had dreamt of this moment. I wondered if the rewind option was a clue that I would see him on television.

During that week I could not get the *Phil Donahue Show* out of my mind. I had been impressed by the young man's energy and was curious about my predictive dream. I finally decided to call the *Phil Donahue Show* and ask the guest's name so I could send a note to him. I got through to an operator and she remembered the show. She told me to hold on while she checked his name. She came back on the line in several minutes. "His name is J. D. England," she said. Again I was struck by the synchronous dreaming of England on the same night. I sent him a note thanking him for his work and recounting my dream. I was gratified to receive a note with a photo in response.

Levitation and the Fox

The following example helped me move more deeply into the unresolved relational issues with my father. This synchronous event features an interesting cast of characters.

My dad was born on November 1 in the astrological sign of Scorpio, the sign of sexuality, rebirth and the occult. Three of my significant male relationships have had the same birthday as my father. My personal issues with him include reclaiming my sexual boundaries, feeling my power in relationships and owning my feminine intuition. He died on November 15, 1988, also in the sign of Scorpio, and my work with him has grown more intimate and rewarding since his passing. Immediately following his death, the lights in my bedroom began to spontaneously flicker on and off. I decided to use the lights to try to communicate with my father. I asked a question and waited for the lights to react. The electrical communication with him stopped abruptly several years after his death, coinciding with my meeting a "Scorpionic" man. The only other electrical activity occurred three years later at the death of my good friend and hairdresser, Tony.

My father's energy still continues to visit me around his birthday. One year the smoke alarm went off spontaneously in the early morning hours on his birthday and four times the phone began to ring in the middle of the night on the eve of his birthday, even when I had it off the hook.

One year I had a string of synchronicities that marked his birthday. It started with a dream. In the dream a visiting yoga teacher named John is teaching a class at the local yoga center, Triangle Yoga. (In actuality he was scheduled to do a workshop at the local yoga studio on my father's birthday several weeks after the dream.) A man of Scorpionic depth and passion, named John like my father, the yoga teacher is charismatic, caring and focused. In the dream he is teaching us levitation. I am doing well and am hovering several feet above the floor. The teacher, John, wearing a robe, is flying about the ceiling demonstrating with ease the art of advanced levitation.

When I awoke from the dream, I was intrigued. I knew that the yoga teacher was playing a healthy, "boundaried" version of my father. Having lived in Hawaii my father wore muumuus in my childhood, so I understood the robe in the dream. Histrionic and dramatic, my father would entertain my childhood friends by eating flaming popcorn. It would be characteristic of him to show off by flying around the room. I recorded the dream in my journal, curious to see what would follow.

The night of the workshop I arrived at Triangle Yoga early. It was Halloween and I decided to bring my extraterrestrial mask for fun. I also put skeleton stickers on my fingernails in honor of All Saints' Eve. I told several of the other students about my levitation dream and they laughed. John, the teacher, arrived soon after, bringing with him a mask of Nixon. Before the workshop began we had fun visiting a few of the other classrooms masquerading as Nixon and an extraterrestrial holding hands. Soon the room was filled with the workshop participants and we started our yoga practice.

As the evening progressed the room became stuffy and John went to adjust the fans. The switch is sensitive and the fans whirled at high speed, bringing a rush of whirling air. John laughed and said, "Well, I guess I'll be teaching levitation this evening!" My friends, remembering my dream, looked at me in surprise.

At the end of the class I noticed I had lost my fingernail stickers. The next day I saw that one of my skeleton stickers had found its way onto John's mat. Another one was stuck to the bottom of his foot. His wife, Suzie (my childhood name), noticed it and pulled it off to show the rest of us. Again we laughed at the synchronicity of it all. I was enjoying the events on a deeper level, too. There was a healing for me as I expressed my playfulness with the extraterrestrial mask and my psychic abilities with the precognitive dream without being shamed or discounted.

The morning of the last day of the workshop I glanced out of my bathroom window into the backyard. There stood a large red fox. I have always felt an affinity for the fox. I had never seen one in my yard and rarely heard of sightings in the area. Again I felt my father's presence, trying in his own way to help me face my fear. The fox looked up at me and our eyes met. He stood staring at me intently for several minutes before he walked slowly into the woods. I raced downstairs to get a last look at him, but he was gone. The message of the fox was clear to me. I was being asked to leave my camouflage abilities behind me. His direct gaze came to me as a challenge to be visible and powerful in my life—a silent challenge to own the gifts I have and deal head-on with the limitations.

Attracting Psychic Dreams

One of the best stimulators of psychic dreaming is reading accounts of precognitive dreaming. I recommend reading dream books before you go to bed. You can reread this chapter of the book as well. It appears that reading about psychic dreaming gives the right brain permission to recall a psychic dream. Reading of another's dream experience can also help alleviate fears and doubts about your psychic nature. You are currently having psychic dreams but not remembering or recording them. The next exercise allows the dreams to enter the conscious memory so that you can benefit from the information.

To request a psychic dream, write the following statement at least five times:

> *I now allow myself to remember and write down a psychic dream.*

Keep your dream journal dated, and reread your dream entries regularly. Look for premonitions of life events. Not every dream is precognitive. It takes time and experience to tell the difference. I have dreams of house fires, break-ins and accidents that seem very real but have not come to pass in physical reality. If a dream is especially strong and persistent, I act as if it were going to happen. With experience you will recognize the unique qualities of a psychic dream.

Mediumship through Dreams

Medium: A person thought to have powers of communicating with the spirits of the dead.

The components of a successful medium are simple—a desire to communicate and an ability to suspend the judgment of the logical left brain. The motivation for contact with the deceased person can be to continue contact, receive information or complete any unfinished business in the relationship. At times the communication is solicited unconsciously. For example, a bereaved husband may have an unexpected dream about his deceased wife. In this case his inner longing to communicate with her draws the dream to him.

Suspending the judgment of the left brain is necessary to allow a mediumship dream. It is unwise to suspend the activities of our left brain if we are operating a vehicle, performing surgery or following a new recipe. The left brain is needed in these activities. However, in communication with discarnate beings, the left brain is not helpful. The left brain needs concrete evidence to comprehend a concept, and the communication style of discarnate beings is neither material nor logical. Since mediumship is intangible and sensory, it is the intuitive right brain that makes the connection and interprets the information. For further study see chapter 6.

Dream Communication

Our intuitive sense can receive a message from a loved one across the country without the use of a telephone. Many of us have known who would be on the other end of the receiver as we picked it up. How did we know a friend was calling when we had not heard from him in three years? There were no concrete or tangible clues to bring us this information. This same natural psychic sense can help us use dreams to communicate with a loved one who is discarnate. Dreams emerge from the subconscious through the right brain. The censure of the left brain relaxes while we sleep. Our unconscious feels comfortable with its psychic abilities and its ability to explore beyond the physical plane. The right brain is not limited by time, space or death.

When a human soul leaves the body, the person's energy is still present—just as a loved one does not cease to exist if she goes to a distant country for an extended stay. She is physically far away yet just as real as when she lived in the same town. It may be more difficult to reach her, but we do not question her existence. She may even change dramatically from her travel experience, but she is still uniquely herself. So it is with our loved ones who die. They have changed form and have gone to a foreign land where the phone service is unique. By understanding the unique communication method of discarnate beings, we can send and receive messages.

Let's look at an example of dream mediumship and explore a technique to develop dream communication:

Katy's Visits

In the spring of 1995 a close friend committed suicide. Katy had struggled for years with constant physical and emotional pain. She was a hard worker and had a gift of humor and wit. After years of resisting the pull to end her constant struggling, she finally chose to leave her body. Pulled by our strong connection, I was drawn to her home and discovered her body. Despite my feelings of shock and grief, I was surprised by the pervasive feeling of peace around her home. I spoke with her spirit continually as the police and ambulance arrived. I reassured her that I loved and supported her in her new form.

I spent the next month helping others accept Katy's death and preparing a memorial service for her. On her birthday, we gathered at her favorite spot on the campus surrounded by large shade trees and flowers. We had a bouquet of her favorite color of balloons to release at the end of the service. We made plans to gather funds to purchase a memorial bench to be placed near her favorite tree. We cried, shared stories and released the orange balloons. We wept as we watched them float up and out of our sight. Knowing the balloons still existed even as we lost sight of them reminded us that Katy was still alive in her new life.

I grieved for my loss. Even though I knew she was safe and happy, I longed for Katy to return to her physical existence. Several months after her death, I received her ashes. I took the ashes home and held them like a baby. As I wept, I thanked Katy and her family for entrusting me with the scattering of her ashes. I would wait until Katy gave me a sign about what to do with them. I told her I loved her and went to sleep. That night I had the following dream.

I am at the airport waiting for a flight out. Suddenly I see Katy come around the corner. Aware that she is dead, I am excited to see her. We share a meal and talk about our lives. She is content in her new life. After our meal, we hug and promise to meet again. I watch her go to catch her plane, and I awake.

Upon awakening, I felt very peaceful. I felt exactly as I would feel after spending time with my friend. I was grateful for this dreamtime connection. The next month when waves of grief revisited me, I asked for another rendezvous with Katy. That night I had this dream.

I am walking along the streets of a strange city. Katy comes walking toward me along the sidewalk. Once again I am elated to see her, and we hug and cry. We chat for a few minutes and then decide to get dinner and go to an Indian movie. Our evening is fun and comfortable. After the movie, we part ways in a large parking deck. Again I watch her go.

I awoke from this dream feeling peaceful and satisfied. I began to ask Katy to meet with me regularly. We have a rendezvous almost every month. Sometimes it takes a few nights after my request to connect with her. It is always a pleasure and a comfort to spend time with her in our dream meetings.

Preparing for a Dream Visit

Your love and connection with the deceased is pivotal in mediumship dreaming. The more you open to your memories and feelings for the deceased, the more you encourage dream communication. It is difficult for the telepathic channels to open if you are holding your grief. Emotions and psychic information use the same channel in the human psyche.

Humans and spirits are both sensitive to significant calendar dates. The birthday, day of death and special anniversaries of the deceased will be opportune times to attempt communication. I often see an increase in psychic phenomena near my father's birthday and day of death. I have had communication dreams on his birthday and day of death. In one dream, my father showed me his new, light body by setting his head afire. This is personally interesting to me because in my childhood he entertained the family by playing with fire. He would light pieces of popcorn and eat them or light the tips of his fingers and extinguish them in his mouth. Both of these dreams exhibit my father's love of drama and his need to be the center of attention.

It is vital to have patience and perseverance to develop mediumship dreams. It may take time for your conscious mind to allow you to remember a spirit communication dream. It can be helpful to write out any fears you have of receiving a mediumship dream. Be as honest as you can. Your honesty will help you open to this powerful healing experience.

Asking for a Dream Visit

Have available any possessions or memorabilia from the deceased loved one. The energy from familiar objects will increase the connection. Take some time to recall memories of your time together. The more vivid and intense the memories, the stronger the energetic connection. Remember that you need to allow your feelings to flow. One of the best preparations for receiving a spirit dream is to cry and release any feelings of grief.

Have a dream journal and pen by your bed. Before you go to sleep, take some time to write a short note to your loved one. Let her know that you want to meet. Feel your heartfelt desire to visit with her in your dreams.

After writing the note, write this statement five times before settling down to sleep:

I now remember and write down a dream of direct communication with _____.

Continue to recite this statement as you are falling asleep to allow the information to soak deeply into your subconscious mind. Continue to write the dream order even if you do not remember any dreams. It takes time to allow the dream communication. When you receive a mediumship dream, write a thank-you note to the loved one and request future visits.

Bad Dreams Are Good for Us

For most of us, a bad dream is unpleasant and frightening. To awaken abruptly with a pounding heart is not something we consider desirable. Likewise, to recall a dream in which we are violent or sadistic is disturbing. However, these uncomfortable dreams can help us work through deep fears and impulses without endangering ourselves through real-life dramatization.

The human psyche must express itself. Our dream life provides a vast and multilevel arena designed to allow us to safely explore the psyche. The human psyche houses the most divine imaginings along with the most shadowy forms of fear. Our dreams provide an arena to acknowledge and experience the complete range of human emotions.

I actively welcome all nightmares into my dreamtime. I am grateful to have a physically safe arena in which my unconscious can expose and process my fears and shadow desires. When I have a frightening or disturbing dream, I work with it, probing the uncomfortable feelings to find the hidden messages. Let's look at an example of a bad dream bringing helpful counsel.

* * *

I had the following dream while I was working as a teacher for a developmental center. I was responsible for the education, care and feeding of small children with severe impairments.

In the dream, I am perched high atop a freestanding ladder that is precariously tilting back and forth. I am using all of my strength to try to keep the ladder upright. Then I am handed one of the children to hold. The ladder leans and wobbles dangerously. I am barely managing to stay upright when another child is handed to me, then another, and another. The dream ends as all the children are falling from my grasp.

I awaken from this dream feeling guilty and horror-stricken. I love these children in my care, and I want to help them, not hurt them. At first glance I think this dream is pointing to my fear of my inadequacy as a teacher. However, on closer examination I see much more.

At the time of this dream I was feeling overwhelmed and burnt-out. After having worked at the center for eighteen months, I needed a change. I was emotionally attached to the children and staff and did not want to think about leaving. However, I was losing my balance and my sense of self by staying. This particular ladder of success was not balanced for me. I looked more honestly at my needs for the future and I faced my reluctance to leave the children. Soon after this dream, I left the center and entered graduate school.

Stop! Thief!

Another example of the benefits of bad dreams is seen in the following series of thief dreams. In the first dream, I am walking in the dark when my purse is grabbed by a man running by me. I scream and scream, but no one helps me. In the next dream, I am in a store and I leave my purse in the cart. When I turn back to my cart, I see a man snatch my purse and run. I yell for help, and people come to help me. But no one can find the man with my purse. In the next dream, I am also in a store. I am near my cart when I see a man reaching into my purse. I jump on him, pin him to the ground and call for the police. A policeman comes and takes him away.

I am encouraged by the progression of these dreams. In each dream, I seem to be finding more of my power. I find my voice and the physical strength to tackle the thief. Even though these dreams are unpleasant and scary, I see I am gaining in strength and courage.

The next dream takes a turn. Once again I am in the store with my purse in the cart. Once again I catch the man with his hand reaching into my purse. This time I am able to tackle him and tie him up. As I am holding him down, I confront him by saying, "Why do you keep trying to steal my money? This has got to stop!" He looks at me genuinely surprised and says, "I wasn't trying to take your money! I was trying to put some money in your purse!" I am so surprised at his answer that I laugh and wake up.

This series of dreams shows us the value of unpleasant dreams. When we face the fears and shadowy forms we project on our world, we find more helpers and assistance than we imagined. In my childhood, I was familiar with men who were secretive and dishonest. Naturally I put this dream figure into the same category of men. Since I generally saw men this way, I was also seeing my own male energy as covert and distrustful. The man in the dream was offering me another viewpoint. Some men are secretive and dishonest, while others are helpful and giving. The series of dreams gave me the opportunity to open to a more balanced opinion of men. In turn, I was able to see my own male energy in a more positive light.

The last dream of the series came months later. Once again I am shopping and see the man at my cart. Out of habit, I pounce on him and feebly call for help. As we are waiting for help I examine his face and shoulders. I am attracted to him and start to playfully touch and caress him. He is mutually interested, and the dream ends in this tender, sensual way. In this dream, I am only mildly alarmed by the man's behavior. I feebly ask for help to remove him. Immediately I am in touch with my interest in him. In this dream I know intuitively that he is not a danger to me. I am then able to open myself up to receiving from him.

Ordering Bad Dreams—Reducing the Real-World Drama

Working with negative dreams can greatly increase self-knowing. So many of our skills and talents are hidden behind fears and painful experiences. Bad dreams can help us reenact these negative messages and patterns so that we can consciously release them to access our personal power.

I often ask for dreams to help me work through my fears. I dream of car accidents, tornadoes, and other high-drama situations. In my dreams, I experience fatal illnesses, paralysis and gunshot wounds. I have given birth numerous times, inflicted a fatal knife wound and fallen to my death.

If you find you are experiencing an inordinate amount of external drama in your life, you may want to try and order a dream to work through your fears. In this way, you ask your dream life to re-create the scenarios you need to face.

Let's imagine that you have a strong fear of having a car accident. You can ask for a series of dreams to help you face and clear this fear. Write the following statement five times before going to sleep.

I now remember and write down one dream to heal my fear of a car accident.

It is helpful to recite the statement as you are falling asleep. Be patient and persistent. It often takes time to absorb the dream order. Continue to write the order at least five times before you sleep. When you awaken, write down whatever you remember, no matter how small or seemingly insignificant. Every part of each dream has meaning and healing within it. You can learn to translate your unique dream language.

The Power of Your Dreams

Psychic dreaming and dream mediumship are natural occurrences. With patience and practice, we can harness the intuitive power of our dreams. Each night we are given the opportunity to look inside the unconscious to view the deepest workings of the psyche. Take the time to investigate this perceptive window into the soul.

Chapter 9
Past Lives Revisited

The doctrine of reincarnation states that this present lifetime and its body, health, fears, desires, talents, relationships, finances and daily events are shaped by many former incarnations. This concept, as metaphor or dogma, gives us a paradigm for comprehending the complexity of our phobias, interests, talents and prejudices. This view can bring meaning to seemingly random encounters and events. Through the study of our distant past we acquire compassion and wisdom. We enter foreign worlds to explore different genders, cultures, professions, environments and historical periods. We comprehend the causes of adverse conditions in our lives and remedies for righting them. We access latent talents and relinquish prejudices. We claim the fuller, richer existence that is our birthright.

Whether or not we believe in reincarnation, we can benefit from this work. Past-life memory reminds us that all people share a common life experience on Earth. What one person experiences, we all experience. The concept of shared consciousness is witnessed daily. While listening to the nightly news, our hearts go out to those in distress. We do not need to live through a tornado to imagine the terror. We do not need to suddenly lose a loved one to touch the pain of grief. By nurturing our ability to walk in another's shoes, we expand our sense of humanity and our ability to love and forgive.

Values of Past-Life Exploration

1. To heal or accept chronic health issues.

2. To understand and improve relationships with family and friends.

3. To reduce judgments and projection of fears onto others.

4. To regain and utilize hidden talents and abilities.

5. To extend compassion to all living beings.

6. To increase abundance in any arena of life.

7. To release prejudice and hatred of specific people or cultures.

8. To understand and release feelings of deep-seated guilt or fear.

Starting the Search

Let's start by accumulating information concerning your past incarnations. Answer the following questions to help you clarify potential past-life experiences:

1. If you could visit anywhere on Earth, where would you go first?

2. Conversely, what country or region do you strongly dislike?

3. What period in history attracts you the most?

4. What period repulses you the most?

5. What are your fears or phobias?

6. How do you feel about your relationship to money and your financial situation?

7. What person (or persons) do you most admire and why?

8. What person (or persons) do you most dislike and why?

9. What ethnic foods do you enjoy?

10. What are your favorite books and movies?

11. If you could be a person in present or past history, whom would you choose? What qualities does this person possess?

By answering these questions, you can see past-life patterns emerge. Adverse reactions to countries or communities of people can represent unpleasant past-life experiences. Strong attraction may indicate positive memories. Unreasonable fears and phobias may reflect unresolved past-life traumas. One clue to past-life exploration is to notice who you judge and dislike. Chances are high that if you abhor it, you have lived it! The more you work with the concept of other lifetimes, the more you will take note of your likes and dislikes.

Map of the World

You can explore your distant past further by using a world map. Place the map in front of you and sit quietly with a pen in hand and your eyes closed. Take several deep and full breaths to clear your mind. Thank your logical left brain for all its hard work and encourage it to rest and relax. It may be helpful to recite: "I now allow my intuition to guide me back into my past."

When you feel relaxed, take your pen in hand. Keeping your eyes closed, draw several small circles anywhere you wish on the map. Take your time. There is no right or wrong way to do this exercise. When you have drawn as many circles as you wish, open your eyes and see what countries you have selected with your intuitive right brain. See if these areas correlate with the information you gathered in answering the questions above. If not, take some time to write down your feelings about the circled areas of the map. Notice any synchronistic events that may follow this exercise. For example, you may find that there is a National Geographic Special currently airing on a region that you circled on your map. You may stumble across a book or movie that depicts life in that particular region. Watch for dreams about one of the countries to gain more insight into your past.

Using the Past to Heal the Present

Your interest and motivation to know your distant past will bring you opportunities to explore your soul's journey. Universal law has an uncanny sense of timely justice. Our human perspective sees only what is before us. We cannot know all of the extenuating circumstances of each event and encounter. It would take an omniscient view to understand the rightness of the universal plan. However, with some insight and willingness, we can see the cosmic sense of balance in our own lives. By embracing a broader perspective of the events in our lives, we can increase our spiritual awareness.

Law of Karma

Karma: The sum and the consequences of a person's actions during the successive phases of his existence, regarded as determining his destiny.

The law of karma is not a law of punishment for crimes committed; it is a law of balance—the righting of inequity through act, deed and word. The idea of being punished for our mistakes is an ego invention. The ego believes in its power to be right and wrong—to be healer and slayer—to be guard and prisoner. The ego does not recognize forces greater than itself that determine justice. The ego does not comprehend a system without victims and without revenge.

The law of karma is designed to teach us what works and what does not work. It is designed to teach us responsibility and the maturity to believe and follow the universal laws that rule us. The universe has a way of putting us in a myriad of experiences where we find ourselves playing many different roles in one play. With the acceleration of awareness on the planet, this phenomenon seems to be happening more often. For example, people involved in a romantic triangular relationship may find themselves experiencing all three positions within a short time. These experiences allow us to feel more of the consequences of our past behavior and to choose differently in future situations.

I have used the power of past lives to heal problematic areas in my life. Let's look at examples of karmic rebalancing with self and others. You can use these examples as springboards to dive into your own personal karmic resolutions.

Healing My Eating Disorder

When I entered college, I was excited and eager to explore being on my own. I went to class, met new friends and experienced the freedom of my new life. Life felt free and fun for the first several months. Then I noticed that I was gaining weight from late-night visits to Dunkin' Donuts. My clothes grew tight, and I felt bulky and heavy. I felt anxious, ashamed and out of control. I decided losing weight was the way to regain my self-esteem. I began to exercise and diet.

For the first few weeks, I ate little and exercised every day. The extra weight began to come off, and I felt lighter. Feeling better, I redoubled my efforts to lose weight. I ate less and less and exercised more. I found it exhilarating to see how little I could eat and how much I could run and swim. I tried to beat my own record each day. My feelings of inadequacy were soon replaced by feelings of elation. Before the end of my freshman year, I went from 120 pounds to 85 pounds. But I still felt heavier than I wanted. I kept checking myself in the mirror to see if I was fat. I remember looking in the mirror and turning sideways and thinking, I will be thin enough when I cannot see myself in profile.

The fasting was soon followed by bulimia. After eating, my guilt would overcome me and I would purge my meal. In 1973, little was known about eating disorders. I had never heard of anorexia nervosa or bulimia. I felt like I was the only person engaged in this cycle. I was shocked when I discovered an article on eating disorders. How did they know exactly what I was doing and how I was feeling? The article described the compulsive exercising, the overachieving attitude, the binging and the purging. It mentioned the controlling nature of the parents of children with eating disorders. I suddenly knew that I was sick and that I needed help to get well.

I found a very understanding and competent therapist to help me. We worked in-depth on the underlying issues of low self-esteem and the drive for perfectionism. I discovered deeply buried feelings of rage at my controlling parents. I uncovered sexual fear and shame in my relationship with my father. My eating disorder was an attempt to control and internalize my intense feelings. I had to rebuild trust with my emotions and learn how to express them. It took years of painful inquiry to unravel the complex tapestry I had woven.

At one point in my therapy, I was eating more normally and starting to regularly express my anger and fear. However, I still felt guilty and ashamed whenever I ate. I started having a reoccurring nightmare of a dirty old man who chased me and tried to molest me. It was natural to turn toward my relationship with my father when interpreting the dreams. However, I was already having explicit dreams about my father and his sexual inappropriateness. The dirty-old-man dream felt different. Since I had been exploring spiritual practices, I decided to ask for a past life to help me heal my eating issues.

At the time, I was reading Shirley MacLaine's book *Dancing in the Light*. Reading about her past-life experiences put me in a receptive frame of mind. With the book by my side, I breathed deeply and relaxed into a meditative state. I asked for any past life that would help me understand my pain with eating.

All at once I was in a huge dining hall with thick, dark wood walls and dimly lit with candles. I saw many men, mostly large, bearded men, with huge steins of beer and wine and plates heaped with food. I saw long, rough tables of roasted pig, fowl, potatoes, vegetables, breads and puddings. The men were eating the food with their hands, gesturing wildly and talking with their mouths full. I was drawn to one man in particular. He was large-boned and corpulent. His hair and beard were long and matted. He was grasping a whole loin of pork, and the grease was running down his arm onto his coatsleeve. He was loud and rude. I was repulsed by his actions, but I could not seem to take my eyes off him. I then saw him grab a servant girl and pull her to him. She resisted, but he laughed and fondled her roughly. He had no regard for her feelings. The more she struggled, the louder he laughed. I knew that he pushed his sexuality on many women with no regard for their feelings. I also knew that he would gorge on food and purge to make room for more feasting.

I remembered the man with the dirty fingernails from my reoccurring dream. I recalled my fear of his unwanted advances. During the eating disorder, I tried to purposefully suppress my sexual desirability by growing thinner and thinner. My menstruation stopped, and my body was thin and flat like a young boy's. All at once I saw myself playing the part of the lusty man. I knew that I needed to embrace and forgive this past experience. I was trying to run from the memory by playing an extreme and opposite role. I was trying to convince myself I was the young maiden victim rather than the persecuting male. I had played the innocent-girl role with my father. Now I needed to look honestly at the part of me that had played my father's role—the overindulging and sexualizing male.

I felt physically ill when I gazed at the bearded man. I felt repulsed by his aggression and licentious air. I took several deep breaths and looked him deeply in the eyes. I faced him and his actions. I began to feel his pain and fear. I saw how far away he was from his soul and conscience. I felt the stirrings of my compassion for him. I spoke to him:

I see your pain. I know you are frightened and hurt. I see how lonely you are. I know you need love and tenderness. I know you are a part of me. I have been running from you. I want you to come home with me. I need you with me to be whole.

In my mind, I reached out to this man and held him. It was very difficult to draw him close to me. I was repulsed and horrified yet drawn to his pain. As I held him in my mind's eye, I felt a rush of warmth and energy. During the eating disorder I felt uncommonly cold. I realized that I had cut off the warmth of my passion for fear of misusing it. Embracing this symbol of my misdirected passion restored my warmth and vitality. I needed this part of my soul's experience to regain my appetite for love and life.

My reoccurring dreams of the dirty old man never returned. From the deep therapeutic work and the past-life exploration, I slowly started to eat more food and my guilt began to wane. I continued to work with the image of this man, repeating my desire to connect and reincorporate him. Whenever I felt harassed by a man in my outer world, I returned to strengthen my relationship with the man from my past life. The more time I spent in understanding and accepting him, the better I related to the men in my outer world.

Facing the Shadow Side

This past-life memory allowed me to penetrate more deeply into my father work by forcing me to face the darker side of my masculine nature. It is convenient to use a present persona to "hide" from one's shadow.

In this lifetime, I am a petite and gentle-natured female. In this particular package it is easy for me to masquerade as someone who has always been sweet, compassionate and nonviolent. I can conveniently keep the darker side of my past-life history a secret. Every human quality expressed by any man or woman belongs to each of us. It may have been centuries since we have had firsthand knowledge of these qualities, yet we all share the same human nature. We can find these cast-off parts of self most easily through our prejudices and judgments of others. The behaviors and qualities that most annoy and inflame us are the ones we have the most difficulty accepting in our own past.

In facing the qualities I most shunned in others, I got in touch with a most difficult and crucial past-life experience. I had written in my journal complaining about the self-righteous, controlling, sexualizing, self-centered nature of the men around me. I asked to understand my resentment by visiting a past life when I exhibited these qualities. The following scene flashed before me.

I saw myself as a minister, charismatic and impassioned. I was so caught up in the passion of preaching that I lost touch with any sense of humility and boundaries. I took sexual advantage of young parishioners, using my position to intimidate and overpower them. I became convinced that I was being asked to determine their destiny and planned a mass exodus by poisoning the parishioners' food.

In this vision I saw that I embodied all of the negative qualities I saw in my father and other men in my life. I knew that I needed to return to this part of myself to improve my relationship with men. By taking responsibility for my shadow masculine side, I would not need men to constantly reflect the rejected parts of my own history.

My next step was to emotionally remember and face the consequences of my past-life behavior. I felt the shame and horror of the abuse and murder. The past life shed a new light on my eating disorder and my fear of food poisoning. I also had a new understanding of my sexual history—including childhood sexual abuse, a date-rape experience and relationships that ended in infidelity and abandonment.

The unclaimed parts of my shadow were showing up in the men that I attracted. I was asking them to play the masculine shadow for me. In this way I could play the "innocent victim" and see them as the "bad guys." As I allowed myself to feel the emotional consequences of my past-life actions, I felt the pain, remorse and sexual compulsion. I expressed my remorse and regret for all the pain and suffering I had inflicted on others. I let the fear and shame run through my body. Over time I felt a lightness of being that follows the deep confrontation of self.

My awareness of this past life has helped me attract healthier men in my life. I am more discerning and can detect inappropriate behavior more quickly. By consciously facing the past, I reduce the need to draw the shadow to me in the present.

Healing Karmic Ties

The next two examples concern healing karmic ties with others. These may be people in your daily life or strangers who come into your life. This technique is helpful for intense and difficult encounters. It can help you understand and heal situations of violence or harassment that seem to come out of the blue. This technique encourages you to let go of the victim stance and to find empowerment in difficult situations.

The Robbery

One spring afternoon, I arrived home with my preschooler and her young friend. We arrived to find the door forced open and the TV, VCR, silverware and some jewelry stolen. After calling 911, I took the children outside to wait for the police. They were agitated and clinging to my legs. I comforted them and got them interested in some outdoor toys. To calm my own fear and sense of invasion, I repeated these statements to myself: "There is no loss. We are safe."

The police arrived shortly, examined the evidence and gathered the necessary information for their report. After they left, I sat down to go more deeply into the meaning of this event. Knowing that every situation has a meaning and purpose for me, I wanted to gain the message from this particularly dramatic lesson.

Closing my eyes to focus, I saw one message clearly. I was working on regaining trust and safety with men. I was finding my sense of boundary with men, and I knew that I still had fear to face and clear. I knew I needed to clarify my right to my sense of physical privacy and sacredness—this robbery being a clear invasion of the boundary of my home. Therefore, I would increase my focus on this issue.

I then asked, "What is the gift of the robbery? What are my lessons?" I received several answers. The first message was that my house was too full. There were clothes and toys that we no longer needed, and I had been putting off delivering them to a needy cause. The outflow was not matching the inflow. This was an imbalance that needed my immediate attention.

Next, I examined the role I seemed to have—one of a victim with loss. So I asked, "Am I repaying an old debt from my past?" Immediately a scene came into view. Eyes closed, I saw a desert scene and a bearded man in loose robes taking a camel from the side of a nomadic tent. I knew that I was that man and that the men involved in the present-day robbery were the owners of the camel I had stolen. From that vision, I received a deeper sense of rightness about the robbery. I felt some relief replacing the fear and resentment. Instead of sending anger and judgment to the robbers, I sent gratitude for the low drama of the break-in. There had been no vandalism or violence to the house or to my family. They had taken the goods and left. I also sent them encouragement and support to face and change their present lives. I knew they must be fearful and desperate to resort to stealing. I also asked for forgiveness for any pain I had caused them in the past.

During the days following the robbery, I also needed time and attention for my feelings of fear, anger, invasion and unsafety. I slept more fitfully and nervously. I had several dreams of break-ins. I spent time writing out my feelings. I vented my anger about the robbery. I also continued to send the intruders compassion and emotional support.

This practice of seeing a broader perspective is not designed to deny normal human emotions. The challenge is to attend to the immediate emotional needs and to recognize the spiritual overview. From this vantage point, we learn to view situations with an increased awareness of our spiritual work and purpose. Let's look at another example of karmic ties with others:

Eight Months Pregnant

I discovered my husband's infidelity in the eighth month of my pregnancy. I had been feeling unsettled and concerned about our relationship for months. I had worked alone with my therapist after my husband's refusal to do a couple's session. The Monday after a tense weekend out of town, I walked into his office space. As if in a trance, I went to one stack of correspondence and pulled out a letter from the middle of the pile. I turned the pages over until I saw the words that confirmed my fears: "You must tell Susan about our affair." The letter was from a woman I knew by sight. I do not know how I knew which letter to choose. Months earlier, I had been aware of her feelings for my husband and had warned him of her intentions. He had discounted my fears.

I moved through the rest of the day in shock and grief. Ironically, my last two clients were involved in extramarital affairs. I was forced to give unbiased and clear counsel to each. I felt as if I were being given a final exam under duress. The synchronicity was poignant and painful.

The following month demanded my complete attention. I moved through as much of the shame, sadness and anger as possible to prepare for the birth. The weekend before I discovered the affair, I dreamt that I gave birth to twins and only one survived. Everyone kept telling me to celebrate the birth of my surviving child, but I was overcome with grief. When I found the letter, I knew that the dream was telling me that I would be celebrating a birth and a death simultaneously. The birth of my daughter was coupled with the death of my marriage. I was grateful for my support system and my ability to express my feelings.

The woman made her presence known in my life. She called my home and office repeatedly and once came to my home. I was appalled by her disregard for my privacy and my marital status. I felt an excruciating mixture of outrage and pain; as if I were the interloper and she, the wife. I was very confused by her boldness. I felt as if I were to blame for the infidelity. I continued to maintain a strong boundary, reminding myself to stay out of the triangular drama.

For months after the birth of my daughter, she continued to call me repeatedly. At times she waited for me after work and followed my car. I remained steady in my resolve to stay detached from the drama. I had no desire to confront her and battle with her. I worked on letting my husband go while releasing my pain and anger. I spent hours and hours using ritual and anger work.

As the intensity of the drama continued, I began to examine my relationship with the woman. On one level she was my husband's lover and my competition—she, the home wrecker, and I, the victim. Yet I knew from the vehemence and passion of her harassment that we had met before in another time. I knew that I needed to face my past life history with her in order to find a peaceful outcome to the nightmare.

I took myself into an altered state for a past-life regression, and I asked to understand on the deepest level my karmic tie with her. I wanted to understand the present situation in light of our past together. The following story unfolded before me like a movie.

I was a wealthy woman of status. I possessed everything that money and position could buy. My only pain stemmed from my inability to bear children. I ached with the desire to mother a child. I saw myself using my money and power to buy a child from a young disadvantaged mother. It was not a mutual decision. I pushed and demanded, using force and intimidation to acquire the child. The young mother was heartbroken and bereft. I turned my back on her and started my new life as the mother of her baby.

I knew instinctively that the young mother was my husband's lover in this lifetime and that the baby held the soul of my husband. Now I understood her possessive tone when she called our home asking for my husband to come to the phone. She was exerting her unfulfilled right as his mother. As a mother in this lifetime, I was appalled by my actions. I can scarcely imagine the agony of being forcibly separated from my child. I wept at her pain. I understood why she seemed to hate me so much, and I did not blame her for this. I prayed to forgive myself and silently asked for her forgiveness.

After this experience I continued to maintain my boundary and keep my distance. My feelings of anger and hatred diminished. I tried to send love and support when she called or followed me. I took time to do loving meditations in her name to help soothe my sense of betrayal. I continued to work on two planes—healing my pain as the victim and owning my responsibility as her persecutor.

In time it became easier to see her around town. Coincidentally, I saw her in town as I was working on this chapter. I had not seen her in nine months. I felt cautious around her but not angry or jealous, and I continued to send her support for her endeavors.

I must emphasize that I did not use the past-life regression to diminish or deny my human reaction to the present-life situation. It is vital to own and experience the present situation. It is then appropriate to delve deeper into the past history. I must also stress that this process took years of work. Unlike a Hollywood movie, where the trauma and resolution happen within two hours time, this process of reconciliation took years of diligent work.

Although my ex-husband was emotionally unavailable for several years, I continued to work on repairing my relationship with him. After years of releasing my anger and grief, I now share a deeper connection with him than I ever did before. I see him and his lover as two of my greatest teachers. I gained more self-love and spiritual understanding from the ending of my marriage than from any other experience to date.

Changing the Channel

At my daughter's fourteenth birthday I revisited the memories of her birth. I was considering having another child, and I was intent on clearing the karmic birth file. The drama and pain around my first birth experience was so intense, I was eager to prevent a reenactment. During these several months of revisiting, I kept running across news stories, books and movies involving children forcefully separated from their birth parents. I also had a rare sighting of the woman involved with my ex-husband fourteen years earlier. I knew the file was activated by these reoccurring synchronicities.

That same evening I was getting my weekly dose of the sitcom *Ally McBeal*. The irreverent zaniness of the program helped me unwind from a hectic day. I was straightening my room as I watched. During a particularly amusing scene, I paused in the center of my bedroom. Suddenly I heard something fall and the channel changed from Fox to CBS. The alarm clock had fallen off the bedside table and hit the channel button on the remote lying on the floor. The program on CBS was *Touched by an Angel*. I sat on the bed curious to find the message in this odd turn of events.

I was amazed to discover the episode involved a family that had adopted a baby under shady circumstances. Desperate to have another child, they had denied the obvious clues that their adopted son came through the black market. The angel works to reunite the birth father with his abducted son. The adopting family must face the devastating consequences of their denial and work to find a healing resolution for the son and his birth father. The subject of the program reminded me acutely of the past life work with my husband's lover. In watching *Ally McBeal,* I tried to escape. The synchronous channel-changing brought me back to the deeper work at hand.

Let's look at a technique to reduce the drama of a current situation by seeing a broader view:

Past-Life Memory

1. Look at a current problematic situation.

2. Examine your current role and the pain, discomfort or feelings you experience in the role.

3. Find the person who seems to be the strongest persecutor.

4. Imagine, invent or create a situation in which the tables are turned and you hold the persecutor's role in equal or greater intensity.

5. Feel your new role—imagine it, face it, live it.

6. State aloud or silently, "I can imagine myself in this role."

7. Embrace, forgive and love that part of you that needed that experience and know that it was appropriate for your soul at that time.

8. Thank yourself for having graduated from that particular role and for not needing to repeat it at the present time.

9. Go back to the current situation and view your feelings toward the persecutor. Note any difference in your feelings. If the feelings have not diminished, repeat the exercise and stay longer in the role as imagined persecutor.

10. When you begin to connect with the energy in this exercise, you will notice more understanding and fewer feelings of victimization.

Past-Life Regression

You may feel as if you are inventing the past-life scenario. The value of the experience will not be lessened. Your right brain is the hemisphere of distant spiritual memory and of imagination. Often psychic hits feel imagined and illogical. These qualities are the characteristics of right-brain activity.

There is a spiritual reason that your intuition brings a particular lifetime into your awareness. Trust yourself and follow it. Remember also that you do not need to know all the details of a past life to benefit from it. The most important points of the life will be given to you.

HOW TO BEGIN

Choose a specific situation or relationship in your present life that may benefit from a past-life memory. The more crucial the situation, the more information you will receive. Write a few sentences describing the present situation. You may want to record the following regression script to guide you through the past-life exploration.

Find a quiet, safe place where you will not be disturbed for at least one hour. You may use a tape recorder to record your past-life journey, speaking into the recorder as you experience the past life. You may also have pen and paper ready for taking notes upon your return. Make yourself comfortable lying down, making certain that your spine is supported.

Begin your relaxation by taking deep, full breaths. As you exhale, note how good it feels to let your physical body rest and relax. Thank your body for all the services it provides you, and thank yourself for taking this time to allow your physical body to rest deeply. Use the focus on your breath to help relax your mind and release the tensions of the day. Follow your inhalations and exhalations with your mind, saying silently to yourself, "Breathing in, breathing out."

Now imagine that you are supported by a soft, fluffy cloud. The cloud is firm enough to support your body weight yet soft enough to allow you to relax completely. Relax deeply into the soft cloud and float. As you breathe, let go of your thoughts and soften the brain. Continue to relax more deeply into the cloud's supportive embrace. Let yourself float and relax.

You are safe and protected as you float. You are floating back in time, to the past life most important for you to experience and remember at this time. You know where you need to go without trying.

When you have reached the past life, the cloud will gently descend. When you are ready, you will sit up and step to the ground. When you step off the cloud, notice your feet. Let your awareness move up your body. What are you wearing? What color is your skin? Are you male or female? Give yourself plenty of time to sense the answers. It is fine if you do not know the answer. Breathe and relax and let the information flow to you.

Now look around you. Notice your surroundings—the temperature of the air, the landscape, any sights, sounds, or smells around you. Take some time to explore your surroundings. Now allow yourself to find your home. Where do you live? Find your way easily to your home and explore the area. Notice any people or animals around you. Are there other people with you in this home? Where do you eat and sleep? Where do you work? How are you feeling in this body in this environment? Take your time and explore your life.

Spend as much time as you like in the lifetime. When you are ready to return, ask yourself these questions: What have I learned? What gift can I bring back from this lifetime? How does this lifetime influence the present one?

To return, lie down on the soft cloud. Allow the cloud to gently float up and move forward in time. Move easily and effortlessly into the present time. You feel relaxed and rested. You feel light and clear. Take your time. When you feel ready, find your fingers and toes and move them gently. Let your eyes open in their own time.

Roll to your side and sit up using your hands for support. Write down your impressions of your past-life voyage. Be aware of your dreams for several nights. Observe any synchronistic encounters that relate to your past-life experience. For further study see chapter 7.

Seeing the Whole Picture

Each lifetime reflects merely a minute portion of each soul's journey. If we examine only the present lifetime, we miss an opportunity to see ourselves wholly. Through the memory of the soul's past, we have the opportunity to embrace the shadow and the light of the human condition. By accepting our humanness, we can learn to express unconditional love for ourselves and others.

Chapter 10:
Communing with the Inanimate

Animate: Possessing life; living. [Latin animare, to fill with breath. From anima, breath, soul.]

Inanimate: Not exhibiting life; appearing lifeless or dead.

All matter on Earth is created from the same building blocks. This material is constantly changing form and expressing itself. The same tree that gives us fruit may eventually be fertilized by our remains. Our bodies die and merge with the soil that creates rocks and trees. These rocks and trees build our homes. Our planet is designed to naturally recycle all elements and create new forms.

As humans, we define animate and inanimate using characteristics discernible by our five known senses. Such a limited view blocks our ability to sense a wider variety of aliveness. In the groundbreaking TV series *Star Trek*, we witness the expansion of previous limits of perception. New life forms are continually being discovered as the starship crew remains open to new definitions of animate beings. No new form is immediately labeled lifeless. They do not judge the new forms by preconceived standards. They are receptive to endless varieties of sentient beings.

Despite an inability to possess life as we know it, inanimate objects have always been an integral part of human existence. We have constant contact with them. Each culture endows specific objects with qualities depending on their purpose. In Africa, a statue of a fertility goddess placed strategically in the home brings the consciousness of fertility into the household. In Native American culture, rocks and mountains are considered sentient. In Hindu culture, there is power in stone statues. In Hawaiian culture, the volcanoes are revered as an animated force. In Western culture, machines and electronic devices are symbols of status and power. The horsepower of a car, the speed of a computer, the smallness of a cellphone—each has symbolic meaning.

As a culture that reveres technology, we have closely linked our collective consciousness with our appliances, communication equipment and vehicles of transportation. Thus the energy of our computers, phone lines and automobiles is influenced by our energetic impulses. We are beings with electromagnetic fields of energy surrounding our physical forms. We see this daily with the effects of static electricity when we

163

receive a gentle shock from a handshake in a carpeted hall. Our bodies are human machines flowing with currents and electrical impulses. Even our vocabulary includes technological terms to describe our moods and states. We can be wired, shocked, overloaded, burnt out, broken down, turned off or turned on.

We are subject to the same electrical influences—positive and negative—as the machinery around us. There are medical studies that prove that our technology has positive and negative impacts on our well-being. From exposure to power lines to the extended use of a cellphone, we are examining some of the possible negative effects of technology on our health. Conversely, we use electrical currents to run life-support machines to keep our bodies alive. We are continuously linked with electrical systems and machinery, and therefore it makes sense to explore how our human electrical currents may influence machinery and electrical systems. It behooves us to become more conscious of our interaction with the inanimate articles in our lives.

Machines Are Our Friends

There is anecdotal evidence of our connectedness to inanimate objects. We know of successful auto mechanics who swear by their ability to talk to the cars they repair, and computer experts who are sensitive to the mood swings of their computers. They find that the more they relate to the cars or computers as mechanical friends, the more easily they are able to diagnose and repair them.

We have intimate and vital contact with machines and electronic equipment in our daily lives. We ask our cars to keep us safe and comfortable while moving us long distances, our computers to keep our accounts straight as well as to send and receive important messages. We ask our household appliances to heat our homes and clean our clothes. We ask our phones to keep us connected to business and personal relationships. At times this equipment needs mechanical attention and repair. Sometimes the reparation is simple and straightforward. At other times, the problem may be difficult to diagnose.

I have found it helpful to intuitively examine electrical and mechanical problems. Occasionally I need to call a repair person to help me. At other times I have been able to fix the problem energetically. In either case, I am able to use the experience to go deeper into my spiritual self. Let's look at an example.

Trick or Treat

I was asked by a local university radio station to be a guest on a Halloween radio program. They wanted me to talk about my life as a psychic and to answer questions from callers. On the scheduled day, I arrived a little early and sat in the waiting area. As I often do before working, I closed my eyes and breathed deeply. I began to focus my energy inward to allow my intuition to come to the foreground. As I relaxed in my chair, I became aware of the agitation of the sound crew. Apparently the main transformer was steadily losing power, and they were having difficulty staying on the air. I opened my eyes and watched the flurry of activity.

Since I am aware that strong energy currents from people influence electrical equipment, I was interested in seeing if I could sense a psychic reason for the electrical problem. A passing crew member explained the situation to me by saying, "We're losing power. We're going to try to go to auxiliary power to keep us on the air. We'll try to start the program as planned."

I was shown into a small room and introduced to my hosts. They were two young men, one tall and outgoing and the other personable and of medium-build. I immediately felt strong emotion coming from the taller man. I sensed that he was going through a personal crisis and did not want to be at work. He was friendly and polite to me, yet I had the strong impression that he was distracted and unfocused. I sensed that he needed to leave the station and have some time to himself. I felt that if he left, the electrical problem would be resolved.

Because we were doing a show on psychic phenomena and Halloween, I asked them if they would agree to explore my idea. They were willing, so I proceeded to gently question the host about his feelings. He shared with us that he was very distracted and did not want to be at the station that afternoon. He was in dire need of some time to rest and think through a difficult personal situation. With the other host's support, he was encouraged to leave and take some space for himself. He left, and we resumed the original format of the show.

I explained that sometimes our strong feelings can influence electrical equipment. This can be witnessed most dramatically in cases of poltergeist activity. There are documented cases in which emotionally agitated teens have moved objects or started engines without physical contact. These are very rare and extreme cases, yet the phenomenon of human energy influencing other energies can be seen daily to a lesser degree. More common examples of this phenomenon include unexplained computer glitches or shutdowns, lights flickering on and off, isolated ringing of the telephone and fluctuations in clocks or watches.

Within several minutes of the host's leaving, we were signaled by the technical crew that the power had resumed. They had found no logical reason for the power outage. After answering some callers' questions, we ended the program. I left feeling amused at the unexpected Halloween trick for the listeners.

Learning from Inanimate Objects

The Halloween radio story is an example of energetic projection. This phenomenon is not unlike its psychological counterpart. In psychology, emotional projection is the unconscious attribution of one's own feelings or attitudes to others. In energetic projection, we are asking our machinery to be the recipient of our unconscious or unclaimed moods.

Let's examine the Halloween radio show story to illustrate this point. The young man was feeling ambivalent about being on the air that particular day. He was abnormally agitated and distracted. His unconscious desire was to cancel work. Without power the radio station would be temporarily shut down, and therefore his unconscious desire for free time would be granted. In this case, we might say that he projected his unconscious desire to cancel work onto the generator. It is very probable that he had not wanted to work at other times yet had not disturbed the power source. However, the combination of the intensity of his distress and my presence as a source of support and understanding, may have increased the likelihood of energetic projection. I was able to sense his distress and allow him to actively claim his need for space. In this instance I could help him consciously own his feelings, and the need for projection dissipated.

We have a unique educational opportunity in examining our relationship with the machinery and electronic equipment around us. We can become more conscious of projecting our own issues onto inanimate objects. We can then reclaim and resolve these issues with awareness. Let's look at a couple of examples:

Where There Is Smoke . . .

When I discovered my husband's affair only a month before giving birth to our daughter, I was thrown into an emotional tailspin. Forced to come to terms with a sense of betrayal and abandonment, I did my best to prepare for birth. Afterward, as I struggled to nurture my infant daughter, my husband's affair continued to intrude upon my personal life. I worked hard to release my feelings of grief and rage.

One evening I answered the telephone to find his girlfriend on the other end. She was calling to complain that my husband was late to meet her. I was appalled at this outrageous invasion. After my husband left for the evening, I released some anger and tried to finish the day's chores.

At bedtime, I was still angry as I fell into a restless sleep. At two o'clock in the morning I was startled awake by the blare of the smoke alarm outside my bedroom. I got up and anxiously checked the house for smoke or fire. During my rounds, the alarm stopped as abruptly as it had started. Finding nothing wrong, I came back upstairs and sat on my bed. As my heartbeat resumed a normal pace, I recalled the earlier phone call. Just as I remembered the call, my anger soared and the alarm let out a loud blast. I took a deep breath in an attempt to release my anger, and the alarm stopped once again. I then wondered if my rage was setting off the alarm. I certainly felt angry enough to set something on fire.

Intrigued, I decided to play with the alarm. I concentrated on feeling my rage, and predictably the alarm went off. I breathed and thought calming thoughts, and it stopped. As long as I remained relatively peaceful, the alarm stayed quiet, but as soon as I disrupted my peace with angry memories, it would emit a loud cry.

Exhausted, I finally fell back to sleep, only to be startled awake again at four o'clock. The alarm had been triggered once again, rousing me from a nightmare in which I was yelling angrily. I got up and expressed more anger through writing and beating the bed, and the alarm accompanied me with its piercing outburst. I finally fell back to sleep at 4:30, and the smoke alarm remained mute. This sort of episode occurred once more during the year. Again, I was feeling intensely angry, this time at my father.

The smoke alarm incidents increased my awareness of my need to recognize and release my feelings of anger. I now remain vigilant of my need to release anger whenever it arises so that I may avoid accumulating an unhealthy backlog of intense emotion. The responsible expression of angry feelings allows trauma to heal and eventually leads to acceptance and forgiveness.

Flat Tires Galore

During a period of seven years, I experienced an inordinate number of flat or punctured tires. This period coincided with my divorce and being a single parent to my young daughter. It was common during that period for me to have at least four tire incidents per year. It never crossed my mind to be without AAA. The tires were usually damaged by picking up nails or sharp objects from the road. It became a source of humor for my friends to find out when my last flat tire had occurred. Needless to say, I was getting weary of the inconvenience and expense, although I was developing a friendly rapport with the local tire company—conveniently located next door to my office.

I knew there was hidden meaning in the flat tires for me, so I decided to begin working with the symbolism of my car and the four tires. In dream language, a car can be synonymous with the body. In this case, the tires would represent feet and legs. Legs and feet work together to ground us and help us move freely in our lives. Flat tires symbolize an inability to move. I felt my part in this drama had to do with my inability to ground myself and my fear of moving ahead in life. Both of these issues deal with the animus, or male energy, of my being.

Archetypically, it is the male who is grounded and realistic and who forges ahead into new adventures. Historically, young girls were discouraged from developing these abilities. It was assumed that they would attract a masculine mate to provide grounding and mobility. At the time, I was consciously working to claim these masculine aspects of myself. My new life as a single parent was forcing me to develop independence. The frequent tire incidents seemed to reflect my fear and reluctance to claim my male qualities. While reviewing the tire saga, I was reminded of my relationship with my father and of a striking memory from my adolescence.

I can vividly recall my first flat tire. I was sixteen and had been driving for several months. I had a flat tire several miles from home with my best friend, Elaine. We called my dad, and he said he would come to help us. I was nervous that he would be annoyed at having been disturbed on a Saturday afternoon. He always listened to a special radio program, and we knew not to interrupt him. However, when he arrived he was unusually upbeat and enthusiastic. As I apologized, he was quick to deny that he was burdened. As I watched him change the tire, I began to see that not only was he not upset by my call for help—he was elated. As I had grown more independent after getting my driver's license, my need for my father had diminished. I wondered if he was feeling left out and unimportant. The flat tire had temporarily remedied that situation. The flat tire had made his day.

By remembering this incident, I was able to go more deeply into my unconscious patterns of needing a man to stand in for my male energy. In a sense, the frequent flat tires were reflecting my reluctance to own my inner father. As a young girl, I had seen my dad become more irritable and distant as I became more mature and self-sufficient. On the day of the flat-tire rescue, I saw him transformed into a warm and enthusiastic father. That day, I unconsciously chose to retain some of my patterns of helplessness in order to stay connected to a more affectionate dad. Later in my life, when I actively began to give up these helpless patterns, I began to draw the flat tires to me. The flat tires represented my unconscious still trying to make the men in my life feel needed in an attempt to stay emotionally connected.

My growing strength and independence played a major role in the ending of my marriage. The increase in flat tires was an automatic reaction to my growing individuation. I was afraid that my increasing strength and independence would push my mate further and further away. I lived out that dreaded drama in my marriage. I began to realize that my independence and strength will only alienate a codependent and insecure man. As I continued to face and release my fear of integrating my male qualities, the tire incidents reduced dramatically. I actively decided I would rather be powerful and single than helpless and married. From four incidents per year, I can now report no tire problems at all for the past five years.

Understanding Energetic Projection

Let's look at some questions to help us decipher energetic projection. When experiencing a mechanical or electrical problem, try taking a few minutes to answer the following questions. Understanding the spiritual components of the incident can allow you to access valuable personal information and help reduce the number of incidents. This exercise is especially helpful for reoccurring problems.

1. Were you agitated, angry, or upset before the incident occurred? Do you feel resentful about your current activity? Are you distracted or unfocused? Honestly assess your emotional state at the time of the mechanical breakdown. Write the statement "I feel . . ." to help clarify your current mood.

2. What is currently happening in your life? Look for problems in health, career or relationships that may be brewing or full-blown. Often the message of the mechanical or electrical problem is related to an ignored, overactive or stressful area of your life. Write down any areas of your life that you are avoiding or that are causing you worry or stress.

3. What equipment is affected? What part of your life is most affected? What is the equipment used for? For example, is it used for communication? transportation? household help? You can use the "Dictionary of Symbols" below to help you decipher the meaning of the affected machinery.

4. What is the nature of the problem? Is the equipment broken down, on fire, flooding or stuck in second gear? You can use the "Dictionary of Symbols" to go deeper into the symbolic meaning of the problem.

5. Is this a reoccurring problem? If so, note the frequency of the problem. Write down as much as you can about any previous experiences. Do you see any noticeable patterns?

6. What is the result of the mechanical or electrical failure? For example, do you need to call someone for a ride? Are you late to an event
   or do you miss it altogether? Do you spend a weekend without television or a telephone? Do you have contact with new people? Is it
   necessary to ask for help or assistance?

7. What is your immediate reaction to the mechanical or electrical
   problem? Do you feel frustration or helplessness? Do you experience
   self-blaming or feelings of powerlessness and abandonment?
   Examine the feelings triggered by this event. Ask yourself when you
   have previously experienced this feeling. Explore the events of any
   relevant memories.

Interpreting the Message

The following "Dictionary of Symbols" lists symbolic interpretations of
common mechanical and electrical problems. It is important to remember that these are possible interpretations. You can learn to collect data
and to find your own personal message from your experiences. Ask your
mechanic or repair person to explain the malfunction. Listen carefully to
the words used to describe the problem. By using this information and
the personal data collected from the questions above, you can begin to
understand the message.

Dictionary of Symbols
Household Appliances

Air-conditioning: Deals with feelings of hot and cold toward people
or areas of your life. Represents dealing with a relationship or situation
that is heating up or too hot to handle. Indicates issues of comfort and
ease in life. Are you confronting the truth about a current relationship?

Central heating: Addresses childhood issues of lack of security and
warmth in relationships and in life. Restimulates feelings of being left
out in the cold. Can indicate a need to nurture and protect oneself.
How can you increase feelings of security and belonging in your current situation? Can you allow yourself to belong to a supportive group
of people?

Clothes dryer: Overheating represents unexpressed anger that
needs to be released. A broken dryer symbolizes feeling unresolved
and incomplete in a situation beyond your control. Laundry has to do

with family secrets. Ask yourself if it is time to admit or expose a family secret that you have been carrying.

Dishwasher: If broken, symbolizes feeling overwhelmed with daily chores. Needing a mom to come in and take care of things. Too much to do and not enough time to nurture self. Can you find new ways to lighten your workload?

Electrical: Loss of electricity represents loss of personal power. How can you gain more power in the present situation and in your life generally? Electrical loss at night can indicate being in the dark about an issue. Can restimulate childhood fears of the dark and memories of abandonment. Can be an opportunity to go inward and develop your inner source of spiritual light and power. Lack of light and electronic entertainment can represent a need to meditate or pray.

Electrical fire: Strong unexpressed anger. Burning with rage deep inside. Find safe, responsible ways to release anger. (See chapter 2.)

Circuit breaker: Moderate anger that needs to be released. Taking care of it now will help you avoid a bigger problem in the future.

Microwave: Represents taking shortcuts and speeding up time. Can be a message to slow down and take time to do things the old-fashioned way. Are you overworking? Take time to breathe and enjoy the process of life.

Plumbing: Frozen pipes represent emotions that are frozen and stuck. Burst pipes or flooding symbolizes strong emotions held in and bursting forth. Fear of being overwhelmed by intense emotions. Need to cry or release emotionally. May indicate an avoidance of developing feminine characteristics, such as yielding, adapting and nurturing. Leaking pipes can indicate a leaking of energy. Are you denying an important feeling? Where are you leaking energy in your life?

Smoke alarm: Alarm sounding without evidence of smoke or fire can indicate unreleased anger. Try writing or vocalizing anger to remedy the problem. May indicate a relationship smoldering under the surface. Examine relationships for passive-aggressive behaviors.

Television/VCR/cable: Represents the overuse of television to escape life issues. May signal a need to reduce television or movie viewing. Indicates a need to go within. Need to balance work and leisure. Are you facing your present duties directly and responsibly? Are you taking a backseat in managing your life?

Toilet: Symbolizes releasing the past. Overflowing can represent difficulty in expressing and letting go of past pain, shame and hurt. Time to write out feelings and let go of outmoded behaviors and beliefs.

Washing machine: Dirty laundry can represent family secrets—something dirty or shameful from the past. Clogged hoses can represent a need to clear past issues in order to move into the present. Are you holding onto an illusion about your past?

Water heater: Represents issues of warmth—being left out in the cold—fear of lack. Can be a spiritual wake-up call.

Well: Well running dry represents a fear of being disconnected from Spirit or the Source. Feelings dried up and unexpressed. Facing fear of lack.

Well pump: Difficulty in accessing the Source available to you. Time to take an active part in activating abundance and emotional flow.

Car

Accident: Depends on the circumstances of the accident. If hit by another car, can indicate the need to strengthen personal boundaries. Can stimulate victim issues—for example, if hit from behind or broadsided. Running into another's car or property indicates a need to become grounded and to honor the boundaries of others. Working on boundary issues helps reduce the risk of car accidents.

Alternator: Feeling powerless. Lack of support around you for your current project or relationship. Look for ways to support and validate your choices.

Battery: If dead, can symbolize feeling run-down or drained. Represents a lack of reserve energy. Can signal a need to stop running around. Can indicate reluctance to move ahead in life. What do you need to recharge your inner battery?

Belts: Represent support and connection. Can indicate a relationship issue. Are you feeling supported at home and work?

Air-conditioner belt: Tired of dealing with a situation that is heating up. Staying in a difficult situation longer than necessary.

Alternator belt: Feeling powerless in a specific area of life.

Power steering belt: Feeling powerless to direct the course of your life. Feeling manipulated or driven by outside forces. Difficulty in steering your life. Fear of relinquishing control.

Timing belt: Symbolizes synchronicity. Are you out of sync with work or a relationship?

Water-pump belt: Overworking and resenting it. No time to cool down and rest between projects.

Brakes: Need to slow down. If bound, may signify fear of moving toward a change. Failing brakes signal feeling out of control in some area of your life. Try to moderate your schedule.

Exhaust valves: Can indicate difficulty in letting go of the past. Pent-up emotions stuck in the body. Take time to clear emotionally.

Flat tire: Fear of moving ahead. Can indicate issues of self-reliance and lack of grounding.

Fuel injection: Can indicate difficulty completing a project or following through with a decision. Feeling stuck and unable to forge ahead. Indicates a need to develop masculine qualities, such as assertiveness and follow-through.

Fuel pump: Can indicate too much or too little pressure in your life. Check for issues of procrastination or pushing too hard.

Hoses: Can be related to digestion. Check for problems with eating or elimination. Look for areas of congestion or clogs in life flow.

Ignition: Can indicate lack of passion or fear of power. Reluctance to give a green light to a current project.

Intake valves: Can be connected with difficulty receiving. Practice receiving help or gifts from others.

Keys: Misplaced or lost keys can symbolize a need to stop running around or overworking. Can be an unconscious desire to stay home. Keys locked in the car may happen when feeling overwhelmed with chores and activities. Keys locked in the car with the engine still running may signal a wish for a chauffeur, i.e., "I wish someone else would drive!"

Lights: Show you the road ahead. No lights indicate the feeling that you are driving in the dark. Feeling uncertain and fearful of the future.

Overheating: Steam or smoke coming from the engine signals a need to do anger work. Clear the air in a personal or work relationship. Need to clear clogged emotions. What feeling(s) are you avoiding?

Radiator: Can indicate a heated issue that is being ignored. Need to slow down and cool off.

Running out of gas: Feeling tired and worn out. Not feeling replenished or renewed by work or relationships. Tired of current responsibilities. Too much going on at once.

Solenoid: Fear of inadequacy in handling current life problems. Can indicate a lack of reserve energy. Rest and restore the body, mind and spirit.

Spark plugs: Deal with the spark of life. Can indicate a lack of vitality and zest for life. Time to eat well, get rest and exercise.

Starter: Deals with the ability to get started. Are you willing to give the green light to a new project?

Transmission: Fear of moving ahead. Indicates difficulty getting in gear to accomplish an overdue assignment. Need to move into higher gear and increase level of commitment, responsibility and productivity.

Communication

Answering machine/voice mail: Losing messages can represent feeling overwhelmed with work. Broken machine represents an unconscious desire to be out of touch—a desire to be left alone.

Computer: Computer problems can come from pent-up frustrations and issues of perfectionism. Too much pressure to finish a project can cause machines to slow down or shut off. The computer acts like a child who is being pushed and dragging her feet, refusing to budge. The computer shutdown temporarily causes the workplace to slow down. Look for resentment about current workload or schedule.

E-mail: Can represent communication problems. If incoming mail is lost, check your current feelings with the correspondent. Do you need to communicate needs or desires more clearly? Are you feeling overloaded or ignored?

Hard drive: Deals with organization and filing systems. Crashing indicates a need to slow down and reorganize. Lost files reflect confusion and inefficiency resulting from trying to handle too much at once. See if there is any "corruption" in your present belief system. Be honest as you assess any changing beliefs.

Memory: Parity problems point to imbalance and confusion. Note if you are emotionally confused or unclear at this time. How can you clarify your feelings?

Printer: Difficulty in manifesting projects. Frustration in completing and solidifying ideas. Represents a block in male energy. Work with releasing inner fears of manifesting your power in the world.

Software: Deals with issues of memory. Are you avoiding dealing with uncomfortable memories? Deals with issues of boundaries and healthy revamping of your current living situation. Are you corrupting your life with unhealthy choices?

Telephone: Problems with communication. Dead phone can represent a reenactment of loneliness and feeling cut off from life or others. Can also reflect too much input and a need to reduce communications. Do you have techniques for limiting the amount of time you spend on the phone?

Help in Setting Up Repairs

When you experience difficulty in setting up a repair, try moving deeper into the issues connected with the equipment. Obstacles in the way of repairs can bring up feelings of failure and powerlessness: "I can't do anything right." Being without a car or major appliance can also stimulate issues of abandonment and lack of support: "There is no one to help me. I have to deal with everything all alone." A complicated and lengthy repair can bring up issues of wanting to ignore personal problems rather than work toward a solution. Use the next exercise to help ease difficulty in setting up repairs. By reclaiming the past issue, you take the focus off the present situation and often the repair will flow more easily.

HOW TO BEGIN

1. When setting up the repair, take notice of who you deal with. Is it a friendly agent or a shaming, judgmental person? Is the treatment cold and distant or warm and supportive? Remember it is not a failure on your part if the person discounts you. It points to an unfinished piece of childhood work coming to the surface for you to clear.

2. Is it difficult to schedule the repair? If so, you may need to take more time to address the emotional issues represented by the equipment. Use the "Dictionary of Symbols" above to help you. Watch your dreams and daily encounters for more clues about your unfinished work.

3. What feelings are stimulated by the situation? How do you feel when dealing with the agent? If you are encountering a delay in the repair, how do you feel about the delay? When in your childhood or adult-

hood have you had similar feelings? You may be transferring unresolved emotions from the past onto the current situation. Write
down your feelings and the connections with your past. If you do
not recall any relevant past history, simply write down your current
feelings. For further study see chapter 2 and 4.

When you have completed the exercise, try to schedule the repair. If
you still experience delays or roadblocks, go deeper into the feelings.
Repeating the exercise at least twice should bring about a significant
shift in the situation.

Getting the Message and Reducing the Drama

While writing this chapter, I met with my best friend, Martha, for
lunch. On the way to meet me, she discovered that her car inspection
sticker was two months overdue. Normally conscientious about keeping
her car inspected, she was surprised to see the overdue date. We talked
about the possible unconscious issue she was enacting.

During our long friendship, we have often talked about being bad
girls. Bad girls break the rules with ease. They are able to do things forbidden by their families. Both of us having been good girls in our youth,
we enjoyed finding safe and adventurous ways to be bad girls. I asked
her if she thought she had unconsciously found a low-drama way to be a
bad girl. She agreed that one of her first thoughts after she discovered
the overdue sticker was of her father's disapproval. Even though she is
an independent and mature professional on her own, the family code
was following her. She unconsciously found a way to break a family rule.
She was able to get in touch with the part of her that wanted more distance from her family. She spoke of her recent decision to miss family
functions and take more time for her activities. She could understand,
validate and support the teenage rebel part of her who had ignored the
inspection due date.

As we parted, she mentioned the inspection sticker again and jokingly
asked if I thought she'd be safe driving home. She indicated that she
would have her car inspected the next day. That night, she called to tell
me that on her way home from the lunch she had run into a roadblock
for a driver's license and inspection check! The officer told her the fine
was $80.00. He also told her that he would not issue her a ticket if she
agreed to get her car inspected immediately.

This is an interesting example of Martha's car assisting her in a piece
of family work. Using the inspection sticker incident, Martha was able to
label the issue, get in touch with her feelings and support herself in her
individuation from her family. When she was caught being a bad girl at

the police roadblock, she found that there was no payment due for her lapse. The police officer acted as a reasonable father who could see her as a responsible and conscientious adult.

No Turning Off the Inner Light

While working on the car section of the "Dictionary of Symbols" in this chapter, I had an interesting car problem. I was attending a powerful yoga workshop with an insightful and expert teacher. He shared information about our bodies and spirits, and I enjoyed the opportunity to grow and expand. As I got in my car on the morning of the last session of the workshop, I turned the key and nothing happened. I called my neighbors, Andrea and Scott. Andrea was at home and offered to help me jump-start my engine. We attached the cables but were unable to get my car to turn over. She kindly drove me to the workshop. I was amused at the timing of this car situation and wondered what I would learn about myself as I found out more about the problem. My ex-husband and daughter picked me up and offered to take me home. Once there, I decided to try jump-starting my engine one more time, and I asked my ex-husband to help. He did, and we were successful. I left the car running for twenty minutes before turning it off and restarting it. The battery seemed fine.

Later that evening, I went out to see if the battery was holding the charge. It wasn't. As I approached the car, I saw that the inside light was on. I could not understand how it had been turned on. I checked the switch, and it seemed to be in the off position. I wondered if I had a short in the electrical system. Once again I called my neighbors. While I was waiting for Scott, the light in the inside of the car flashed on and off. Once he arrived, we were able to get the car going.

I felt especially motivated to examine the interpretation of this latest car problem. I felt it was noteworthy that I was unable to jump-start my car when I was helped by a woman but was successful when assisted by the two men. This followed the same pattern revealed in the work I had down with my father and the flat tires. I also found it interesting that the problem stemmed from the car's inner light.

The symbol of inner light is a very important one for me. My work is to connect others with their inner light. In the past, I have felt rejected and alienated because of my natural ability to connect with my own inner light. I have felt self-conscious and embarrassed about my abilities. In the workshop, I had felt safe to openly share my present path.

If I let my inner light shine consistently and strongly, I am afraid that I will scare away a man. I fear that I must choose either power and mobility in the physical world or my inner light. I fear I cannot have both. I know spiritually that my inner light will recharge my energy system. I am still questioning whether I will be allowed to maintain my inner light and still be accepted into the relationship club.

Appreciating Our Inanimate Teachers

Take time to examine and analyze the details of mechanical and electrical problems. Let the daily encounters with your household appliances, cars and other equipment teach you more about your spiritual lessons. In Bali there is a special ceremony designed specifically for the blessing of household appliances and automobiles. They take time regularly to thank the machinery and electrical devices in their daily life.

Design your own blessing ceremony to honor the inanimate objects in your life. Try talking to your car, computer or aging washing machine. Expressing gratitude to the inanimate beings in your life reminds you of their constant support and assistance. When you have a problem, consciously work to reclaim any projected emotions and issues to gain personal insight. This increased awareness can help reduce the number of incidents, increase the ease of reparation, and prevent reoccurrences.

Telekinesis

Telekinesis: The movement of objects by scientifically unknown or inexplicable means, as by the exercise of mystical powers.

As I began to respect material objects and spend time trying to understand and interpret them, they began to reward me with interaction. I had increased the energetic connection between myself and the material world by studying and writing about inanimate objects. This rapport seemed to follow a pattern similar to human relating. Two strangers come together with a smile or a shy hello. After a handshake and a quick exchange of names and identities they talk. This leads to lunch and a deep conversation that lasts for hours. They both extend to establish a connection based on mutual interest and respect. My interest in the inanimate sent out a call that was answered by spontaneous and unexplained movements. The inanimate objects were responding to me as if to say, "Hello. We want to play."

The following telekinetic episodes (with the exception of spoon bending) have several elements in common. These include a relaxed state, a feeling of openness, a direct, yet softened gaze and a distance of approximately four feet from the object. When my left brain is in gear trying or expecting the movement, I cannot achieve it. The movement comes when I am open and fully experiencing life in the present moment.

Move!

When I was young I practiced telekinesis on toothpicks. I sat for long sessions staring at a toothpick and willing it to move. I would stare pointedly at the tiny wooden stake silently repeating the command "Move!" I felt the harder I concentrated the more likely the toothpick would succumb to my command. I abandoned the telekinetic project after some months with no success.

My first experience with a spontaneous movement happened many years later. My friend Lorraine and I were at her home sitting on her couch. We had been discussing a spiritual topic when suddenly the play button on the portable tape recorder clicked into the on position. A tape began to play and we froze in our seats listening carefully. Ironically it was a recording of a spiritual group meeting. We sat still listening to the message and then slowly walked toward the recorder to examine it. Lorraine had not played the recorder that day. We could not figure out how the button was pushed down. We gave a silent thanks to the energetic impulse that turned on the spiritual message.

Spoon Bending

On the last evening of mediumship training at Delphi University, we gathered for spoon bending. Our teacher, Patricia, explained the technique. We were going to demonstrate the power of intent and focus on influencing material objects. We were each handed a silver spoon and told to rub the shaft while chanting "Bend!" After several minutes of chanting and focus, the silver would seem to melt. The goal was to twist and bend the spoon as much as possible before the metal rehardened.

I was excited and nervous as I sat willing my spoon to soften. Suddenly I felt a softening of the metal in my hand. I swiftly and deftly began to twist and wrap the spoon around itself. Then as suddenly the silver rehardened, and I was left staring at the misshapen silverware. We did the exercise several times. I found it worked best when I felt silly and playful. The more I joked and horsed around with fellow classmates the more stunning the results. I brought home silver flatware that was no longer flat. Spirals, humps, twists and turns made them look like eccentric art pieces for museum display. The lesson clearly demonstrated the influence we have over the physical world. I was excited to think about the possibilities for using this energy to heal the physical body. The spoon bending exercise gave concrete evidence of our intimate link with the material world.

Remote Control

One early evening, I was talking animatedly to my friend Sarah Louise. My day had been filled with synchronous events and an especially powerful healing session with a rolfer (bodyworker). As I was describing the insights I had experienced during the session, I stood facing the blank, still screen of the television. Suddenly the television turned on. Startled, I stopped talking for a moment and looked to my left. The remote lay on the bedside table. I told Sarah that I would call her back and I turned my attention to the program on the set.

The program was a nature show about volcanic islands. Many of my trips involve the exploration of volcanic islands. I am intrigued by the landscape and the energy of these varied islands. I sat and absorbed the beauty of the islands on our planet. As I watched, I wondered about the unexplained turning on of the television. My body was buzzing with an increase of energy from the bodywork and subsequent emotional clearing. I wondered if my energy was exceeding normal amounts—enough to influence electrical equipment to this degree. I left the question for further exploration and called Sarah to finish our talk.

The Message in the Bottle

One month later I stood under steaming hot water taking a relaxing shower. It felt good to wash away the stresses of the day, and I sighed deeply. I was gazing at the myriad of shampoos and shower soaps on the ledge in the shower, my mind open and clear. Suddenly one bottle tipped back and then eased back in place. I blinked, wondering if I had imagined the deliberate movement. If I had caught the movement out of the corner of my eye I would have discounted it, but in this case I had been gazing directly at the bottle. Without touching the bottle, I focused my energy on it. When nothing happened, I peered at it from above to see if it could have been leaning on another bottle. There was ample space around the bottle, so the leaning theory did not explain the tipping backward and forward. I finished my shower wondering about this particular "message in the bottle."

Knock. Knock. Who's There?

The following month, I attended a yoga retreat in Mexico in a small town by the sea. On the third day, my friend Molly and I swam in the sea and walked the beach strand. Back in our room after a relaxing warm shower, I was standing in front of a vanity dresser with three small drawers with metal knockers. Combing out my wet hair, I stood staring at the drawers. Suddenly one of the metal knockers lifted up and came down striking three distinct knocks. Her back to the vanity, Molly turned to see what had made the noise. I told her what I had witnessed. We waited reverently for a few minutes to see if there was any more movement. Then we walked gingerly toward the drawer and timidly opened it. We wondered if something heavy had fallen inside the drawer and shifted the contents. Inside were two cotton yoga tops. There was nothing hard enough to cause the rapping. Even though I was certain that I had seen all three knockers in place before the noise, I tried to perch the metal knocker up to see if it had fallen. The design of the drawers prevented this possibility. I knocked hard on the inside of the drawer to see if I could make the knocker produce three distinct sounds. I could not replicate the three separate raps even when using my fist. This event followed so closely on the heels of the bottle tipping, I became excited at the prospect of developing regular interaction with the inanimate world. When I arrived home from the retreat I was greeted with another telekinetic mystery.

Moving Ganesha

Ganesha, with his human body and elephant head, is a well-loved Hindu god. The son of Shiva and Parvati, he is revered as the remover of obstacles. He is a symbol of power and strength, symbolizing fertility and therefore the preservation of life. Several years ago, I visited Bali and found a three-foot statue of Ganesha for my garden. Since his arrival by ship, he has faced my front door with his grounding presence.

My yoga teacher and artist, Victor van Kooten, has a special affinity for this god and often sports a T-shirt with a hand-painted depiction of Ganesha. He and his partner, Angela Farmer, hosted the yoga retreat in Mexico. When I drove into my driveway upon my return from Mexico, I was startled to see Ganesha facing the drive. The statue had rotated 180 degrees in my absence. I knew that he had been facing the house when I left on my trip the week before.

That evening I walked outside and squatted in front of the statue. It was vibrating with energy. I asked him to help me receive the message of his new position. I felt him telling me to turn and face the world directly. I knew it was time to move outward, risking more as I ventured out from the known safety of my inner world. As the remover of obstacles, Ganesha was pointing the way beyond the fears I envisioned on my life path.

I do not know how Ganesha changed direction. I live in a remote area in the countryside where visitors are rare. It could have been a prankster, a lawn maintenance person or unexplained phenomena. Nevertheless, it is interesting to me that Ganesha changed his stance as I began to move into a more visible and confrontational role in my own life.

Chapter 11

Weathering the Earth's Changes

Geological and climatic changes activate profound issues. Unpredictable weather and the instability of the earth's core bring us face to face with a loss of control. Since our survival depends on the stability of the earth's surface, when it quivers and quakes, we face potential injury and death. When the waters rise or the winds whip, we face the possible destruction of our homes and resources. These lessons of impending death and loss are graduate-level courses—the letting go of safety, security and of life itself.

Earth is accompanying us on our spiritual journey, and as she changes, we receive opportunities to evolve. The more we learn how to listen to the language of nature, the more easily we can weather the changes ahead. Thus it serves us to learn as much as possible from our teacher, Mother Earth.

Lessons from Mother Earth

Let's look at the issues stimulated by extreme weather and geological conditions. After each issue listed below, there are simple practices that can help you understand these issues. Voluntarily addressing each of them daily can prepare you for the courses taught by Mother Earth.

1. *Seeing:* viewing life from a new perspective

   • Sit and watch night fall or day break.

   • Find something good to say about someone you judge.

   • Hang upside down off your bed.

   • Stare at a small patch of earth and watch the grass and insects.

2. *Changing:* interrupting the routine of life

   • Try relaxing and sending healing energy when you hear a siren.

   • Drive a different way to work.

   • Sit in a radically different seat at the cinema.

   • Take a class on something you know nothing about.

3. *Letting go:* humbling the ego and dealing with issues of control and loss

- Let someone in line in traffic or at the grocery store.

- Take something off of your to-do list.

- Forgive yourself and one other person for a transgression.

- Write down a worry and throw it away.

4. *Uniting:* bringing people together for cooperative work and play

- Talk to a stranger.

- Visit a neighbor just to say hello.

- Go to a different church.

- Smile at everyone in the elevator or on the bus.

5. *Appreciating:* enjoying the present moment

- Slow down and breathe.

- Laugh for no reason at all.

- Be grateful for the red traffic light.

- Say thank you to Mother Earth.

The Four Elements

We share a system of elemental qualities with our planet. The four basic elements are fire, earth, air and water. Each contains specific characteristics necessary to maintain a balanced, healthy organism, and each has unique qualities that enhance the life of the organism. If any one of the elements is lacking, the organism's health may be compromised.

All weather and geological conditions contain one or more elements. Since we also contain these elements, we can use current conditions to alert us to imbalances in our own energy. The more we understand the symbolic meanings of the four elements, the clearer the message. The clearer the message, the easier we can ride out the earth's changes. Let's look at the characteristics of the four basic elements.

Fire: energy, creativity, transformation, manifestation, regeneration, passion

Earth: survival, stability, property, physical health, procreation, nurturance

Air: ideas, plans, foresight, organization, conceptualization, logic

Water: emotion, dreams, intuition, cleansing, healing, nurturance

Dictionary of Weather and Earth Changes

Following are some symbolic interpretations of weather and geological conditions. The appropriate element is noted after the condition. Use the characteristics above to determine the nature of the lesson. Add your own ideas from personal experience or intuitive knowing. Also notice if your deams contain any of the weather or earth conditions. When you face the following changes in your life, use the ordeal to attend to any neglected areas of yourself.

Blizzard (Water/Air): Stop in all action. Feeling lost and confused. Cannot see what is in front of you. Stop and ask for help. Move with caution. Feeling powerless to move ahead. Frozen projects or feelings. What feelings are frozen and how can you thaw them?

Drought (Air): Absence of feelings. Need to go within and feel. Creative juices dried up. Find time to express your creativity. Use feelings generously.

Earthquake (Earth): Deep revolution. Need for core changes. Foundation shifting. Old beliefs changing from the ground up. Grounding yourself in spiritual life rather than material life. Anchor your core beliefs. Focus on spiritual foundation.

Flood (Water): Overwhelming emotions. Time to release pent-up feelings and to move on. Need to go with the flow of life. Immerse yourself in intuition, creativity and feeling.

Fog (Water/Air): Lack of clarity. Inability to see into the future. Groping along. Need to clarify beliefs and goals. Reexamine motivation for a current project or relationship.

Forest fire (Fire): Need to let go. Major rebirth. Phoenix rising from the ashes. Dramatic burst of energy. Time to say goodbye to an old way of life and to start over. Express the anger inherent in grieving the past.

Hail (Water): Unexpected surprise. Stuck in a rut. Need to see things anew. Situation not as you expected. Let go of judgments and expectations and see with a child's eyes.

Hurricane (Air/Water): Emotional housecleaning. Time for a clean sweep to remove ungrounded elements and to discard outmoded concepts. Stuck in old ways of thinking and being.

Ice storm (Water): Stop! Be still and go deep within. Thaw out old frozen emotions. Take no more steps forward until you take personal inventory. Honestly survey your motivation and tactics.

Mudslide (Earth/Water): Mobility. Precarious grounding. Time to move. Instability. Issues and relationships unclear. Check the feelings and the facts. Need for some distance and objectivity. Time for a drying-out period.

Rain (Water): Letting down and flowing. Need to cry and flow with any feeling. Cleansing and purifying. Clears the dust; the old and the stale. Need to take time out to grieve the past before moving into the future.

Snow (Water): Stilling energy. Need to go inside. Slow down and listen to your inner voice. Meditate and commune with your spiritual self. Feelings are frozen. Needing to thaw out and let your emotions flow.

Thunderstorm (Fire/Air): Release of pent-up emotions. Need to clear the air. Time to make a move in an area of your life. Need for physical activity.

Tidal wave (Water): Overwhelmed by intense emotion. Fear of the power of passion. Letting go of control. Surrender to current lifestyle.

Tornado (Air): Letting go of control. Facing impermanence. Need for selective change. Time to clear out old order. Destiny in action. Restructuring.

Volcano (Fire/Earth): Passion and anger. Emotional eruption. Need for creative expression. Deep transformation. Need to change the landscape. Laying fertile soil for new creative ideas and expression.

Wind (Air): Sweeping change. Need for new beliefs. Old ideas are blown away. Clear the air and begin anew. Revolution of thought and ideas.

Ritual Release

The past can hold us captive in many ways. Emotionally, we hold onto old hurts and painful memories. Mentally, we maintain outdated views of our skills and abilities. Physically, we store pain and tension in our bodies and create imbalance. The more painful our past, the deeper we may try to bury it inside. Our bodies are not built to provide the burial grounds for the pain of the past. Sooner or later we begin to manifest symptoms that reflect the buried memories. The symptoms may appear as physical illness, troubled relationships, financial problems or a myriad of other unhealthy guises. When we suppress our pain unconsciously, we re-create painful situations that mirror the past.

Ritual release takes the burden of the past off the body and psyche. By volunteering to dig up our old burial grounds, we can exhume and cremate the skeletons of our past. Once we acknowledge and release the past, we can project healthier energy into the future. Using the elements of fire, earth, air and water, we can prepare meaningful rites of passage to heal the past and claim the future. Simple practices such as lighting a candle, walking a path, bathing in petals and throwing a leaf to the wind can feed the human need for ritual.

Fire Element

Fire is an ancient symbol of death and rebirth—the phoenix consumed in flames to rise again. The fire ritual is a powerful transformative experience. Watching the flames consume paper and wood, reminds us to use the energy of the past to fuel the future. When we have difficulty letting go of a stage of life, fire ritual can quicken the process.

This ritual is designed for releasing a relationship, job, home or other significant life situation. We can use the burning of the symbols to help release the old and prepare for the new. By releasing the symbolic representations of the past, we can live more fully in the present and move freely into the future. This ritual is designed to release the emotional charge and to ease the transition.

Fire Ritual

You will need paper, pen, candle and matches. Find a private space indoors or outdoors where it is safe to have a lit candle. You may use a metal bowl for burning paper.

Gather symbols of the significant life situation. For example, if you are releasing a job, you may use copies of photos, letters, documents or objects that directly relate to the work situation. These items act as symbolic representations of the past. Light the candle. Write the statement "I now release _____." Fill in the blank appropriately.

Take time to look at the items. Experience the sadness, anger or relief of the ending of the stage. Use this time to feel as deeply as possible. Use the paper and pen to vent emotions. You can also rip copies of the photos or documents or beat a pillow to release anger. You may feel like crying or laughing. Give yourself permission to experience any and all feelings.

Finish the ritual by burning the release statement and any documents or photos. If you have large items, you can give them away, sell them or throw them out. When you have released your feelings, sit and breathe. Feel your heart beating and your breath moving in and out. You may feel lighter after releasing emotions. You may feel drained or energized. If at any time you feel a wave of feeling, follow it. Come into the present moment as much as possible. Keep your breath moving so that your energy may flow. Let's look at an example:

A Wedding and a Funeral

When my marriage ended after four years, I was shocked and bereft. I was aware of problems in the marriage, and although I worked on my issues in therapy, my husband was reluctant to go to a marriage counselor. When he left the marriage, I had hoped for reconciliation. My vision of the future did not include a divorce. At the end of the first year of separation, however, I received the divorce papers and was brought face to face with the inevitable death of my marriage.

During the first year of separation, I spent time releasing my illusions about my marriage. I faced my denial of the early warning signs of a troubled relationship. As I faced my unhealthy desire to stay married at any cost, I began to understand how women are able to stay so long in untenable situations. Since my husband left the marriage, I had no choice but to release my grip on it. I decided a release ritual would help me bury the past.

One rainy afternoon I gathered symbolic items from my marriage. I chose the most poignant symbols of my marriage—my wedding skirt, blouse, sash, shoes and wedding ring. I lit a red heart-shaped candle and burned copies of the wedding invitation and photos. I recalled memories of the courtship and engagement. I remembered my excitement and nervousness as I dressed for the wedding. I cried as I grieved the death of my dreams.

My naivete died with the death of the relationship. The wedding band symbolized my naive trust and the broken promise. I needed to release the gold band in order to let my marriage rest in peace. I blew out the candle and placed the ring deep into the hot, soft wax. I placed the candle, ring and clothes in a large box and drove to the garbage dumpster near my husband's office. I flung the box into the deep, green bin to be burned. The burial was complete. I felt emotionally drained but lighter of heart as I drove back home to work toward my new life.

Earth Element

The earth is our foundation. We depend on its firmness and stability to support us as we step into the future. As we take our first steps as toddlers, the earth is patient and supportive. It feeds us physically and emotionally. It teaches us to honor each stage of life from birth to death. The earth's energy grounds and centers us as we walk our spiritual path. Earth rituals include walking, gardening, sitting and playing sports.

Walking is an ancient practice for entering a sacred space of contemplation. The act of taking steps reminds us of the steps we must take when conceiving of and completing a physical project. Walking soothes the central nervous system and clears the mind of worries. You can use this practice when a busy, hectic schedule leaves you feeling anxious, worried or nervous. By walking, you are taking the time to shift your focus to your inner guidance.

Earth Ritual

To begin, find a place indoors or outdoors where you can construct a walkway. You can build it using seashells, stones, paper or pieces of bark, or you can use a stick to mark a path in the dirt or sand. Use any design you wish: serpentine, spiral, circular or linear. Choose the design to fit your mood.

You can chant or sing while you walk the path. You can affirm aloud your wishes or goals. You can release hurts or resentments. You can offer healing for yourself or another. At the end of the walk, kneel or squat and touch the ground in gratitude. Acknowledge the earth element for supporting your spiritual path.

The Spiral Walk

I once had the opportunity to practice yoga and explore the beauty of the island of Hawaii with a group of women. We visited the active volcano and ancient stone carvings called petroglyphs. The petroglyphs depict figures and ancient symbols. Inspired by the stone carvings, we constructed a ritual pathway by placing stones in a spiral design. That night, under the waxing moon, we gathered around the walkway. At the start of the path, each woman described her vision of a dream project. She then walked the spiral pathway while imagining the manifestation of her dream. We applauded and cheered as each woman found her way to the center of the spiral to symbolically birth the project. She then retraced her steps to return to the community of support.

When I returned home, I designed a spiral walkway. Whenever I feel tired, confused or depleted, I walk the spiral inward and outward to help shift my perspective. In this way I remind myself to become grounded and to trust the natural unfolding of events. I honor the natural process of taking steps to manifest goals. I allow the earth's energy to help me focus my energy so that I might realize a physical project.

Air Element

This ritual uses the natural phenomenon of wind to help release old patterns. Wind has been defined as the harbinger of change—by its very nature it sweeps up old leaves and seeds and moves them to new ground. Wind is nature's moving company. When the wind visits your home, it can signal a good time to sweep out the cobwebs and allow change to move you. Standing in a strong wind can help you release old tensions and tired beliefs. Ask the wind to carry away your outdated beliefs. Close your eyes and listen for the new thoughts and beliefs it brings.

Air Ritual

Take a felt pen and go outside. As you walk around, pick up any leaf, petal or piece of wood or bark that attracts you. Notice the quality of the air around you. Is it windy? Is there a gentle breeze? Is the air still and calm? Remember to breath and to let your instinctual self move freely. Suspend the thoughts of your logical left brain and let your body go wherever it pleases. When you have collected several natural objects, find a place to sit.

Using the pen, write on the objects. You can write words and draw pictures or symbols. Let your imagination be free and expressive. Write down any words that come to mind. Do not try to analyze them. Trust your intuitive right brain. For example, during one air ritual, I chose a leaf, a petal and a piece of bark on which I wrote the following:

Leaf: Money, control, let go of past, start anew.

Petal: Love, sex, release, femininity.

Piece of bark: My community supports who I am.

After you have written your words, sit and hold the object. Breathe and embrace any feelings that may arise. Close your eyes and silently honor the power and force of the winds of change. Give the wind permission to clear you. Ask it to take the object from you and to help you release the past. When you are ready, hold out your hand and let the wind pick up the object. If the air is calm, leave the object on the ground for the wind to move later. Stay as long as you like, to feel and observe your thoughts.

The message of the wind is to let go and change. Normally change is difficult for the human ego to accept. Connecting and aligning with the wind can help you persevere during difficult transitions.

El Niño

When I was attending a yoga workshop in Mexico in March 1998, the warm currents of El Niño were affecting the weather. Strong and incessant winds moved across the small Mexican town, and the weather was unseasonably cool. I felt the wind asking me to release any old and weary patterns. Its unrelenting quality seemed to be saying, "More, release more!"

During class I connected with one of the men in the group and we decided to exchange energy work. He suggested that we use the wind to help us. One evening after class, we stood and faced the wind. It was very strong and cold. As we breathed, we could feel the wind sweeping us clean. At one point he stood directly behind me and we breathed in unison. Eyes closed, we breathed with the wind. Suddenly I felt my physical body melt as the wind seemed to pass through both of our bodies. I felt it pass through my belly and back. Strong emotions from my past welled up inside me, as I felt my fear of connecting deeply with a man. Over the next few days, I continued to feel my fear. My dreams were numerous and intense.

On the last day of the workshop, the yoga teacher helped me find a more open position for my tighter left hip. At the end of the class, I asked my friend to sit behind me and support me. The open hip position opened old grief and sadness surrounding the birth of my daughter. Having discovered my husband's affair one month before her birth, I had felt alone and unsupported during labor and delivery. During the celebration of my daughter's birth, I had been grieving the death of my marriage. With the help of my new friend, as he sat behind me and supported me, I was able to relive the birth of my daughter. The wind helped me change enough so that I could experience the presence and support of a sensitive man.

Water Element

The emphasis of the water ritual is on cleansing, purifying and soothing the body, mind and spirit. The water washes away fatigue, soreness and toxicity from daily life. Immersion in water reminds us of the security and comfort of the womb. Water's fluid nature keeps us in touch with the flow of our emotions. Emotions, like water, need to continue flowing in order to stay pure and clean. Free-flowing emotions feed creativity and joy.

Sixty-five percent of our physical body is made up of water. Without water, we would wither and die. Just like plants, we need to be watered—physically and emotionally. The water ritual reminds us to trust the flow of life. Whenever we feel challenged in life, we can use the healing properties of water as a balm for our body and soul. We can then reenter the world feeling refreshed and rejuvenated.

Water Ritual

A water ritual can be performed anywhere and is especially comforting when you are feeling tense and tired. If you are near a lake, stream, river or ocean, you can use that body of water in the ritual. You can also use a rainstorm, a sprinkler, your own bathtub or shower, a hot tub, a fountain, a puddle or a bowl or basin.

Let the water rinse away any fatigue, sadness or jitters you may feel. Dip into the restorative water—add salt, petals, leaves, scents or floating candles. Cry into the water. Pour the water over your head. Dip your hands, your feet, your face, your elbows into the water. Run through the water, splash and play. If weather and privacy permit, go naked into the water. Jump into the water and let it catch and carry you away. Feel the support of the water. Float and drift. Breathe and allow the water to restore you—body, mind and spirit.

River Walk

During a woman's yoga retreat that I participated in, the group stayed in a peaceful abbey in Louisiana. The abbey stands near a shallow, sandy-bottomed river. The group organizer, who lives on the river, suggested we take a river walk. Walking to the river's edge, we left our shoes on the bank and waded into the cool water. As we started to move upstream, the current pushed against our legs. Light filtered through the trees, and the air was clear. The flowing water seemed to draw the tension and worries out of our bodies. We laughed and joked as we walked.

Our guide, Sharon, took us to some banks of natural clay. Stripes of purple, yellow, white and red clay lined the banks. We dug our hands into the clay and began decorating our bodies with the vivid colors. We laughed at each other and admired the decorations. We giggled and played like young girls discovering their mother's makeup kit. Without actual mirrors, we were able to reflect to one another the beauty of our artwork. I experienced the freedom of feeling beautiful without feeling judged. Our inhibitions fell away as we took turns decorating each other with colorful markings.

We walked downstream adorned and light of heart, collecting bits of driftwood and lumps of colorful clay. As we walked, the sun dried the clay on our skin. Before getting out of the water, we bathed and cleansed our bodies. Our skin felt silky and soft from the clay. Leaving our inhibitions and cares in the river, we made our way back to the abbey.

Group Ritual

Each of us needs support and affirmation from others in order to step into the fullness of our unique power. Many of us lack families who support our chosen beliefs, professions or lifestyles. Therefore, we need to create our own family group to stand witness to our growth and development. Group ritual provides a gathering of supportive, like-minded people to anchor and comfort us as we step beyond our previous limits.

Growth is a process of continually entering new stages of development. Our completion of the required work in one stage automatically moves us to the next. There may be fear and uncertainty as we move from the known and familiar to the unknown and foreign. It is during this time of uncertainty and insecurity that we can use the support and affirmation of others.

The following group ritual is designed to acknowledge and honor the completion of a stage and to provide emotional support for welcoming in the next stage. The size of the group may vary—two or more people can do this ritual with powerful results.

* * *

Each person in the group will need a pen and a piece of paper. The group begins by sitting in a circle and taking a few moments to focus its energy by using a silent prayer, a chant, a song or by holding hands in silence. When the group feels connected, each person takes a few minutes to identify a life stage that he or she is ready to complete and release. After identifying the stage, each person selects a new goal.

For example, Carol is ready to leave an unfulfilling job and go back to school to earn a degree. She writes:

I am now ready to release the security of my present job.
On the other side of the paper she writes:

I am now ready to receive the financial support to earn my degree.
Bill has chronic symptoms that prevent him from enjoying life and exploring new options. He writes:

I am now ready to release feeling sick and tired.
I am now ready to receive health and vitality in my life.

Annie is dealing with a string of unsuccessful and unsatisfying relationships. She writes:

I am now ready to release my dependency on others.
I am now ready to receive self-love and approval.

Each person uses the following format:

I am now ready to release _____.
I am now ready to receive _____.

After each of the cards have been completed, the group goes around the circle and each person reads her or his card aloud. This important step allows the group to witness and affirm the steps being taken. After all of the cards have been shared, the group may close with a prayer, song, chant, inspirational reading or silence.

This ritual emphasizes the power of group energy. I suggest gathering the cards and symbolically releasing them. You may wish to have a bonfire and let everyone place their card in the fire. You can also throw each card into a common trash can. The energy of the group continues to support and affirm each member in his or her new path of growth.

One Month to Live

This exercise is designed to help you let go of the physical body. By imagining that you are living your last month on Earth, you can confront your beliefs about your life and death. Death is an obligatory event for living beings, and rehearsing your death can be a transformative process. People who have consciously faced death have spoken of an increased awareness of their surroundings. You may have noticed this if you have spent time with a loved one before a long separation. You truly look at them as if to drink them in. You notice sounds and sights that have always been present but that you have never before noticed. You become more aware of the present and feel each moment as deeply as possible.

You may choose a shorter time for this experiment—for example, imagining that you have one week or one day to live. I found that a month gave me time to move through more stages of transformation.

* * *

Begin by answering the following questions:

If I had one month to live . . .
- *Who would I contact?*
- *What unfinished business would I want to complete?*
- *Who would I call to say "I love you" or "I'm sorry?"*
- *How would I choose to spend the thirty days?*
- *Would I end any present relationships?*
- *Would I quit or change my work situation?*
- *What worries would become irrelevant and fade away?*
- *How would my priorities change?*
- *How would my daily routine change?*
- *How would my awareness of people and the world around me change?*

Answering these questions will help you cut away the deadwood in your present life. Examine the changes you would make if you had one month to live. Ask yourself which of these changes may be appropriate for you to initiate now. Facing death helps us move more honestly into the present and reevaluate our choices.

Next, simulate the emotions that you imagine feeling—shock, anger, sadness, fear, grief, relief, panic, disappointment, disbelief, detachment, etc. You may be surprised which feelings arise. Even though this is an exercise and not a reality, you can still touch the human emotions that accompany the passage into death.

You may also wish to keep a diary during the month. Write your thoughts and observations. The heightened awareness you encounter can carry over into your daily life once the month is completed. The exercise of rehearsing your death can bring you more fully into your present life. Death is inevitable and can be welcomed as a timely conclusion to our visit on Earth.

What Difference Can We Make?

The increasing problem of pollution and waste disposal leaves many of us feeling frustrated and disheartened. We try to recycle and be conscientious consumers, yet the problems increase with each passing day. We feel powerless to make a significant dent.

We can help clean up the earth by volunteering to deal with our emotional garbage. We can address our inner storms and emotional droughts rather than wait for the external drama to awaken us. We live in the Age of Aquarius—the era of the individual choosing an inner revolution that brings outer change. Access to the power of this age is found in the recognition that inner change precedes outer manifestation. Now more than ever we are impotent to bring about change in the physical world until we address our numerous inner conflicts and imbalances.

We cannot expect the earth to reflect a peaceful, clean and harmonious environment until we create our own inner balance and harmony. Each of us must make the choice to address our inner work. Each person who chooses to clean the earth from the inside out becomes a model for others who may eventually make the same choice.

We must start with an honest assessment of our backlog of personal garbage. Are we addressing and clearing out feelings of rage, sadness and fear? Do we take out our own emotional garbage—daily, weekly or even monthly? For most of us the answer is clearly no. And our negligence is being reflected in our physical world.

It is vital that we continue outer recycling and be conscientious consumers as we begin to address our inner pollution and garbage. Recycling and regular emotional cleansing (see chapters 2 and 4) have the power to significantly affect the health and cleanliness of our planet.

Healing the Earth

Alan Shephard, the first American man in space, had the opportunity to travel to the moon during his career as an astronaut. In a recent interview, he spoke of his first look at Earth from the moon's surface. He was amazed to see the blue of the water, the green of the terrain and the white of the snow caps. He was most struck by the earth's vulnerability and fragility as it hung in the sky above the moon. He said that tears came to his eyes when he realized how lucky we are to reside on this beautiful planet. He also felt sad that we had not yet found the awareness to love and care for its resources or for each other. From his vantage point, Shephard was able to see the limits of Earth's resources. From our perspective, these resources seem infinite. If each of us had the opportunity to view our home planet from outer space, how would our awareness grow and evolve? How would this awareness affect the environment and world peace?

This next exercise gives us the opportunity to travel outside the limits of the earth and its atmosphere. From this cosmic vantage point, we can revise our limited views and prejudices. We can open our minds to treating ourselves, our fellow humans and our planet with greater care and compassion.

HOW TO BEGIN

You can do this meditation alone or with a group. You can tape the meditation or have someone read it aloud. Find a quiet place to sit or lie down for thirty minutes. After closing your eyes, take several deep, full breaths. Let out a sigh. Feel your physical body let go of any tension.

Become aware of your position in the room. Feel the space around you. Sense the walls, the ceiling and the windows. Continue to breathe deeply as you allow your mind to travel out of the room and onto the roof of the building. Next, allow your consciousness to travel above the building to view the other buildings of the neighborhood. Look down at the treetops and the roofs below. From this vantage point, continue rising until you can see the entire town or city. As you move further and further into space, you can see more of the world beneath you. The city grows into the state, the state into the country, the country into the continent. Finally, you can see several continents and bodies of water below you. Keep breathing as you move further and further above Earth. From this vantage point, you can travel quickly to any part of the globe.

As you hover above your world, open your heart and send love and comfort to the inhabitants below you. Pay special attention to the parts of the world experiencing war or strife. Imagine the soldiers in the war zones putting down their weapons and crossing borders to embrace the opposing soldiers. Remind the soldiers that they are brothers and sisters. Send love to the leaders of the countries to help them reclaim their projections in order to enable a peaceful resolution. If the area is experiencing a natural disaster, send your comfort and healing prayers. Feel your love and concern traveling through space to enter the countries, cities, neighborhoods and houses in the troubled region.

After you have spent time with the inhabitants, take some time to observe the natural resources. See the bodies of water running clear and clean, the air purified, all species of plants and animals thriving and the soil rich and balanced. Feel the harmony between the earth and its inhabitants. Take time to visit the oceans, deserts, rain forests, snowy mountains and plains. Relax your mind and send healing energy from your heart.

When you are ready, slowly come back toward Earth. Seeing your continent from above, move closer to your home. Bring your consciousness into your country, state and city. Continue to breathe and relax as you find your way back to your neighborhood and finally to your building. Come back into the room and to your position in the room. Take a few minutes to settle back into your body. Feel the fullness in your heart. When you are ready, move your fingers and toes. Slowly open your eyes and look around the room. Notice any changes in your perception or feelings. Write down any impressions or experiences from the meditation.

Appreciating Mother Earth

It is easy to forget that Mother Earth is our hostess and that we are her guests. She is gracious and generous in providing us with air, food, lodging and beautiful surroundings during our stay. It is important that we do not abuse her hospitality. Take time to sit outside and listen to our Mother's heartbeat. She whispers messages to us through the wind, washes away our shame with rain showers, quiets our mind with the snowfall, shakes us out of our stupor with thunder and illuminates our denial with lightning. The more we understand and know ourselves, the more we support the health and well-being of Mother Earth and all of her inhabitants.

Epilogue

Congratulations! In completing the courses described in this book, you have earned a degree in spiritual awareness. Your third eye has been invited to open and see beyond your past limitations. This degree of consciousness entitles you to an increasing knowledge of your rights and privileges in this lifetime. You are now eligible to breathe into the present moment, honor your emotions, listen to your physical body and make time for your inner child. You have reclaimed your right to redefine relationships and to access psychic abilities and dreams as you appreciate countless synchronicities. Past-life knowledge, communication with discarnate beings, animals and inanimate objects and sensitivity to geological and climatic changes are now part of your daily existence.

As you navigate the world with heightened sensitivity, you will see that there are as many paths to consciousness as there are people on the planet. Your tolerance of others will reflect your mastery of spiritual awareness and will return to you as grace and joy. Enjoy your stay on Earth and learn as much as you can before you go.

Bibliography

Andrews, Lynn V. Jaguar Woman and the Wisdom of the Butterfly Tree. San Francisco: Harper & Row, 1985.

Bernstein, Morey. The Search for Bridey Murphy. Garden City, N.Y.: Doubleday, 1956.

Capacchione, Lucia. The Power of Your Other Hand: A Course in Channeling the Inner Wisdom of the Right Brain. North Hollywood, Calif.: Newcastle Publishing, 1988.

———. Recovery of Your Inner Child. New York: Simon and Schuster, 1991.

Hay, Louise L. Heal Your Body A-Z: The Mental Causes for Physical Illness and the Way to Overcome Them. Carlsbad, Calif.: Hay House, 1982.

Johnson, Robert A. Inner Work: Using Dreams and Active Imagination for Personal Growth. San Francisco: Harper & Row, 1986.

Kapit, Wynn, and Lawrence M. Elson. The Anatomy Coloring Book. New York: HarperCollins College Publishers, 1993.

Morris, William, ed. The American Heritage Dictionary of the English Language. Boston: Houghton Mifflin, 1981.

Sams, Jamie, and David Carson. Medicine Cards: The Discovery of Power through the Ways of Animals. Santa Fe, N.Mex.: Bear & Company, 1988.